D1540282

During her annual physical examination, a nurse friend of mine mentioned that she had been depressed. Her hurried physician tried his best to say something empathic: "So, who's not depressed? If you work in health care, you're depressed."

Americans live in the age of industrialized medicine, and everyone—inside and outside of health care—is now in the same boat. Doctors are financially pressured to be speedy mechanics, and patients often receive assembly-line treatment, which can be a painful reminder of their assembly-line lives. While most Americans manage to go to work and pay their bills, more than a few struggle just to get out of bed, and growing numbers feel fragile, hollow, hopeless, and defeated.

In 1998, Martin Seligman, then president of the American Psychological Association, spoke to the National Press Club about an American depression epidemic: "[W]e discovered two astonishing things about the rate of depression across the century. The first was there is now between ten and twenty times as much of it as there was fifty years ago. And the second is that it has become a young person's problem. When I first started working in depression thirty years ago . . . the average age of which the first onset of depression occurred was 29.5. Essentially middle-aged housewives' disorder. Now the average age is between fourteen and fifteen."

Despite the unparalleled material wealth of the United States, we Americans—especially our young—are increasingly unhappy. What is happening in our society and culture? How is it that the more we have come to rely on mental health professionals, the higher the rates of depression? And are we in need of a different approach to overcoming despair?

During the course of our lives, it is the unusual person who does not have at least one period of deep despair. The majority of depressed people do not choose professional treatment but many do, and my intent is not to create discontent among patients satisfied with their mental health treatments. This book is for people who believe that any approach to depression that does not confront societal and cultural sources for despair becomes part of the problem rather than a sustainable solution. Standard mental health treatments routinely ignore the depressing effects of an extreme consumer culture, and for people who feel alienated from such a culture, it is my experience that conventional treatments can actually increase their sense of alienation and contribute to their despair. This book is also about providing hope and a practical path for people who have lost faith in psychiatric orthodoxy, often because it has failed them or their loved ones.

I am in my third decade of working with people who have not been helped by standard psychiatric treatments. I have found that while the majority of such "treatment resisters" do not identify with any political party, most share these political views: they are deeply pained by a society that focuses on increasing consumption rather than celebrating life; they believe that powerful corporations rather than individuals and communities dictate public policy; they suspect that many of those authorities and institutions—including those in mental health—that inform Americans have been corrupted and hijacked by corporations whose singular goal is increased profit; and they consider it common sense that an alternative approach that threatens the societal status quo will be ignored or derided by those who financially profit from the status quo.

I recall one such treatment resister, a middle-aged man who was dragged into family counseling by his wife because of their daughter's self-destructive behaviors. On his own, he had valiantly struggled to overcome rage and despair that he attributed to job stress caused, he said, "by a new CEO whose only loyalty is to stock share value." He made clear that he disliked manipulative managers and know-nothing mental health professionals as well as the term *depression*. He said, "I know what helplessness and hopelessness are, and I know what shutting down my pain is, but the diagnosis of depression is some damn shrink psychobabble." He explained that the word *depression* didn't do justice to his experience and only irritated him. In contrast, when I used the word *hurting*, it touched him deeply.

I have found that the words people use to describe their conditions

Advance Praise for *Surviving America's Depression Epidemic*

"While *Surviving America's Depression Epidemic* is an excellent self-help book, it is not just for the clinically depressed. This well-conceived and researched book illuminates the general malaise tinting the canvas of our lives and validates the background of unhappiness inherent in our contemporary lifestyles—a background often mislabeled as pathological. We are all trying to survive this epidemic. The book is empowering, energizing, and provides a road map to greater psychological health, motivation, and fulfillment."

— Stuart Shipko, M.D.,
author of *Surviving Panic Disorder*

"If you've ever smelled a rat in the way corporate America tears down community with one hand and pushes antidepressant drugs with the other, this book is for you."

— Will Hall, co-founder of
Freedom Center (Northampton, MA)
and staff member, The Icarus Project

"*Surviving America's Depression Epidemic* bravely connects much of the overwhelming despair in our society to society itself, and offers innovative remedies. I encourage anyone who has ever asked, 'What are the alternatives to the current mental health system?' to read this book. Bruce shows us an array of specific, practical options to fight the good fight on our increasingly demoralized planet. As a psychiatric survivor, I highly recommend that mental health professionals read this book."

— David W. Oaks, Director
MindFreedom International

"This well-written and insightful book locates depression where it should be situated—in the dehumanization of American culture and the corporatization of psychological health and well-being. Moreover, Dr. Levine offers insights into what we've lost sight of and what we can do about it."

— David Walker, Ph.D., Associate Professor,
American School of Professional Psychology

"This is a terrific book. Bruce E. Levine argues convincingly that our modern depression epidemic is the result of a demoralized society. He integrates critical thinking about psychiatry, extensive clinical experience with clients diagnosed as depressed, and a refreshing look at the factors that affect our morale—alienation, consumerism, and spirituality. Highly recommended."

— Jeffrey Lacasse, MSW, Visiting Lecturer,
College of Social Work, Florida State University

WITHDRAWN
FROM THE RECORDS OF THE
MID-CONTINENT PUBLIC LIBRARY

"How does a sane person find meaning in a world gone mad? The question is not a new one, but Bruce Levine offers timely insights about the social and cultural causes of demoralization. In this, the Dark Age of the pharmaceutical-military-industrial complex, Levine gives a much needed wake-up call that challenges each of us to find our own antidote in the healing aspects of integrity, nature, self-transcendence, and community."

— Grace E. Jackson, M.D.,
author of *Rethinking Psychiatric Drugs*

"Unlike pharmaceuticals, this book is an anti-depressant that works. When depression is a reaction to a depressing culture, all the drugs in the world can't numb us to the truth that health—whether mental, physical, or spiritual—is about wholeness. This is the message we should be getting from our preachers, politicians, doctors, teachers, and therapists. What a rare, welcome, and timely message."

— Rev. Davidson Loehr,
author of *America, Fascism, and God*

"Bruce Levine exposes our unhealthy way of life. He argues convincingly that modern medicine—marvel that it is—cannot save us from the pains and struggles that come with living and dying. His is a trenchant, though not ideological, critique of 'powers and principalities' that prey upon depression, powers that have greatly increased in our lifetime. His simple calls to restore lost communal and personal practices ring true. I plan to share this book with church members fighting depression or tempted to despair."

— Rev. Randy Cooper,
United Methodist pastor (Ripley, TN)

"*Surviving America's Depression Epidemic* offers a fresh perspective on what ails America, the 'community malnourishment' that fuels dispirited morale, disconnectedness, and a frantic search for meaning. Dr. Levine challenges us to look past diagnoses and labels, reminding us that community and horizontal connections inherently offer the balance with which our souls can be nourished, helping us discern lasting paths to healing and wholeness in American life."

—Rabbi Lewis H. Kamrass,
Isaac M. Wise Temple (Cincinnati, OH)

"Levine is the smartest, most level-headed guy around when it comes to depression, and it comes from years of clinical practice, not ivory-towered theory."
— Kirkpatrick Sale, contributing editor for *The Nation*
and author of *Human Scale* and *After Eden*

Surviving America's Depression Epidemic

MAR   2008

362.1968527 L578
Levine, Bruce E.
Surviving America's
 depression epidemic

MID-CONTINENT PUBLIC LIBRARY
North Oak Branch
8700 N. Oak Trafficway
Kansas City, MO 64155   **NO**

NO 2

Surviving America's Depression Epidemic

How to Find
MORALE, ENERGY, AND COMMUNITY
in a World Gone Crazy

BRUCE E. LEVINE, Ph.D.

CHELSEA GREEN PUBLISHING COMPANY
WHITE RIVER JUNCTION, VERMONT

MID-CONTINENT PUBLIC LIBRARY
North Oak Branch
8700 N. Oak Trafficway
Kansas City, MO 64155

NO

MID-CONTINENT PUBLIC LIBRARY - QU

3 0003 00025547 9

Copyright © 2007 by Bruce E. Levine. All rights reserved.
No part of this book may be transmitted or reproduced in any form by any means
without permission in writing from the publisher.

Project Manager: Collette Leonard
Copy Editor: Nancy King
Proofreader: Nancy Ringer
Indexer: Melanie Piper Krueger
Designer: Peter Holm, Sterling Hill Productions

Printed in the United States
First printing, August 2007
10 9 8 7 6 5 4 3 2 1

Library of Congress Cataloging-in-Publication Data
Levine, Bruce E., 1956-
  Surviving America's depression epidemic : how to find morale, energy, and
community in a world gone crazy / Bruce E. Levine.
     p. ; cm.
  Includes bibliographical references.
  ISBN 978-1-933392-71-4
  1. Depression, Mental—United States. 2. Depression,
Mental—Treatment—United States—Evaluation. 3. Self-acceptance. I.
Title.
  [DNLM: 1. Depressive Disorder—therapy—United States. 2.
Culture—United States. 3. Depressive Disorder—epidemiology—United
States. 4. Self Concept—United States. WM 171 L665s 2007]

  RC537.L479 2007
  362.196'8527—dc22

2007023897

Our Commitment to Green Publishing
Chelsea Green sees publishing as a tool for cultural change and ecological stewardship.
We strive to align our book manufacturing practices with our editorial mission and to
reduce the impact of our business enterprise on the environment. We print our books
and catalogs on chlorine-free recycled paper, using soy-based inks whenever possible.
This book may cost slightly more because we use recycled paper, and we hope you'll
agree that it's worth it. Chelsea Green is a member of the Green Press Initiative
(www.greenpressinitiative.org), a nonprofit coalition of publishers, manufacturers, and
authors working to protect the world's endangered forests and conserve natural
resources.
   Surviving America's Depression Epidemic was printed on 55# Natures Natural, a
50 percent post-consumer-waste recycled, old-growth-forest-free paper supplied by
Maple-Vail.

Chelsea Green Publishing Company
Post Office Box 428
White River Junction, Vermont 05001
(802) 295-6300
www.chelseagreen.com

Contents

lead them down certain paths. The term *depression* so pervades our culture that I cannot escape its use. However, when I am in emotional pain and without the energy to act constructively, I consider myself demoralized rather than depressed. *Depression* reminds me that I am depressing my pain and my being—this I need no reminder of. *Demoralized* reminds me that I am lacking morale, and *morale* is exactly the word I need to be reminded of when I am down in the dumps. It heightens my awareness to that which is energizing and inspiring. Morale is the emotional experience of cheerfulness, confidence, and zeal in the face of hardship. Without morale, difficult tasks seem impossible to accomplish; with morale, those same tasks can feel challenging and fun. When I think about morale, I am reminded that an individual can inspire a community, a community can energize an individual, and we can all remoralize one another.

Much of what I will spell out is increasingly neglected in the education of mental health professionals. Today I would give most professional training programs failing grades in the following areas necessary for revitalization:

- *Regaining morale.* The demoralized need people skilled at the craft of transforming immobilization to energy, and they need to learn the craft of self-energizing.
- *Understanding depression.* Depression is a "strategy" for shutting down pain, a strategy that can result in the depressing of one's being and a vicious cycle of more pain and repeated depression.
- *Healing the source of depression.* The unhealed need helpers skilled at the craft of healing emotional wounds, and they need to learn the craft of self-healing.
- *Distinguishing self-acceptance from self-absorption.* While the self-absorption associated with extreme consumerist society is one source of depression, self-acceptance provides the security necessary for connecting with the whole of life, which is an antidote to depression.
- *Teaching the essentials of relationships.* Beyond simplistic communication skills, depressed people often need a

deeper wisdom about friendship, intimacy, family, and community.

- *Reforming society.* Whether people are successful or not in shaping a less depressing world, they are often rewarded with community and vitality when they go beyond their private sphere.

Many people I have known who are diagnosed with depression are more gentle than the world around them. It saddens me when unhappy people who have become so despondent that they consider suicide view themselves as weak or sick. If death feels more attractive than life, it means nothing more than the fact that one's present pain feels unbearable.

There is no more scary topic for mental health professionals than suicide. The book *Suicide: The Forever Decision* (1992) by psychologist Paul G. Quinnett is not only compassionate but candid about mental health professionals' anxiety: "[M]ost of us do the conservative thing when we have an actively suicidal person on our hands; we lock him or her up. Whether this is always for 'their own good' or 'our own good,' I can't say—maybe it is a bit of both." In many nonconsumer cultures, a person seriously considering suicide would be watched by loved ones until the self-destructive impulses had passed; but in societies where moneymaking is prioritized over all else, hospital or prison staffs are employed to guard against a suicide attempt.

Books about depression often start off with a disclaimer such as this: "If you are considering suicide, immediately seek help from a mental health professional." From my experience, it would be only with great sarcasm that suicidal people would respond: "Gee, what a valuable suggestion! Why didn't I think of that?" I suppose instructing suicidal people to seek professional help makes the author *appear* responsible to those people not considering suicide. However, if suicidal, you usually know what you are *supposed* to do but are overwhelmed by pain. The last thing you need is another's anxiety, and if you're paying for it, it's enough to make you even more hopeless and angry. When your pain feels unbearable, it is likely that you desire someone who can bear your pain.

In the United States, if you are considering suicide, you are not alone. In 2000 it was estimated that every year, 750,000 people make a suicide attempt. That's over two thousand every day who give suicide a try. The U.S. Surgeon General, focusing on mental health in 1999, reported that suicide was the eighth leading cause of death and the third leading cause of death for teenagers and that the rate of teen male suicide had tripled since the 1960s. While many Americans are reluctant to criticize our way of life, it is clear that Happy Meals are not quite doing the trick.

I have talked to many extremely demoralized adults and teenagers who have been diagnosed with depression. When we humans are seriously depressed, no matter what our age, we routinely become self-absorbed. While depressed adults can pretend to care about another's presence, depressed adolescents are usually more genuine, and their self-absorption is often straightforward. Adolescents' blank faces and one-word replies make clear the futility of my probing. When I stop torturing them with questions, they usually stop torturing me with nothingness.

One day, instead of firing questions at a sixteen-year-old boy, I started to rant and rave about my views on society. He appeared relieved, as my pontifications meant less pressure on him to perform. He could remain silently self-absorbed in his own pain. I told him that I was ready to give a commencement speech at his high school. This got his attention. "Bruce, I don't think the principal will allow it. You'd probably start off your speech with that Mark Twain quote you like. The one that goes 'Never let your schooling get in the way of your education.'" I was pleased to discover that he had been listening to me. He agreed to hear my proposed commencement speech, and I began, "Parents, faculty, and students, there are two types of adults, and one day you students will become one type or the other. Type one, the vast majority of adults, spend all day thinking about two things: how to get other people's money, and how to keep other people from getting their money. Type two, the other kind, are . . . homeless." He laughed, and guessed that while most parents and teachers wouldn't appreciate this speech, most of the kids would like it—they wouldn't feel quite so badly about themselves for being scared of the world.

Before I met this young man, he had been treated by two other doctors with different antidepressants and his condition had worsened, the severity of his diagnosis deteriorating from "mild depressive disorder and doing poorly in school" to "major depression and suicidal ideations." It was heartbreaking for his mother to listen to her intelligent son say that he felt like a failure. The first time we met, he told me, "I must be unfixable, one of those incurable cases. I mean I've talked to other doctors and have had all different kinds of medicine." I told him that his conclusion of being incurable was only one possibility, but a more likely possibility was that none of those doctors took the time to get to know him, which could have made him even more depressed. He considered that for a few seconds, and agreed. He and his mother were convinced that medication had been a failure, and he wanted to stop taking his current antidepressant. I explained to them the dangers of abrupt withdrawal from antidepressants. Pharmaceutical companies once denied this withdrawal problem but today accept it and term it *antidepressant discontinuation syndrome*. To prevent potentially debilitating withdrawal symptoms, he cut back gradually.

Two months off his antidepressant, he was no longer demoralized, suicidal, or feeling like a failure. This is not to say he was walking around with a chronic grin. The opposite of depression is not so much happiness as vitality. He continued to dislike school and was distressed by his parents' ugly divorce, but he came to believe that his pain made sense, and he was no longer immobilized by it. He got a good part-time job, passed his classes, and made mature career plans. I took the time to get to know him, and I'd like to believe that I helped him with what I will talk about in the following pages, but it would be hubris to say this for certain. Science cannot unravel whether I helped him, or whether he would have gotten his act together without me.

In reflecting on the empirical research on depression, on my work with depressed people, on the memoirs and essays of people who have experienced depression, and on my own personal experience with demoralization, immobilization, and despair, it is difficult to deny the power of faith and belief—what scientists term "expectations" and the "placebo effect." In a 2004 study on the influence of patient expectations on the effectiveness of an experimental antidepressant, it was found that among depressed patients who expected that medication would be *very* effective, 90 percent had a positive response; while among those expecting medication to be *somewhat* effective, only 33 percent had a positive response. No depressed people were included in this study who expected the experimental drug to be *ineffective*, but such nonbelievers rarely tell me about having a positive response with antidepressants.

It has been my experience that to the extent that one has faith in the efficacy of *any* treatment or approach, one's likelihood—at least temporarily—of overcoming depression increases. By contrast, an absence of faith in anything is associated with chronic depression. People can choose to have faith in religion, philosophy, art, dietary supplements, or exercise. I have seen many different belief systems work to reduce despair. However, I do not advocate that you believe in *anything* for the sake of belief. *What* we believe in matters a great deal. The beliefs we choose determine in no small way what kind of people we are, what kind of friends we have, and what kind of effect we have on society.

The faith encouraged by consumer culture is a faith in money, technology, and consumer products, and it is a faith that often has significant adverse side effects, including addiction and withdrawal. Americans who don't share the faith of such a culture will likely feel alienated from society, and alienation—from either one's humanity or one's surroundings—is painful and can be a source of depression. I believe that many people feel alienated in consumer culture, and it is my hope that this book will help energize them to find others who share their beliefs and then together create community.

In the United States, mental health treatment is increasingly shaped by two powerful industries: giant pharmaceutical companies, often collectively referred to as Big Pharma (the industry's trade association is Pharmaceutical Research and Manufacturers of America or PhRMA), and insurance companies (and their managed-care bureaucracies). It is in the best interest of Big Pharma if people are prescribed drugs, and it is in the best interest of insurance companies if treatment is extremely brief. In addition to encouraging doctors to prescribe drugs, insurance companies also pressure psychotherapists to focus narrowly on what is easiest to do in a few sessions. Commonly, this means teaching "rational thinking" and "social skills." Ironically, these simplistic techniques require little in the way of a therapeutic relationship and can be learned through a book. Prior to the current era, psychotherapists were free to choose among many options. For example, one therapy—now threatened with extinction in the time-pressured world of managed care—consists of helping depressed people find *meaning* in their lives. Once, it was routinely accepted that meaninglessness was an important source of depression, but today, managed-care time restraints have resulted in denying and ignoring this reality.

Historically, the mental health profession has been a joke of sorts when it comes to morale boosting. Specifically, I recall the old joke: "How many psychiatrists does it take to change a light bulb? Only one, but the light bulb must want to change." Even before the time pressures of the managed-care era, many mental health professionals were quick to abdicate responsibility for patient immobilization. Today, most of them spend little time being frustrated. They simply write a prescription or refer to a drug prescriber. The new joke—not quite as funny—is, "How many psychiatrists does it take to change a light bulb? Only one, but the light bulb must be medication compliant." If you are immobilized and behaving self-destructively, I don't assume that you are irresponsible or in need of medication. One strong possibility is that you are not around anyone—even if you are seeing a mental health professional—who has the capacity to energize you.

What about the craft of healing? Mental health professionals increasingly view themselves more as technicians who provide medications and skills rather than healers who care about wholeness. Despite that, relationships still do occur in psychotherapy, and occasionally, sometimes even accidentally, so does healing. However, in our time-pressured era, even more prevalent than simplistic therapy is a procedure called *medication management*. A typical "med management" session consists of checking symptoms and updating prescriptions, and recipients tell me that they are usually in and out with a new prescription in ten or fifteen minutes. They also tell me that it's common for med managements to be scheduled every two or three months, and that during these appointments, the doctor often needs to peek at their files to remember their names. In such assembly-line treatment, there is virtually no chance of a relationship forming, and gone is even the accidental possibility of healing through another's humanity.

In the training of mental health professionals, the revitalizing component of reviving community is all too often neglected. There is no greater antidepressant than focusing beyond one's private sphere to a societal concern. Whatever the scale, mental health professionals need to encourage community building of some kind. People who engage in life-affirming change have a greater chance to connect with like-minded others, and they are rewarded with greater vitality.

A major reason for writing this book is my conclusion that standard psychiatric treatments for depression are, for many people, unsustainable. The latest research shows that antidepressants often work no better than placebos or no treatment at all, can cause short-term and long-term adverse effects that may be as or more problematic than the original problem, can result in drug tolerance (an increasing need for higher dosage), and can promote dependency on pharmaceutical and insurance corporations. Moreover, antidepressants and other mental health industry treatments divert all of us from examining the unsustainable aspects of society that create the social conditions for depression. In this book, I am speaking to those who feel alienated from an increasingly extremist consumer culture and who are seeking genuine community. And I am speaking to those who have already rejected standard psychiatric theories and treatments of depression and are seeking alternative explanations and solutions.

The U.S. Surgeon General reported in 1999: "Nearly two-thirds of all people with a diagnosable mental disorder do not seek treatment." The reason for this, Americans often hear, is "the stigma of mental illness." This is certainly the explanation provided by the American Psychiatric Association, the National Alliance for the Mentally Ill, and other mental health institutions that are financially linked to pharmaceutical companies—collectively referred to in this book as "the mental health establishment." However, a recent poll suggests that the reason for this disinclination toward psychiatric treatment, at least for some Americans, is simply a lack of confidence in psychiatrists. A December 2006 Gallup poll asked Americans about the "honesty and ethical standards" of different professions. The percentage of Americans reported to have a positive opinion of nurses was 84 percent, and for clergy it was 58 percent; but for psychiatrists it was only 38 percent—much lower than the 69 percent positive rating for other medical doctors.

While some of what I will say is not controversial, much will be cultural and professional heresy—but I believe it is necessary. How else can this epidemic of depression be turned around without letting go of cultural arrogance and professional pretensions?

Surviving America's Depression Epidemic

We're Lost, but We're Making Good Time: Marketing, Myths, Science, and Society

Many critics of the pharmaceutical industry's undue influence retell this allegory: A drunken professor, having lost his watch, searched a single area of the street that was illuminated by a streetlamp until a young man confronted him.

"Your watch is obviously not where you are looking for it," said the young man.

"I know," said the professor. "I think I lost it on the other side of the street."

"Then why do you continue to look here?" asked the young man.

"Because that's where the streetlamp is."

I begin by describing how most of the "streetlamps" used by the general public and doctors to illuminate mental health information are powered by the pharmaceutical industry. I then discuss the myths and realities of antidepressant medications, talk therapy, characteristics of depressed people, and the "chemical imbalance" theory of depression. The impact of society and culture on mental health is routinely neglected in standard psychiatry books, and therefore much of this chapter is devoted to examining what in American society (and other consumer cultures) may be contributing to escalating rates of depression.

Drug Marketing

In 2000 an ABC News poll found: "One in eight American adults had taken Prozac or a similar antidepressant. . . . Among nonusers, moreover, 25 percent reported that a close friend or relative had taken such medication." Today if you were to tell a physician in the United States that you are depressed, you may not leave that appointment with a prescription, but it is likely that you would be apprised of the antidepressant option.

"Ask your doctor" drug commercials started flooding the public airwaves in 1997. That year the U.S. Food and Drug Administration (FDA) changed the rules for broadcast advertising, no longer requiring *full* information about side effects (which had previously made it problematic for drug companies to run a thirty-second spot). It was a great victory for Big Pharma, which was well aware of studies showing that the majority of physicians are likely to comply with requests for drugs from patients who have seen media advertisements.

In 2001, the Associated Press ("Drug Firms Turn to Celebs: Spots Blur Line between Ads, News") reported how celebrities are paid to mention specific drugs in media interviews: "In one campaign, former gymnast Bart Conner was paid to discuss how he was treating his osteoarthritis with Celebrex, made by Pfizer . . . [but] ABC's *Good Morning America* did not make clear that Mr. Conner was paid. Todd Polkes, a spokesman for ABC, said his operation was unaware of the relationship. Pfizer also has paid Julie Krone, a former female jockey who retired last year, to promote Zoloft, an antidepressant."

Less-than-candid celebrity spokespeople are not illegal, and neither is the drug-company practice of funding advocacy organizations such as the National Alliance for the Mentally Ill (NAMI). But in 2002, one drug company moved from the legal-but-morally-questionable to a new realm. With Prozac's patent having run out, its manufacturer, Eli Lilly, began marketing a new drug, Prozac Weekly. Lilly sales representatives in Florida gained access to "confidential" patient information records and, unsolicited, mailed out free samples of Prozac Weekly. Though they targeted primarily patients diagnosed with depression who were receiving competitor antidepressants, at least one Prozac Weekly sample was mailed to a sixteen-year-old boy with no history of depression or antidepressant use. While American society has grown cynical of corporate manipulations, this was so over the top that it resulted in a *60 Minutes II* story and lawsuits.

Marketing to patients is just the tip of the promotional iceberg, as the bulk of drug-company marketing dollars is spent directly on doctors. The majority of antidepressant prescriptions are written by physicians other than psychiatrists (especially primary care physicians such as family practitioners and pediatricians), and drug companies have been very effective in gaining their trust. In one study, 58 percent of family practitioners reported that the sales representative from the pharmaceutical company was their source of information for the last drug they prescribed (four times more than any other source mentioned).

In addition to sales representatives delivering free samples and gifts along with their pitches, there are many other powerful techniques that pharmaceutical companies use to ensure that doctors and researchers remain on their piece of the street. These techniques have been documented by many journalists as well as Marcia Angell, physician and former editor in chief of *The New England Journal of Medicine*, in her book *The Truth About the Drug Companies* (2004), which includes chapters with titles such as "The Hard Sell . . . Lures, Bribes, and Kickbacks" and "Marketing Masquerading as Education."

One of Angell's examples of drug-company influence on psychiatrists is the head of the psychiatry department at Brown University Medical School, who made over $500,000 in one year consulting for drug companies that make antidepressants. Angell remarks, "When *The New England Journal of Medicine*, under my editorship, published a study by him and his colleagues of an antidepressant agent, there wasn't enough room to print all the authors' conflict-of-interest disclosures. The full list had to be put on the website."

These are a few of Big Pharma's streetlamps:

- Funding university psychiatry departments. In 2005, the *Boston Globe* reported that Harvard Medical School's psychiatry department at Massachusetts General Hospital received $6.5 million from four drug companies.
- Sponsoring conferences and continuing education for doctors in attractive locales; providing transportation, lodgings, and meals; and, according to the *Washington Post* in 2002, offering cash gifts as high as $2,000.
- Advertising in professional journals to such a degree that many of these journals are highly dependent on Big Pharma dollars.

- Funding events and activities for professional organizations such as the American Psychiatric Association.
- Paying well-known physicians and researchers to be speakers and consultants.
- Funding research that is likely to produce favorable results for the pharmaceutical company's product and suppressing negative results that show its drugs to be ineffective or unsafe.
- Providing high-paying industry jobs to former helpful governmental officials, such as those from the FDA, the National Institute of Mental Health (NIMH), and Congress.

Increasingly, the streetlamps by which all Americans—including doctors—get mental health information are lit and powered by drug companies. However, we do not necessarily have to be at the mercy of drug companies. While money dictates the flow of information in our society, it cannot yet completely bury truths.

The Battle over Antidepressants

Prior to the Prozac media blitz that began in 1988, far fewer Americans who picked up a book such as the one you're reading would have been interested in antidepressant drugs. A 1986 poll showed that only 12 percent of American adults were willing to take medication for depression, while 78 percent were willing to live with depression until it passed; but by 1998, 41 percent said they would take medication for depression (though when pollsters in 2000 informed Americans that safety studies on long-term use of antidepressants had not been conducted, only 28 percent were willing to take antidepressants for depression for an extended period of time). Between 1987 and 1997, the percentage of Americans in outpatient treatment for depression more than tripled, and of those in treatment, the percentage prescribed medication almost doubled. By 2004, U.S. antidepressant annual sales had grown to $11.2

billion, a dramatic increase from 1985, when annual sales were only $240 million.

On June 30, 2002, the *New York Times* reassessed the value of Prozac-type antidepressants, the so-called SSRIs (selective serotonin reuptake inhibitors) that include Zoloft, Paxil, Celexa, Lexapro, and Luvox. The lengthy front-page article discussed how these drugs no longer deserve the *miracle* label: "Yet even as the numbers have grown, it has become clear that the drugs are more prone to side effects and in some cases less effective than many people assumed. Many SSRIs cause sexual dysfunction. . . . Other patients complain of apathy and emotional flatness. 'All it did was make me feel like I had no emotions,' said Zachary Howard, 22, of Boston, who took Zoloft for a month in high school. 'I felt like a zombie.'"

For those who are neither prescribers nor users, it may be difficult to understand how this article could be so enraging for antidepressant advocates. Mental suffering has had such a long history of being trivialized or viewed as sin or weakness that some get defensive when they hear any criticism of mental health authorities and their treatments. They confuse criticism of mental health institutions with a belittling of mental suffering. So let me say this very loudly: Quite the opposite from trivializing or belittling it, I think mental suffering can be so horrific that I have spent much of my life trying to understand and alleviate it. I am not trying to persuade anyone to stop using drugs. I strongly believe in the freedom of informed choice. I believe that doctors have an obligation not only to be completely open and honest about the scientific value of drugs, the downsides, and alternative paths but also to reveal personal values that might create bias.

There are many people who feel their psychiatric medications are helpful. They are quick to point out that numerous drugs have side effects and that the benefits outweigh the adverse effects. Andrew Solomon's *The Noonday Demon* (2001) articulates the message of this group. Solomon, a writer, is to be commended for divulging, "It is hard for me to write without bias about the pharmaceutical companies." (His father, to whom the book is dedicated, is the CEO of Forest Laboratories, U.S. distributor of Celexa.) Solomon reports, "I have been on, in various combinations and at various doses, Zoloft, Paxil,

Navane, Effexor, Wellbutrin, Serzone, BuSpar, Zyprexa, Dexedrine, Xanax, Valium, Ambien, and Viagra," and he adds that a specific "cocktail" (Solomon's term) of Effexor, Wellbutrin, BuSpar, and Zyprexa allowed him to write *The Noonday Demon*. Solomon strongly believes that for himself and others who suffer from serious depression, medication is usually required. Writing about drug critics such as psychiatrist Joseph Glenmullen, author of *Prozac Backlash* (2000), Solomon minces no words: "[T]he ludicrous assertions made in such stridently foolish books as *Prozac Backlash* cannot be taken for more than pandering to the cheapest fears of an apprehensive audience. I deplore the cynics who keep suffering patients from the essentially benign cures that might give them back their lives." This echoes psychiatrist Peter Kramer, who, in *Listening to Prozac* (1993), describes critics of antidepressants as afflicted with "pharmacological Calvinism."

In another camp, there is a significant number of professionals who have mixed feelings about antidepressants. Psychologist and antidepressant user Lauren Slater gives voice to this group in *Prozac Diary* (1998). Slater describes her initial experience of taking Prozac as "miracle tinged." Although this euphoria soon wore off, she reports that Prozac reduced her depression and anxiety for several years. However, Slater also tells us how tolerance developed, which her doctor called "Prozac poop-out," and she had to increase her dosage from 20 mg to 80 mg to get the same effect. Slater is clearly angry about not being told at the onset of treatment about the tolerance or poop-out phenomenon. She comes to see herself as "drug dependent" and is troubled by diminished sexual desire, memory difficulties, and other intellectual deficits. But by book's end, she remains ambivalent: "My cognition may be fraying, my libido may be down, I may lose language. Prozac is a medicine that takes much away, but its very presence in my life has been about preserving as well as decaying." At one time, psychologists were more critical of psychiatric drugs than psychiatrists, but Lauren Slater is representative of a great shift that has taken place among psychologists. The American Psychological Association is fighting to gain prescription rights for psychologists, and in 2002 psychologists won that right in New Mexico.

A third camp is represented by Harvard psychiatrist Joseph

Glenmullen (whom Solomon excoriated). Glenmullen, an SSRI prescriber, came to believe that Prozac and other SSRIs are not, as Solomon describes, "essentially benign cures." In *Prozac Backlash*, endorsed by a former president of the American Psychiatric Association, Glenmullen has this to say about Prozac and other SSRIs: "Withdrawal syndromes—which can be debilitating—are estimated to affect up to 50 percent of patients." Even more ominous, based on his own clinical experience and review of the research, Glenmullen warns about the long-term effects of SSRIs: "Neurological disorders including disfiguring facial and whole body tics, indicating potential brain damage, are an increasing concern with patients on the drugs." However, Glenmullen continues to prescribe antidepressants—albeit with much trepidation.

There is a fourth camp that has no ambivalence in its denouncement of antidepressants. Perhaps the most well-known spokesperson for this group is psychiatrist Peter Breggin. Breggin, a former teaching fellow at Harvard Medical School and consultant with the NIMH, is unequivocally opposed to calling Prozac and other antidepressants "medication," and he assists patients who choose to withdraw from them. A decade before Glenmullen, Breggin warned the public in *Toxic Psychiatry* (1991) of the tolerance, dependency, withdrawal, and brain damage associated with antidepressants and other psychiatric drugs, and he further detailed his findings in *Talking Back to Prozac* (1994). Breggin sees a psychiatric profession that is now less than benign, having virtually merged with the pharmaceutical industry and created what he terms a "psycho-pharmaceutical complex." He has testified against pharmaceutical companies in lawsuits and opposed the mental health establishment in congressional hearings.

I listen to what Solomon, Kramer, Slater, Glenmullen, and Breggin have to say because each represents a significant constituency (and I believe it highly unfortunate that the mental health establishment has attempted to smear and marginalize its critics). However, my perspective has been most formed by the empirical research on depression, by my clinical work with depressed people, by my own personal experience of depression, and by my observations of an increasingly depressing society and culture. Although I am critical of antidepressants, my greatest passions are not aroused by the drug issue. Having read pro-drug books by both patients and doctors, I've discovered that it is far more than just drugs we disagree on—it is the very nature of life (which I will detail). And having read antidrug books by both patients and doctors, I've discovered that many of those who are unbridled in their criticism of psychiatry are far too tame in their criticism of society and culture. While I am clearly troubled by the enormous increases in the use of antidepressants and other psychiatric drugs, I am not advocating a prohibition of them. I am for abolishing the hypocrisies that surround these drugs—hypocrisies that not only hamper the development of individuals but also sabotage the rehumanization of an increasingly dehumanizing society (more later on these hypocrisies). I try never to criticize those who believe in drugs as right for themselves, as I strongly believe in the philosophy of "live and let live." However, when drug enthusiasts proselytize others and withhold information in order to encourage the use of drugs, I think that is a very different matter.

Antidepressant Realities and Misconceptions

In the spring of 2002, while waiting for my wife at her physician's office, I spotted a drug representative. He worked for Pfizer and his product line included Zoloft. I told him, "Things must be a little tough for you these days with that *JAMA* study that just came out. Isn't it hard to sell Zoloft when the study shows that the placebo did slightly *better* than Zoloft—and the Zoloft did *no better* than St. John's wort?" If looks could in fact kill, I would have been a dead man.

In April 2002, the *Journal of the American Medical Association* (*JAMA*) published a study that addressed this question: While many people report effectiveness for Zoloft and the herb St. John's wort, are these substances any more effective than a sugar-pill placebo? The *JAMA* study reported that a positive "full response" occurred in 32 percent of the placebo-treated patients, *better* than the 25 percent positive full response of the Zoloft-treated patients or the 24 percent positive full response of the St. John's wort-treated patients.

The scientific effectiveness of all antidepressants—not just Zoloft—is now in serious doubt. In July 2002, *Newsweek* reported on still another research investigation on antidepressants: "A new study concludes that America's favorite antidepressants are little better than sugar pills." This investigation, reported in the American Psychological Association's journal *Prevention & Treatment*, was an analysis of forty-seven studies that had been sponsored by drug companies on Prozac, Paxil, Zoloft, Effexor, Celexa, and Serzone. Many of these studies had not been published but all had been submitted to the FDA, so University of Connecticut psychology professor Irving Kirsch and his research team used the Freedom of Information Act to gain access to the data. Kirsch discovered that in the majority of the trials, the antidepressant failed to outperform a sugar-pill placebo (and in the trials where the antidepressant did outperform the placebo, the advantage was slight). Kirsch titled this *Prevention & Treatment* article "The Emperor's New Drugs."

Many people swear by their antidepressants, but in order to separate what part of a reported positive effect is caused by the drug from that which is brought about by mere expectations, science requires that the drug be compared with a *proper* placebo. What makes matters worse for antidepressant advocates is the fact that in both the *JAMA* study and the studies analyzed in *Prevention & Treatment,* the dice were loaded in favor of the drugs and against the placebo. Specifically, proper drug research requires that neither subject nor experimenter knows who is getting the drug and who is getting the placebo (a true double-blind control). The studies mentioned above used *inactive* placebos such as sugar pills (which don't create side effects), and subjects could more easily guess whether they were getting the actual drug. In order to make it more difficult to guess correctly, an *active* placebo (which creates side effects) should be used. In 2000, a *Psychiatric Times* article concluded: "In fact, when antidepressants are compared with active placebos, there appear to be no differences in clinical effectiveness." The use of improper placebos is just one technique that drug company studies use to make drugs look more effective than they really are, but even with such dice loading, antidepressants have not fared well.

In March 2006, the NIMH triumphantly announced that 50 percent of depressed people saw remission of symptoms in a two-step treatment study (which ultimately would include four steps) that it called Sequential Treatment Alternatives to Relieve Depression (STAR*D). Specifically, depressed patients who failed to respond to Celexa in step one then received, in a second step, other drugs in place of or in addition to Celexa. STAR*D researchers, who received consulting and speaker fees from the pharmaceutical companies that manufacture the antidepressants studied in STAR*D, acknowledged that the treatment provided in STAR*D was exceptional, as there was a "relentless effort to optimize the dose." Despite this, at each treatment step of STAR*D, remission occurred in less than a third of the patients. In every STAR*D treatment step, remission rates were lower than or equal to the customary placebo performance in other antidepressant studies, but to the exasperation of many scientists, there was no placebo control in this $35 million U.S.-taxpayer-funded STAR*D study. And in the same time it took to complete steps one and two of STAR*D—slightly over six months—previous research shows that depressed people receiving *no treatment at all* have a spontaneous remission rate of 50 percent. So the NIMH's loudly trumpeted results of the first two stages of STAR*D were in fact no better than the results of a placebo or the results of no treatment at all. STAR*D researchers then offered a third and fourth treatment for patients who failed prior ones, but for each of these steps, remission rates plummeted to below 14 percent. However, in November 2006, STAR*D researchers again exasperated many scientists, this time by failing to incorporate the *relapse* rate (for patients who at previous steps were considered to have been successfully treated) into their overall results. If one takes into account STAR*D's extremely high relapse rate, the actual cumulative remission rate of the four treatment steps was no higher, and probably lower, than 43 percent.

In clinical practice, it is a common occurrence for doctors to switch antidepressants after a patient reports that his or her first antidepressant didn't work or when a second one stops working. And patients often don't inform their doctors when their third or fourth drug fails. Why? One reason is simple politeness—not wanting to be seen as ungrateful or to cause frustration for their doctor. Another less common reason is that some patients are aware that the next recommended step after multiple medication failures may well be electroconvulsive therapy (ECT), commonly referred to as shock treatment—which they want no part of.

What I hear from many people reflecting years down the road on their antidepressant treatment are some positive testimonials and some horror stories, but most commonly they tell me: "It worked for a while but eventually did nothing for me" or "It was mostly a waste of time." On July 16, 2005, *BMJ* (formerly known as the *British Medical Journal*), in a major review article ("Efficacy of Antidepressants in Adults"), summarized the research on the long-term outcome of antidepressants this way: "Antidepressants have not been convincingly shown to affect the long-term outcome of depression or suicide rates."

Today antidepressants are increasingly used by Americans who are not severely depressed, and they are being prescribed on a long-term basis. The previously mentioned 2000 ABC News poll reported that 46 percent of antidepressant users had taken them for a year or more. Some doctors are troubled by this because of the adverse effects and prefer prescribing them only to the seriously depressed for short-term usage.

The theory of short-term usage is that while using antidepressants as a jump-start, one is *also* in counseling or therapy, learning healthier thoughts and behaviors, and that one can then utilize this new learning when off the drugs. A similar rationale was offered in the 1980s by a group of marital therapists who used Ecstasy to help spouses open up with one another. No doubt some antidepressant users may feel, as an advocate of this school of thought describes, "less easily derailed by setbacks and rejection." However, I am not convinced that drug-induced experiences get integrated into one's personality when off drugs. I have rarely met a shy alcohol abuser who, having taken interpersonal risks when using alcohol, could then integrate those skills when sober; and of those using psychiatric drugs, I see few changes that are retained when they are no longer taking these drugs. But this is an increasingly moot debate, as the ABC News poll on antidepressant use also reports: "Most of those who've taken such drugs—59 percent—say they have not had counseling or therapy along with the medication."

Perhaps the most dangerous misconception is that the seriously depressed can better be prevented from suicide by antidepressants than any other therapeutic technique. Not only is there no such proof, but SSRI antidepressants actually increase suicidal thoughts and behavior for some patients. In 2004, the FDA ordered that antidepressants carry a "black box" warning, the government's strongest warning, alerting consumers to the risk of increased suicidal thoughts and behavior among children and teens taking them. Research data, previously unpublished, revealed that children given antidepressants were almost twice as likely to have suicidal thoughts and behaviors as those who took placebos. In 2003, the British Medicines and Healthcare Products Regulatory Agency (the MHPRA is the British equivalent to the FDA) had gone further, telling physicians that depressed patients under eighteen should not be prescribed most antidepressants; the MHPRA concluded the lack of safety far outweighed any evidence of effectiveness. Recently, the FDA has been pressured by media exposure to focus on the effects of antidepressants on adult suicidality. In December 2006 an FDA expert panel accepted new research that showed antidepressants more than doubled the risk of suicidal behavior in patients aged eighteen to twenty-four (though the FDA panel believed that risks diminish as adults age); and in May 2007 the FDA proposed that antidepressant manufacturers include a black-box warning of increased suicidality during initial antidepressant use for this eighteen to twenty-four age group. Critics of the FDA questioned how it could be that at age twenty-five the suicidality threat would disappear.

One explanation for increased suicidal thoughts and behaviors is that some antidepressant users experience the adverse side effects of *mania* or *akathisia* (an intense restlessness and agitation), which, when combined with despair, can result in destructive or bizarre behaviors. While some people who make a suicide attempt intentionally use alcohol for "liquid courage," antidepressants can unintentionally also provide a disinhibiting function.

Some antidepressant users who have behaved bizarrely report that their very "self" disappeared. Fifty-year-old former Major League relief pitcher Jeff Reardon is one example. After the death of his son,

Reardon began taking antidepressants and other psychiatric drugs. He soon became emotionally unstable and ultimately robbed a Palm Beach, Florida, jewelry store in December 2005. When he was apprehended at a nearby restaurant, he offered no resistance. An embarrassed Reardon said, "I don't think I've ever had a speeding ticket before, for crying out loud," and he blamed his actions on the medication he was taking for depression. Reardon had made over $11 million in his baseball career and was reported not to be having financial problems. The court found him not guilty by reason of insanity.

Politically Correct and Politically Incorrect Drugs

The Spanish conquistadors discovered that the Incas, whom they had conquered and enslaved, chewed coca leaves when they were lacking food and needed energy for a task or when they simply wanted to feel better. When the conquistadors initially forbade the use of coca leaves, this reduced the Incas' productivity in the silver mines. Eventually, the prohibition was withdrawn and coca use for the Incas was encouraged. Ritalin, Adderall, and other amphetamines affect the same chemical messengers (neurotransmitters) as do coca leaves, cocaine, and crack, and all of these drugs are called *psychostimulants*. I have talked to many teenagers who because of their lack of interest in school had been prescribed Ritalin-like medications. Upon hearing about the Incas, these young people often identify with them.

In the history of psychiatry, alcohol as well as several drugs that are now illegal were once considered "medication." Sigmund Freud used cocaine as medication to treat depression. Later, amphetamines were used. Alcohol was a recommended treatment for anxiety as late as the 1940s. In the 1950s and early 1960s, psychiatrist Oscar Janiger used LSD to treat the neuroses of Hollywood stars and other celebrities. As noted, Ecstasy was used in marital counseling during the 1980s, and today researchers are studying it as a possible treatment for post-traumatic stress disorder.

Chemists consider psychiatric medications, illegal mood-altering drugs, and alcohol all to be *psychotropic* (or *psychoactive*) drugs. The mass media strives for political correctness and seldom reports that prescription psychotropics, illegal psychotropics, and alcohol are actually all in the same category.

SSRIs such as Prozac, Zoloft, Paxil, Celexa, Lexapro, and Luvox enhance the neurotransmitter serotonin. Ecstasy also enhances serotonin, although by a different mechanism (you won't likely feel the same using SSRIs as you would using Ecstasy in part because Ecstasy has a quicker, shorter-lasting pop). Both cocaine and amphetamines enhance the neurotransmitters norepinephrine, serotonin, and dopamine. The antidepressant Effexor enhances norepinephrine and serotonin, and the antidepressant Wellbutrin enhances dopamine, and it's not uncommon (as in the case of Andrew Solomon) to be prescribed Effexor and Wellbutrin at the same time. Effexor in combination with Wellbutrin enhances the *same* neurotransmitters as cocaine (you won't likely feel the same, mainly due to the quicker impact and shorter half-life of cocaine).

In 1975, psychiatrist Lester Grinspoon in *The Speed Culture* astutely predicted: "Drug companies probably will continue to produce increasingly sophisticated and disguised amphetamines, and these 'new' drugs undoubtedly will be greeted with initial enthusiasm by the medical establishment until it is recognized that any drug with amphetamine-like CNS [central nervous system] stimulating properties almost invariably is just as toxic, potentially addictive, and therapeutically limited as [the amphetamines] Benzedrine or Dexedrine."

The mass media often reports positively on people who have used prescription psychotropics to help them function. However, it is politically incorrect to report on those who use alcohol and illegal psychotropics to help them function. But the word does get out. Author and journalist Eric Schlosser, investigating the meatpacking industry, discovered this: "The unrelenting pressure of trying to keep up with the line has encouraged widespread methamphetamine use among meatpackers. Workers taking 'crank' feel charged and self-confident, ready for anything." Social psychologist Stanton Peele has detailed how many professional athletes performed quite well when they were abusing alcohol and illegal drugs, and how some saw their performance statistics deteriorate following treatment and sobriety. Cary Grant described himself as a "horrendous" person who became a better one—"born again" in his words—by using LSD approximately one hundred times. In 2004, the mass media covered Miami Dolphins star running back Ricky Williams's announcement that he had found marijuana to be "ten times more helpful than Paxil." What made Williams's declaration difficult to ignore was that he had been a celebrity spokesman for GlaxoSmithKline, manufacturer of Paxil.

I have worked with many people who believed their alcohol and illegal psychotropic drugs helped them function. They often used them as sleep aids and to divert them from the unpleasantness of their jobs. I remember one factory worker telling me, "Yeah, I know I am an alcoholic, but I've got less of a problem than most everybody else working the floor. You try working for those bastards without using something. I went to rehab for alcohol and pot, and the first thing they do is give me some Valium and then Prozac. I know I was doing some bad shit, but they put me on some worse shit, so when I got out, I just went back to my old shit."

When I was getting a new roof, I noticed most of the crew smoked marijuana before they climbed to the top of my house. I was curious as to why they wouldn't be afraid of becoming uncoordinated, and I asked a friend in the construction business about this. He chuckled and said, "Once in a while they do fall, but mostly they know what they're doing and take just enough of a hit to reduce their fear. In my experience—which I can't claim is scientific—more than 50 percent of roofers are just a little stoned." In 2004, researchers Roger Nicoll and Bradley Alger detailed in *Scientific American* ("The Brain's Own Marijuana") how "the brain makes its own marijuana, natural compounds called endocannabinoids." In 2002, Lidia Wasowicz, the senior science writer for UPI, speculated ("Pot-Like Chemical Helps Beat Fear") about the future development of pot-like psychiatric drugs (related to the THC found in the cannabinoids marijuana and hashish) as a treatment for anxiety. Neuroscientist Pankaj Sah notes, "[I]t's worth considering that people [who] constantly use cannabis may be doing it for other reasons than just to 'get high'—perhaps they are experiencing some emotional problems which taking cannabis alleviates. Much the same way as some people drink alcohol to relieve anxiety."

One woman I know very well used Paxil when she was going through an abusive relationship that almost financially destroyed her. Another woman I know very well, in a similar situation, used cocaine. When I asked both what the drugs did for them, they had the same answer: "It took the edge off and helped me function." Both women worked in health care and knew the long-term dangers of psychotropic drugs, noticed the decreasing effectiveness of their drugs, and stopped taking them as soon as their luck and their circumstances changed.

Journalist and author Michael Pollan is a longtime critic of America's hypocrisy around psychotropic drugs. In 1999, in the *New York Times Magazine,* he wrote: "Historians of the future will wonder how a people possessed of such a deep faith in the power of drugs also found themselves fighting a war against certain other drugs with not-dissimilar powers. . . . The more we spend on our worship of the good drugs ($20 billion on psychoactive prescription drugs last year), the more we spend warring against the evil ones ($17 billion the same year). We hate drugs. We love drugs. Or could it be that we hate the fact that we love drugs?"

I have compassion for people who temporarily choose psychotropic drugs to "take the edge off." However, I have little respect for professionals who maintain hypocrisy, labeling one set of psychotropics as "modern medicine" used in "treatment" and the other set of psychotropics (which affect the same neurotransmitters) as "deadly drugs" used to "get high." What's troubling—besides the withholding of information on effectiveness and safety—is societal hypocrisy around their use. When we recognize that psychotropic prescription drugs are chemically similar to illegal psychotropic drugs and alcohol, and that all of these substances are used for similar purposes, we see two tragic hypocrisies: First, the classification of millions of Americans as *criminals* for using certain drugs, while millions of others, using essentially similar drugs for similar purposes, are seen as *patients.* And second, a denial of the societal realities that push increasing numbers to use these drugs at all.

Talk Therapy

I make a living providing talk therapy (psychotherapy), but what I am about to say may upset many of my fellow practitioners. It's the kind of stuff that most of them usually only admit privately. It's not that I think psychotherapy cannot be helpful, but I believe it is not a standardized, scientifically proven treatment. Rather, a psychotherapist's effectiveness is far more similar to a teacher's. Connect the right teacher with the right pupil, and all kinds of wonderful learning can happen; make a bad connection, and a pupil can be turned off from a subject for life. Likewise, when a patient connects with the right psychotherapist, good things can happen, while mismatches can be nonproductive or even counterproductive.

The research shows that mental health professionals with an MD, a PhD, or an MSW have no more success at talk therapy than nonprofessionals. The specific technique or school of psychotherapy is not all that significant when it comes to success rates. There is a great deal of research that confirms the commonsense idea that psychotherapy is more effective when there is a positive relationship between therapist and patient (referred to as *client* by some mental health professionals). If I get better results than other psychotherapists, it's not because I'm a PhD and a licensed clinical psychologist but because I have been rather clever about whom I take on as clients. People who seek my help often know something of what I am about, either through my books and articles or through referral sources who know me well. Common sense and the research tell us that *all* learning—and psychotherapy is essentially a certain kind of private tutoring—is much improved when teacher and pupil are on the same wavelength.

Most of the research I have seen comparing psychotherapy to antidepressants shows that both work about equally on depression, and when these treatments work, psychotherapy results in a somewhat lower relapse rate than antidepressants. Widely reported by the media in 2002 was a major NIMH-funded study comparing Paxil to cognitive therapy (one kind of psychotherapy). In this study, researcher Robert DeRubeis, chairman of the psychology department at the University of Pennsylvania, and his coresearchers found the following:

After four months, the improvement rates were identical for depressed patients treated with either Paxil or cognitive therapy. Ultimately, however, those who had improved with cognitive therapy had a lower rate of relapse than those who had improved with Paxil.

Although some reviews of the psychotherapy research conclude that there are benefits from therapy, similar to the research on antidepressants, other reviews show that psychotherapy works no better than the passage of time with no treatment at all. In science, if treatment works no better than a placebo or no treatment, it is considered ineffective. In life, if something has worked for you, then you consider it effective. So of course there are psychotherapy recipients who praise psychotherapy.

Psychotherapy advocates were delighted when *Consumer Reports* reported in 1995 that of patients polled on their past psychotherapy, approximately 90 percent said it was helpful. However, over the last thirty years, I've been doing my own polling among friends and acquaintances, and my personal results are a lot different from those of *Consumer Reports.* My findings are that the percentage of therapists described as truly helpful is roughly equivalent to the percentage of high school teachers who inspired the love of learning—which is to say that a minority of therapists had great things said about them by their former patients. I can only guess why my results are so different. Of *Consumer Reports'* 180,000 readers, only 7,000 subscribers responded, and of those, only 4,100 saw mental health professionals. Most people I've known who did not have a positive experience with psychotherapy would not have responded to *Consumer Reports'* lengthy one-hundred-plus questions—even with compensation.

Psychotherapy is difficult to study scientifically. While psychotherapy—like *any* treatment—often has a positive outcome, *scientific* effectiveness requires that a treatment be superior to a placebo. However, researchers have never solved the dilemma of how one creates a "psychotherapy placebo"—an event that appears to the patient, therapist, and researcher to be psychotherapy but is not psychotherapy. Another scientific problem is that research requires standardization, and any attempt to standardize psychotherapy alters the nature of it. Simply put, if you force a psychotherapist to behave in a uniform way, you have removed much of what is potentially beneficial about the therapeutic relationship. The uniqueness and complexities of human relationships are such that healthy relationships—ones with respect, trust, and affection—will never be achieved through any standardized formula.

Perhaps the most popular school of psychotherapy today—at least if one counts the titles of books published—is some form of *cognitive-behavioral* therapy, an array of techniques for confronting self-defeating thoughts and behaviors and replacing them with more positive ones. Increasingly rare are *Freudian* and *psychoanalytic* therapists who interpret the free associations of their couched patients, although many psychotherapists have a *psychodynamic* perspective that familial relationships and unconscious drives are important. Other major schools that have waxed and waned in popularity in the past thirty years include *client-centered* therapy, which emphasizes empathy, nondirective reflections, and creating a warm and accepting atmosphere; *interpersonal* therapies, which concentrate on relationships, including the interaction between the patient and the therapist; *gestalt* therapy, an array of techniques designed to engage the whole patient in the here-and-now; and various *existential* therapies, focusing on discovering purpose, meaning, and identity. Many therapists describe themselves as *eclectic*, borrowing from more than one of these and other schools.

I believe that therapists practicing any of these approaches—similar to musicians who are "covering" someone else's song—had better put their own being and style into it if they want to genuinely connect and have an impact. So whether I'm covering another school or doing my own original material, I always focus on being as authentic, transparent, and spontaneous as possible. The common complaints that I hear from people for whom previous mental health treatment was nonproductive or counterproductive are that their doctor or therapist was disengaged, impersonal, or even robotic; they were treated as objects; and rather than showing a concern for their whole person, the doctor/therapist focused entirely on their symptoms, which were labeled with different diagnoses and treated with behavioral manipulations and/or drugs.

What is truly therapeutic? My subjective experience is that it consists of authentic curiosity, compassion, and respect, and that it includes genuine reactions that validate a person's emotionality and humanity or that confront self-defeating and self-destructive actions. My style certainly cannot be codified into standardized procedures, laws, or dogma, as what I say is specific to a given person at a given moment in time. It is my experience that if I approach clients with authentic curiosity, compassion, and respect, even if my candid reactions are occasionally insensitive, clients usually cut me some slack.

One week during this writing, I met for the first time with two women in their early thirties, each of whom had previous mental health treatment.

One of these women was in emotional turmoil following a major loss, and she was concerned about her increased use of alcohol. She began crying while disclosing that when she was an adolescent, during her father's alcohol rehab hospitalization a social worker had told her, "Given your father's alcoholism, it is extremely likely that you will either become an alcoholic or marry an alcoholic." My genuine reaction to that story—which I told her—was, "Geez, given the choice between becoming an alcoholic and marrying one, I'd probably choose to become an alcoholic." With tears still rolling down her cheeks, she burst out laughing, and she had taken the first step in both releasing her fear of being doomed as well as healing some of her shame over her difficulty committing to an intimate relationship. She thanked me for not thinking she was so crazy that she needed drugs.

The other woman had been diagnosed with depression in her teens and since then had had multiple counterproductive psychiatric hospitalizations, which she resented and was embarrassed by. I was curious as to whether, during her hospitalization, she had been asked standard questions such as, "On a scale of one to ten, how depressed are you?" and if hospital staff were still attempting to get patients who were suicidal to sign a contract agreeing to tell someone if they were suicidal. When I asked if she had experienced those interventions, she responded, "All the time. I'd usually lie to them. You'd think they'd worry about the possibility of patients lying to them, but they just wrote down my response, and they would give me more drugs if I said higher numbers on the scale or they'd release me from the hospital if I signed the contract. It all seemed kind of silly to me." Her response made me chuckle, and my curiosity and genuine reactions encouraged her to tell me several funny stories about her psychiatric hospitalizations, which became less a source of resentment and embarrassment and more a source for a comedy routine.

It's my personal and professional experience that there is nothing more potentially therapeutic than a human relationship. But relationships need not be labeled as *psychotherapy* to be therapeutic. And relationships that are officially sanctioned as psychotherapy are often not therapeutic.

Depression, Critical Thinking, and Wisdom

One of the most renowned psychologists in American history is William James (1842–1910). James, who spent a considerable part of his life depressed, once wrote, "I take it that no man is educated who has never dallied with the thought of suicide." The modern American psychologist Martin Seligman concludes, "There is considerable evidence that depressed people, though sadder, are wiser."

Psychology and philosophy professor David Livingstone Smith reported in *Scientific American Mind* in 2005, "Several classic studies indicate that moderately depressed people actually deceive themselves less than so-called normal folks." These studies show that depressed people are *more* accurate than nondepressed people both in their assessment of their control over events and in judging people's attitudes toward them. Researchers Lauren Alloy and Lyn Abramson, studying nondepressed and depressed subjects who played a rigged game in which they had no actual control, found that nondepressed subjects overestimated their contribution to winning and only believed they had little control when losing, while depressed subjects more accurately evaluated their lack of control when losing or winning. And researcher Peter Lewinsohn found that depressed subjects judge other people's attitudes toward them more accurately than nondepressed subjects.

While many depressed people are critical thinkers, their rigid attachment to this mode can create difficulties for them. Critical thinking and an absence of self-deception are traits crucial for success in many areas of life, but they can result in two problems: First, a more accurate notion of how truly powerless one is in a situation (such as family or an organization) can result in a greater feeling of helplessness and depression. Second, this can also make one stubbornly resistant to much of what helps others. To the extent one has uncritical faith in a treatment, it is far more likely to be experienced as successful. To the extent that one is more skeptical about the effectiveness of treatment, one is less likely to experience its benefits.

I believe a wiser attitude to take toward the power of belief and faith is not to belittle it as *merely* a placebo effect. Rather, I think that a large part of transforming depression has to do with faith and belief. The good news is that today some doctors have adopted a new attitude toward faith, belief, and the placebo effect. They've come to realize that this phenomenon is so powerful that it can make all the difference with mental suffering and even in some cases of severe physical illness.

Many intelligent depressed people are not so wise when it comes to the issue of faith and belief. They want to *know*—not merely believe in—every aspect of their life. And they may know, statistically, that treatments for depression are not any more effective than a placebo. This can render these treatments ineffective for them. There are certain facts that people must accept, but there remains another part of the human experience that is open to belief and faith.

William James ultimately dealt with his despair by utilizing his capacity for *both* critical thinking and wisdom. While James embraced scientifically proven facts, he also came to accept that the "fact" of whether life was or was not worth living could not be proven by science. For such truths, James concluded that "faith in a fact can help create the fact" (in his famous essay "The Will to Believe"). James scholar John McDermott notes, "Having rejected suicide in favor of the possibility of a creative life unsupported by certitude, James developed a doctrine to sustain such belief." James came to "believe in belief," let go of his dallying with suicide, and wrote, "Life shall [be built in] doing and suffering and creating."

Chemical Imbalances and Dominoes

In 2002, the *New York Times* reported: "Researchers knew that anti-depressants seemed to raise the brain's levels of messenger chemicals called neurotransmitters, so they theorized that depression must result from a deficiency of these chemicals. Yet a multitude of studies failed to prove this precept."

The American Medical Association Essential Guide to Depression stated in 1998: "[T]he link between low levels of serotonin and depressive illness is unclear, as some depressed people have too much serotonin." Elliot Valenstein, professor emeritus of psychology and neuroscience at the University of Michigan, in *Blaming the Brain* (1998) pointed out that it is just as likely for people with normal serotonin levels to feel depressed as it is for people with abnormal serotonin levels, and that it is just as likely for people with abnormally *high* serotonin levels to feel depressed as it is for people with abnormally *low* serotonin levels. Valenstein concluded, "Furthermore, there is no convincing evidence that depressed people have a serotonin or norepinephrine deficiency."

Yet the general public continues to hear (through antidepressant commercials and from many mental health authorities) about the neurotransmitter deficiency theory of depression, and so it was news to many Americans when *Newsweek,* in a February 26, 2007, cover story about depression, reported: "For decades, scientists believed the main cause of depression was low levels of the neurotransmitters serotonin and norepinephrine. . . . [However, a] depressed brain is not necessarily underproducing something, says Dr. Thomas Insel, head of the National Institute of Mental Health—it's doing too much. . . . Instead of focusing on boosting neurotransmitters (the function of the antidepressants in the popular SSRI category such as Prozac and Zoloft), scientists are developing medications that block the production of excess stress chemicals." Pharmaceutical companies, however, have been so effective at marketing the neurotransmitter deficiency theory of depression that even though the NIMH has now retreated from this view, the general public and many doctors continue to believe it. The mental health establishment has not yet zealously publicized its newer depression theory—that excess stress chemicals (such as cortisol) can cause nerve cell damage—perhaps because it would confuse millions of patients who continue taking neurotransmitter-enhancing drugs (it would certainly upset the pharmaceutical companies that manufacture them).

Stress can stimulate the release of cortisol, which can negatively affect both body and mind. And many other medical conditions (such as anemia) can also result in symptoms of depression. However, the American Psychiatric Association's diagnostic manual, the *Diagnostic and Statistical Manual of Mental Disorders* (*DSM*), states that a patient should *not* be diagnosed with depression when the symptoms of depression are due to the "direct physiological effects of a substance (e.g., a drug of abuse, a medication) or a general medical condition (e.g., hypothyroidism)." If hypothyroidism is considered a medical condition, it's unclear why the overproduction of cortisol leading to nerve cell damage would not also be considered a medical condition.

A more glaring contradiction in the diagnosis of depression was brought to the public's attention on April 3, 2007, by both the *New York Times* ("Many Diagnoses of Depression May Be Misguided, Study Says") and the *Washington Post* ("Criteria for Depression Are Too Broad, Researchers Say"). Specifically, the *DSM* states that depression should *not* be diagnosed if the temporary symptoms of depression are caused by the death of a loved one; yet if the cause of depression is the loss of a relationship or the loss of a job, a person *can* be diagnosed with depression. This distinction appeared to the media as especially odd after a study published in April 2007 by the *Archives of General Psychiatry* showed that the symptom profiles for these two groups, who have experienced different kinds of loss, are virtually identical.

What about brain anomalies and depression? Soon after each announcement of a brain-scanning breakthrough that links depression to brain structure, other researchers have detected methodological flaws in these studies. In October 2005, the *New York Times* ("Can Brain Scans See Depression?") concluded, "After almost thirty years, researchers have not developed any standardized tool for diagnosing or treating psychiatric disorders based on imaging studies . . . imaging technology has not lived up to the hopes invested in it." Certainly, depression symptoms can be associated with the presence of drugs or certain brain abnormalities, but that is very different than saying that scientists have discovered a chemical or biological marker specific to the cause of a psychiatric disorder.

Though the American public continues to hear that depression, like diabetes, is caused by a chemical imbalance, even some antidepressant advocates such as Andrew Solomon have acknowledged that this is unproven. Solomon correctly points out, "Depression is *not* [his emphasis] the consequence of a reduced level of anything we can now measure."

Disease advocates say that though the scientific community has not yet established biochemical markers that can be used to diagnose depression, it would be irresponsible to wait until such markers are scientifically established before calling depression a disease, since that would make it difficult to get funding to continue scientific research.

While some mental health professionals and patients remain certain that depression will one day be firmly established as a disease with measurable biochemical markers, others believe that the terms *illness* and *disease* are metaphors—figures of speech used to describe a condition that people should consider *as serious as* an illness or disease. Among those who believe that it is metaphorical to call depression an illness, there is still another debate: Some believe it is a helpful metaphor; others believe it is not helpful.

Some people believe that although depression is not really a disease in the same manner as diabetes or cancer, it's still a good idea to call it a disease. They point out that in our society, if a problem isn't labeled as a disease, it becomes trivialized and insurance companies will not reimburse for treatment. They also believe that by calling something an illness, the suffering of shame and stigma can be mitigated. For some people, labeling a problem as a disease or illness does remove intolerance—at least temporarily. A friend once told me, "I don't think that ADD is really a physical disease because my kid can pay attention to what he's actually interested in. But when he does not listen to me or his teacher and I think he is just being stubborn, I want to strangle him. When I label his inattention as a disease, I don't take it so personally." A couple of months later, I asked my friend whether terming his son's inattention a disease was still providing him with increased tolerance. He said, "Not any more.

Now I want to strangle my kid and his damn ADD." The good news is that without any Ritalin or other psychostimulant drugs—or strangling—my friend's son grew out of his annoying behavior and did well in school, and the two now have an excellent relationship.

I don't oppose the use of metaphors. A metaphor can be very powerful. The right metaphor can take that which is confusing and help us see it more clearly. However, people should be very careful not to misuse metaphors. That's the moral of the following two pieces of history. When Hitler first began annexing territories, it would have been great if world leaders had invoked the metaphor of European countries toppling like dominoes. The domino metaphor or domino theory is very applicable to imperialistic nations and expansionistic corporations. With each territory or market they conquer, they grow more powerful, making it easier to conquer the next territory or market. The metaphor of dominoes toppling helps us see vividly a certain reality. Unfortunately, the domino theory was not applied early on to the Third Reich but was employed a generation later to a very different situation. During the Vietnam War, politicians and media who favored American involvement claimed that Vietnam was a domino in danger of being toppled by the Soviet Union and China, and if America let it fall, it would topple the Japan domino, which in turn would topple the Australia domino, ultimately toppling the Hawaii domino, the California domino, and so on. Critics who opposed the Vietnam War claimed that it was a civil war, not an imperialistic one, and that the domino metaphor falsified rather than illuminated reality. After North Vietnam toppled South Vietnam, it did not try to topple Japan or cause any other such domino effect that had been predicted. When applied to the Vietnam War, the domino metaphor distorted reality and contributed to the tragic deaths of nearly sixty thousand Americans and approximately two to three million Vietnamese. While the right metaphor can help us see a certain reality more vividly, the wrong metaphor can distort reality and result in tragedy.

I have met many people who were not helped by viewing their depression as a disease or illness. They tell me that shock treatment did nothing but destroy their memories, or that hopelessness ensued when one medication after another did not help. Patients who have been failed by such treatments talk about the adverse physiological effects of their treatments, but they also talk about something else. By becoming compliant patients to a doctor authority, they describe losing control over their lives. Depression is an experience of helplessness and hopelessness, and for these people, accepting depression as a disease made them feel even more helpless and hopeless.

Labeling their depression as a disease gives some people relief and others grief. Many people who believe depression is a medical disease often claim that those who reject this belief are guilty of trivializing depression. Ironically, people who believe that depression is not a disease—but rather a deeply painful and potentially tragic human reaction—think that those people who claim that depression is simply the result of faulty neurotransmitters are the ones guilty of misunderstanding and trivializing it.

Are Society and Culture Irrelevant to Depression?

During the years of intensive removal of German Jews to concentration camps, their rate of suicide is estimated to have been approximately fifty times higher than the rate for non-Jewish Germans who were not forced into concentration camps. Psychologist Roland Chrisjohn in *The Circle Game* (1997) notes: "In truth, does not the history of Jewish suicide during the holocaust, like the histories of suicide in the Arawaks, the Home Children, and the Marshallese Islanders, and countless other oppressed groups, teach us that suicide is in part a *normal human reaction to conditions of prolonged, ruthless domination?*" (Chrisjohn's emphasis.)

In the United States, Native Americans have the highest suicide rate among all ethnic groups, and suicide is the second leading cause of death among Native American adolescents. Prior to colonialism and their subjugation, suicide was a rare event among aboriginal peoples, restricted to the sick or elderly who felt they could no longer contribute. For Native Americans, social and cultural upheaval has resulted not only in depression and suicide but also in alcohol abuse and other destructive behaviors.

Societal disruption has not affected just aboriginal peoples. The rate of suicide for European nations at the beginning of the Industrial Revolution was significantly lower than it was when the Industrial Revolution shifted into high gear. For example, in France the suicide rate increased 355 percent between 1836 and 1890, and significant increases in suicide rates for this time period were also recorded in Prussia, England, and Sweden.

In the United States by the mid-1800s, per capita insanity was increasing at a higher rate than in European nations, according to the *Southern Literary Messenger*, a major periodical of that era, which in 1844 attempted to explain this phenomenon: "Life in our republic has all the excitement of an olympic contest. A wide arena is thrown open, and all fearlessly join in the maddening rush for the laurel wreath, or gold chaplet . . . [resulting in] sickness of hope deferred, ambition maddened by defeat, avarice rendered desperate by failure." By 1903 in the United States, approximately one in 500 was considered "disabled mentally ill," a number that increased by 1955 to one in 300, and sharply increased by 1987 to one in 75. And by 2003, one in 50 was considered disabled mentally ill.

In 2001 the director of the World Health Organization noted there was a greater prevalence of depression in high-income nations compared to poorer ones. Psychologist Oliver James points out that affluent, industrialized societies encourage rising expectations, but "when expectations outstrip real outcomes, we feel either aggressively resentful or depressed."

As Mexican immigrants accommodate to American society, their rate of "mental disorders" dramatically increases. In 1998, researcher and professor of public health William Vega found twice the rate of mental disorders among Mexican Americans born in the United States compared to recent Mexican immigrants (and compared to Mexicans who remained in Mexico). With respect to depression, Mexican Americans born in the United States were almost three times as likely to have had a "major depressive episode" than recent Mexican immigrants. Vega discovered that the rate of mental disorders steadily grew after immigration, so that Mexican immigrants who had been in the United States for more than thirteen years had nearly the same rate of mental disorders as native-born Americans. Vega concluded, "Mexicans are coming from a much more integrated family system. There are tremendous benefits of that in terms of everyday psychological resilience. . . . They are much more likely to be in a situation where people help each other out. . . . There is a cost for this greater personal and economic freedom. The cost is loss of reciprocal support."

Postpartum depression occurs in 10 to 20 percent of women in the United Kingdom and the United States but is considered rare in China, Fiji, and some African populations, according to a 2004 *BMJ* article ("Learning from Low Income Countries: Mental Health"). Based on a review of the literature, the authors concluded, "Structured social supports after childbirth are described in groups of women with low rates of postpartum depression."

Psychologist Michael Yapko notes, "As other societies westernize, i.e., become more like America, their rates of depression typically go up," and he observes that in societies where depression is less prevalent than in the United States, there is less emphasis on technology and consumerism and greater emphasis on family and community.

No one has been more successful in industrialization than Americans, perhaps because no one has more rapidly and completely adopted industrialization's value system: the worship of efficiency, productivity, consumption, and growth. When one worships industrialization, one also worships speed. And for high-speed production, one needs standardization, as this enables the assembly line to move faster. The American assembly line does not call for a standardized race, religion, ethnicity, or sexual preference; it recognizes that in the modern world, the crucial component is standardization of personality.

William H. Whyte in *The Organization Man* (1956) was one of the first to call attention to the transformation of the United States to a society demanding a more uniform personality. Whyte observed that corporations and other bureaucracies were increasingly taking over American society and requiring a more conformist personality. He concludes his book with the section "How to Cheat on Personality Tests," suggesting, "[G]ive the most conventional, run-of-the-mill, pedestrian answer possible," and repeat to yourself such lines as "I like things pretty much the way they are." Whyte is troubled by such conformity but does not advocate rugged individualism. He reminds us that de Tocqueville (in the early 1800s) observed that Americans' special genius was in cooperative actions among those who respected individual differences.

A healthy society is composed of neither isolated nor conformist individuals, but rather it consists of voluntary cooperation among nonstandardized personalities. People are not all the same, not all meant to fit into the same uniform school, corporation, or other such bureaucracy. American society has attempted to have everyone fit into increasingly standardized environments, and I believe that this has contributed to increasing numbers of Americans feeling alienated, inadequate, and depressed. Whyte concludes: "The quest for normalcy . . . is one of the great breeders of neuroses." When this normalcy, or standardization, is imposed on individuals possessing different personalities *and* different values—for example, aboriginal peoples—it is basic common sense that it will result in even more dramatic self-destructive behaviors.

I believe that a one-dimensional worship of industrialization is an important cause of increasing depression because this singular worship comes at the expense of other components necessary for mental health. One such component is autonomy—or the experience of some control over one's life. Another component is community—face-to-face contact with emotional and economic interdependence. These are two significant antidotes to mental difficulties that have long been known. The revolutionary French referred to autonomy and community as *liberty* and *fraternity,* while today the American Indian Movement calls them *sovereignty* and *support.* Americans have increasingly lost autonomy and community, liberty and fraternity, and sovereignty and support and have acquired something I call *institutionalization*: the domination by gigantic, impersonal, bureaucratic, standardized entities—visible in large corporations, government, the workplace, health care, shopping malls, schools, airports, and much of our lives. This institutionalization has made many Americans feel small, isolated, helpless, hopeless, scared, angry, bored, alienated—and depressed.

Technology Worship and Scientific Sham

The faith of our culture is that technology is omnipotent. On my way to getting a PhD, I learned about behavioral technologies, about cognitive technologies, and about biochemical technologies. I learned to think about depressed human beings as broken objects that needed to be fixed. After experiencing the futility of this type of approach, I learned a completely different way of thinking.

I do not oppose technology per se. I merely oppose the uncritical worship of it. My concern is not unique; it echoes that of Ralph Waldo Emerson, Lewis Mumford, and many others. Human beings have always had technology of sorts—some sort of tools and techniques to make their lives easier. The difference today is that technology has increasingly become the supreme value of American culture.

Technology is all about control, and the more we Americans singularly worship technology, the more we singularly worship control. Our society is increasingly dominated by *megatechnologies*—huge, complex technologies that most of us neither understand nor can control. Human beings pay a psychological price for any technology that controls them more than they control it; they can actually feel more powerless. And the feeling of powerlessness is highly associated with depression.

Uncritical worship of any value or belief leads to extremism and fundamentalism. Henry David Thoreau, another early critic of technology worship, lamented, "Men have become the tools of their tools." He knew that a society that worships technology would spend little energy assessing its ultimate value, resulting in what he described as "improved means to unimproved ends." Beyond its attribute of control, technology has no meaning, and if people singularly worship it, they will have meaningless lives. A meaningless life, like a powerless life, is a depressing one.

The consequences of technology fundamentalism are no less comical and tragic than the consequences of antitechnology fundamentalism. The belief that technology is the solution to all of life's problems is no less naive than to believe that technology is the source of all of life's problems.

American mental health culture has increasingly become a technology fundamentalist one. Drugs have become a first option for many doctors, electroconvulsive therapy has made a comeback, and psychosurgery is no longer frowned upon. Technology fundamentalists demand speed and efficiency. By the early 1990s, two-thirds of doctor visits were less than fifteen minutes, and a 2001 RAND Corporation survey revealed that the majority of physicians were diagnosing depression in less than three minutes. In a culture that worships speed, I suppose this is considered progress, but a culture that truly respects life would view this quite differently.

In a society that worships technology, the authority of *science* provides any given technology with legitimacy, and so there are great incentives to convince the public that the techniques used to measure depression are scientific. However, the technology for assessing depression lacks the basic elements of science—including objectivity and verifiability.

One of the most common depression measurement techniques used in researching the effectiveness of antidepressants and other biochemical treatments is the Hamilton Rating Scale for Depression (HRSD). The HRSD was the primary measure of depression in the NIMH STAR*D study, and it is routinely used in antidepressant studies evaluated by the FDA for drug approval. However, even the *American Journal of Psychiatry,* the American Psychiatric Association's own journal, concluded in 2004, "Evidence suggests that the Hamilton depression scale is psychometrically and conceptually flawed." And the *Journal of Clinical Psychopharmacology* noted in 2005, "When looking closely at the construction and content of the HRSD, it is clear that this is a flawed measure." When legitimate scientists examine the HRSD, they immediately notice its biases in how depression is defined, the arbitrariness of a point total for qualifying a person as depressed, the arbitrariness of what qualifies as remission of depression, and the subjective nature of how responses are interpreted and evaluated.

In the HRSD, clinicians and researchers rate subjects, and the higher the point total, the more one is deemed to be suffering from depression. There are three separate items about insomnia (early, middle, and late), and one can receive up to *six* points for difficulty either falling or remaining asleep; however, there is only one suicide item, in which one is awarded only *two* points for wishing to be dead. The HRSD is heavily loaded with items that are most affected by psychotropic drugs, and thus it is not surprising that pharmaceutical-company-sponsored researchers use the HRSD in their antidepressant studies. And it is therefore especially damning for antidepressants that even with such measurement dice loading, these drugs routinely fail to outperform placebos.

Even with depression measures that reflect the standard psychiatric view of depression more accurately than the HRSD, there are interpretation problems. Standard depression symptoms such as depressed mood, loss of interest and pleasure, sleep difficulties (too little or too much), activity difficulties (agitation or lethargy), lack of energy, guilt and self-reproach, poor concentration, indecisiveness, and suicidality are not objectively quantifiable in a scientific sense (and weight gain or loss, a standard symptom that can be objectively measured, is routinely assessed via interview—without a scale or baseline weight). I have talked to people who, while eating a sandwich, report that they have no appetite, and I've talked to others claiming a good appetite who in reality have not eaten in days. People routinely deny they are suicidal when they are in fact so, and vice versa. And I've known people who had poor concentration because they were passionately in love, and people with excellent concentration who were considering suicide.

There can be some value in interviewing or polling people on their subjective experience of "unhappiness," "depression," or "number of depressive episodes" and comparing the responses of different populations. However, only someone who knows nothing about the objective nature of real science could take seriously an arbitrary point total on a subjectively interpreted questionnaire and conclude it to be a scientifically conclusive criterion for diagnosing a person as suffering from the disease of depression (or declare that another arbitrary point total is scientific evidence for remission from the disease of depression). Yet such is common practice in the mental health establishment.

A worship of technology rather than a respect for its power and limitations has also resulted in denying or ignoring phenomena that are obviously nonquantifiable. However, if one dismisses all phenomena that are not measurable, some of the most significant aspects of humanity are simply not discussed. Science cannot accurately quantify the emotional impact of a given trauma on any given person or the love required for healing that wound. And authenticity, spontaneity, compassion, and other variables involved in morale and healing are too subjective to be captured with any scientific certitude. But rather than acknowledging the limitations of quantification, powerful nonquantifiable antidotes to depression are too often simply neglected.

U-Turn from the Wisdom of the Ages

Throughout history many seekers, thinkers, and prophets have taught about overcoming despair. However, it would be difficult to top the greatness of Buddha, Spinoza, and Jesus. All three were rebels and heretics. All three rejected societal norms and religious orthodoxy. Buddha rebelled against both the caste system and religious rituals. Spinoza rebelled against hypocrisy in his community and certain aspects of accepted theology. Jesus rebelled against a materialistic society and religious authorities. Buddha gave up royalty and wealth, Spinoza was excommunicated and nearly assassinated, and Jesus sacrificed his life.

Buddha, Spinoza, and Jesus all came to a similar conclusion about despair—quite a different one than that reached by the modern mental health establishment. Although each described it differently, Buddha, Spinoza, and Jesus concluded that the source of our misery is avarice, material attachment, and self-absorption. While each used different language, they all provided a path away from torment and toward well-being. Buddha taught how to release oneself from narrow self-interest and craving. Spinoza taught how to liberate oneself from greed and other irrational passions. And Jesus taught, very simply, about love.

Modern mental health culture classifies depression as quite a different matter from the despair spoken of by Buddha, Spinoza, and Jesus. However, while modernity has resulted in different sources of pain, human beings and their responses to pain can hardly have changed so dramatically. And so to believe that Buddha, Spinoza, and

Jesus would have dealt only with mild and moderate unhappiness and left debilitating depression for future mental health professionals to tackle seems quite unlikely.

Buddha, Spinoza, and Jesus were not alone in their understanding of the importance of moving beyond self-absorption. In more recent times, their message has been echoed by many others, including psychoanalyst and social critic Erich Fromm (1900–1980). Fromm argued that the increase in depression in modern industrial societies is connected to their economic systems. Financial success in modern industrial societies is associated with heightened awareness of financial self-interest, resulting in greater self-absorption, which can increase the likelihood for depression; while a lack of financial self-interest in such an economic system results in deprivation and misery, which increases the likelihood for depression. Thus, escaping depression in such a system means regularly taking actions based on financial self-interest while at the same time not drowning in self-absorption—no easy balancing act. In Fromm's culminating work, *To Have or to Be?* (1976), he contrasts the depressing impact of a modern consumer culture built on the *having mode* (greed, acquisition, possession, aggressiveness, control, deception, and alienation from one's authentic self, others, and the natural world) versus the joyful *being mode* (the act of loving, sharing, and discovering, and being authentic and connected to one's self, others, and the natural world).

Fromm's penetrating social criticism of an alienating society resulting in increased depression was, during his lifetime, widely respected by many mental health professionals. Today, however, the mental health profession has come to be dominated by biopsychiatrists: those who see depression as a matter mainly of brain chemistry. Fromm, if alive today, may well have labeled this as "microscopic self-absorption." And he most certainly would be sad that mental health treatment has increasingly become a component rather than a confrontation of modern consumerism.

The Unhappiness Taboo

There are many possible reasons for the increasing rate of depression among Americans, but I believe that one important cause is a culture that *demands* happiness. The pressure to be in a good mood can make people ashamed of not being in one. This "pain over pain" can then result in normal low moods becoming prolonged bouts of despair.

Why did this unhappiness taboo take hold so strongly in the United States? One possibility is a societal distortion of the right to "the pursuit of happiness," which has come to mean the expectation of being in a good mood all the time. The irony here is that the signers of the Declaration of Independence signed their death warrant had the American Revolution failed, and it is difficult to imagine Thomas Jefferson telling them, "Don't worry, be happy." It was once accepted that experiencing uncomfortable feelings was often necessary to achieve an ideal.

The unhappiness taboo has dominated the United States since it became a nation primarily of consumers rather than citizens, a gradual process that accelerated with the ascent of advertising in the beginning of the 1900s, and which dramatically spiked with the consumer boom following World War II. The belief that people should be either happy or trying to be happier is a fundamental principle of modern consumerism—the never-ending search for products and services to bring happiness and prevent unhappiness.

In a culture of consumerism, people are forever trying to buy happiness, and sellers are expected to appear happy so as to inspire confidence in what they are offering. There are few businesses that are not in some sense selling happiness or the relief from unhappiness—and thus there is enormous pressure to maintain the appearance of happiness.

The perversion of the pursuit of happiness to mean that it is our duty to be chronically upbeat has, according to psychologist and journalist Lesley Hazleton, resulted in the labeling of anxiety and depression first as weakness and now as illness. In 1984 she published *The Right to Feel Bad*, which confronts this unhappiness taboo: "Feeling good is no longer simply a right, but a social and personal duty. . . . How are we to see depression as a legitimate emotion? How are we to avoid calling ourselves sick or wrong when we feel it? How are we to reclaim it from the clutches of those who claim that anything but feeling good is bad? . . . Seeing depression as pathological—that is, as illness—is a useful way of invalidating it. . . . If we were allowed to be depressed—if we could allow ourselves to be so—we might find it much easier to tolerate." Hazleton convincingly argues that depression is a normal human reaction, and if we cannot accept it, we become ashamed and alienated from ourselves, and this is what makes depression so lethal.

Is it the stigma of depressive illness that we need to eliminate, or rather the stigma of being depressed? Instead of viewing being depressed as weakness or illness, we Americans might better decrease depression by understanding it as a normal human reaction—to be taken as seriously as all other dimensions of our humanity, but neither shamed nor pathologized. When people label a natural component of their existence as "sick," they run the risk of alienating themselves from a part of who they are, making that component far more problematic than it naturally is. By contrast, when we accept the whole of our humanity, we are often rewarded with greater joy—and almost always receive increased wisdom about life.

Morale and Energy

This chapter is about morale and the craft of transforming immobilization to energy. Morale in itself is not the complete solution to depression but a necessary first step to other sustainable approaches.

This chapter is *not* about healing emotional wounds, self-acceptance, satisfying relationships, or public passion. These powerful antidotes to depression require significant energy, and attempting them when you have little energy often results in failure and increased demoralization. When I have little energy, I have learned that it makes no sense squandering what I do have condemning myself. If you have little energy but have used some of it to read this book, I doubt that you are essentially "lazy" or a "resistant patient." More likely, you are doing the best that you can, given what you know. In later chapters, I will talk about understanding destructive behaviors, healthier habits, intimacy, connecting to life beyond oneself, and reviving community—but forget about all that for now. For now, the focus is only on relighting your pilot light.

Freedom from the Demoralization Box

With morale, people can attempt almost everything. Without morale, they lack the energy to try anything. And without morale, they lack the energy to regain morale. This is why the demoralized can feel stuck in a box.

The fear of depression is quite reasonable. Nowadays, depression is worse than simply an unpleasant condition. In modern industrial society, should you remain immobilized for even a short length of time, you can be disposed of. You can, for example, lose your job, have no energy to get another one, and find yourself homeless or institutionalized.

In another era, around 560 B.C., Siddhartha Gautama of the Sakyas was born in northern India into wealth and royalty. In his twenties he became deeply discontented, and at age twenty-nine, he rejected his entire life and society. He took the next six years to deal with his despair. One evening Siddhartha Gautama sat under a fig tree, which has since become known as the bo tree (short for *bodhi* or enlightenment). He vowed not to rise until he achieved spiritual and intellectual illumination. With a combination of meditation, rigorous thought, and mystic concentration, he remained in a rapture of sorts for forty-nine days. When he opened himself to the world again, he was no longer simply Siddhartha Gautama of the Sakyas. He had become Buddha, the Enlightened One.

Think what would become of a rich young man today who rejected his family and his class for homelessness, then wandered unhappily for six years, and finally resolved to sit under a tree for several weeks until he was enlightened. Most likely he would be picked up by the police, given a psychiatric evaluation, hospitalized, drugged, and perhaps electroshocked. In an assembly-line society, there is simply no time to allow anyone six years or six months or even six weeks *just to be*. Many Americans feel like cogs on a great wheel, and they are under great pressure to remain on the wheel. This is why many people turn to psychotropic drugs—prescription or illegal—which can dull pain and facilitate remaining on the wheel.

It is not uncommon for friends and family of depressed people to be frightened, frustrated, and even angry with them for being immobilized. Nondepressed friends and family often say with their words or with their eyes, "Stop feeling sorry for yourself. Pull yourself up by your bootstraps." This of course makes matters worse. If you can't deal with your own pain, you certainly can't deal with the pain of others—especially if you are the one putting them in pain.

It's futile and often counterproductive to tell the immobilized to "work a program" for which they lack the energy. Friends and family sometimes become frustrated when I don't immediately tell the immobilized to take significant actions. However, for extremely depressed and immobilized people, discovering that which requires almost no energy but which provides more energy often means starting extremely small.

I recall one depressed man who felt guilty about the pain that he was inflicting on his friends and family. This guilt, rather than motivating him to take constructive actions, resulted in increased marijuana smoking to dampen his pain. What tiny action could he muster that might reduce others' pain about his condition, which would in turn reduce his pain and reduce his need to depress and dampen his being? He disliked self-help books but his wife loved them, and he believed that she would become more hopeful if he was reading such material. I gave him a brief self-help article, which he left where his wife could discover it, which lifted her spirits, which in turn eased his pain, resulting in him having enough energy to actually read the article!

If you are immobilized, and all your struggling to move out of that place has failed, perhaps it is because your struggle is born of fear, and nature wants you to find an energy supply that is not fear-based. So for now, don't try to change your mood, your thinking, your behaviors, your relationships, your job—or the direction of Western civilization. For now, just try to stop beating up on yourself, and forget about fighting against your immobilization. Take the pressure off. Give yourself permission to just hang out where you are until you find a healthier source of energy.

When people are demoralized, they lack the energy to heal the source of their fear. So they fight their fear or surrender to it. Either way, the focus is on fear. Without healing, fear overcomes them, and they sink into depression and immobilization. Since the fear is often quite reasonable, a distraction from it is what I call *wise unreasonableness*.

There are also many unwise distractions. Psychotropic drugs—legal and illegal ones—may work temporarily to help deny one's hunger, fatigue, and negative emotions and to stimulate one to action. However, the potential of psychotropics for abuse and dependency makes them physically dangerous, and these drugs often block healing and are impediments to learning. Thus, it is my experience that psychotropics—as used in American culture—are often unwise distractions. Is it possible to get out of the demoralization box without drugs? Can you experience stimulation without swallowing, smoking, or snorting something? My experience is that the answer to these questions is yes.

No matter how depressed I get, Beethoven's Ninth Symphony or

Pink Floyd's "Another Brick in the Wall" can resonate with me and energize me. Mikhail Gorbachev said that Mahler's Fifth Symphony saved him from depression during his darkest hours. Others view a painting or watch a movie and get energized. Have you ever felt tired, but then listened to a speaker and felt pumped up? People can derive energy from a passionate orator if they can connect with what is being said. The capacity to touch the core of many people is one definition of genius. There are rehumanizing geniuses and dehumanizing geniuses (such as demagogues, who resonate with those feeling victimized and powerless and energize them to do horrific things). Part of wisdom means being receptive to those who care about life, while rejecting those who are resonating to our darkest, most destructive side.

In this chapter, I describe various nondrug stimulants, but keep in mind that these do have something in common with drug stimulants. The power of nondrug stimulants is also short-term, and if you don't do something positive during that brief interval, the energizing effect is wasted. Cocaine's half-life (the time it takes for half of the drug to leave our system) is between 30 and 90 minutes, amphetamine's half-life is 3 to 6 hours, and Paxil's is approximately 24 hours. I can't tell you the length of the half-lives of the nondrug stimulants. But I can tell you that changes made under the influence of nondrug stimulants, because they are more attributable to *your* actions and not the drug-induced action, are far more likely to be integrated into your being than those that occur while you are on psychotropic drugs.

Creating a wise distraction from fear is part of the craft of remoralization. It's unlikely that you can afford Buddha's wise unreasonableness. It's a pretty safe guess that your boss won't give you six years of paid leave to find yourself. You probably can't even afford to sit under a bo tree for a week. However, there are other forms of wise unreasonableness.

Risk and Faith

While wise unreasonableness and nondrug stimulants may take minimal energy, they still have certain requirements. Openness to anything new requires a certain *risk* and *faith*.

How can you make changes in your thoughts, behaviors, relationships, and life if you can't even find the energy to get out of bed? In order to discover answers, I was drawn to study psychology. I received no answers in my undergraduate psychology classes, and I hoped that I would find some in graduate school. I was accepted into a highly selective American Psychological Association–accredited PhD program in clinical psychology and took more than twenty courses in the first two years—but found no answers. (My program did provide more clinical experience than the typical ones, so I was at least able to begin the struggle to find my own answers.) I jumped through the hoops required for my PhD, discovered how it feels to be dispirited for a long period of time, and learned—from the inside—about the limitations of mental health professional training.

The nondepressed may have difficulty understanding how it could be valuable for depressed people who have not been helped by their treatments to see the limitations of mental health professionals. However, if you are demoralized, the insight that you didn't fail your treatment but that your treatment failed you can be "hope fuel" for your empty tank. Even more important, it is crucial that the immobilized become more conscious of both the buzz-killing and the energy-creating power of the people they are with.

Mental health professionals do know something about the attitudes, habits, and communication skills associated with well-being. However, if I were completely demoralized, I would be wary about turning to most of them. Of course there are exceptions, but they are strikingly different from the average psychiatrist, psychologist, social worker, or counselor. Most mental health professionals are impotent in remoralizing the demoralized because they lack the most important attributes necessary for the craft. They—at least those who have not rebelled against their professional socialization—are not risk takers, and they have little faith.

Risk taking is a necessary component of helping another person and helping yourself. Risk taking provides energy for you and for others. Those professionals who take no risks also provide no models of risk taking. From helpers, I want not only their energy but also their example.

Students who gain acceptance into medical school or doctoral psychology programs are, for the most part, straight-A students. I know what it takes to get straight As. It's compliance, not risk taking. If a risk taker happens to slip through the gates, a good part of his or her "training" consists of learning to fear taking chances. Mental health professionals are heavily socialized to fear lawsuits and the sanctions of licensing boards, managed care, and professional associations. Policing institutions' fear of a risk taker embarrassing the profession far exceeds any desire for the wise risk taking necessary to help an immobilized person make a breakthrough.

When I take a risk with a demoralized client, my career is on the line, and so it can be easier to take a risk with a depressed *nonclient*. For example, the teenage nephew of a friend of mine had experienced a great deal of neglect and abuse in his life, much of which he felt was the fault of mental health professionals, and he consequently harbored a great deal of anger. Knowing that I do radio interviews, he asked to go on the air with me to tell the world what had happened to him. He risked my rejection of his request, and he was willing to risk publicly embarrassing himself. His aunt had custody of him and gave her permission, and a talk show host agreed to make it happen. The teen spoke articulately, handled himself maturely, and—to my relief—did not slander anyone or disclose anything he regretted. Moreover, he said that the experience was very helpful for him. At a minimum, he felt that some adults cared enough about him to provide an opportunity that he really wanted. Although I do take risks with my clientele, I would never have taken this public one with a client because the potential for adverse consequences—legal or professional—is simply too great.

In addition to the fear of taking risks, there's another reason why most mental health professionals would be the last people I'd turn to if I were demoralized and immobilized. Regardless of what they may say in public, my experience is that in private, the majority of them pay only lip service to faith. If a doctor does not have faith in that which cannot be seen, a doctor will take appearances far too seriously. This means a doctor will focus only on symptoms and will move quickly into trying to control them—which these days often means prescribing drugs.

How does one get faith? There is no formula for how one learns to "believe in belief." It helped me to read about critical thinkers such as William James (discussed earlier) who ultimately gained faith. And I've found it helps others to be around people who have a genuine faith that provides them with an antidote to despair. You need not copy their specific beliefs, but you may be inspired to seek a belief in something.

Faith and risk go hand in hand. It is difficult to take risks when one is dominated by fear. But faith can dislodge fear, and then occupy the void so that fear cannot easily return.

So as I am not misunderstood, let me repeat: There are mental health professionals who are wise risk takers and who have great faith. However, the number of this kind of mental health professional is on the decline. People who are risk takers and who have great faith just aren't the sort of people who are attracted to the mental health profession. And the profession is certainly not very accepting of them.

When people have become immobilized, I have found that sometimes the only nondrug stimulants that can get their adrenaline flowing are truths about why their standard treatments failed. It is also my experience that the immobilized desperately want to be inspired, and often they are receptive to and energized by models of risk taking. I have found answers to my question of how to get energy when demoralized, but these have, for the most part, come from outside of my professional training.

Outrageousness and Morale

My first memory of morale-boosting genius came when I was fourteen years old in Junior High School 198 in New York City. Nobody could remember the last time our school soccer team had scored a goal, and most were pretty sure we had never won a game. My friends and I decided we would join the soccer team. After all, it couldn't get any worse, and nobody really cared if it did. This was 1970, the days before American kids cared about soccer. We knew lots about hockey, baseball, football, and basketball, but not soccer. Not only did we have few soccer skills, we didn't even know all the rules. In hockey, we "played the man," which means when an opposition player had the puck, we bodychecked him so he'd lose control of it. When we bodychecked opponents on the soccer field, the referees not only blew the whistle but some got really ticked off. Thus, it's fair to say that not only were we winless and goalless, we were also an imminent danger to others.

One day we were playing a team that was so amused and so frightened by our style of play that it had managed to score just a single goal, and we were losing only 1–0 late in the second half. At that point, for a reason beyond our comprehension, our coach decided to remove our best player, Mitchell. Our coach was an unathletic history teacher who seemed to know even less about soccer than we did. He didn't appear to realize that Mitchell was our only player who could actually control the ball. The coach's last name rhymed with *barrel*—I'll call him Mr. Carrel.

When Mitchell—whom we all assessed had a fifty-fifty chance of graduating and a better than fifty-fifty chance of ending up in prison— heard Mr. Carrel order him to the bench, he screamed back, "Shut up, Carrel, you big fat barrel!" I was on the field near Mitchell, and I looked back at Mr. Carrel, who had turned red. Alongside Mr. Carrel was our assistant principal, who was now angrily screaming along with Mr. Carrel for Mitchell to leave the field. Mitchell looked at us, and we, never having heard such an outburst at a teacher, were grinning. He then looked back at Mr. Carrel and the assistant principal, who were both now screaming even louder for him to leave the field. Mitchell repeated his initial assertion, thought for a second, and added, "I'm staying in and I'm scoring a goal!"

I can't remember a time in my life being more remoralized than I was by Mitchell's outrageous display of blatant rebellion and confidence. The entire team was inspired. We stopped seeing ourselves as unskilled losers. We were revolutionaries. We just had to get Mitchell the ball. I've always imagined that the silver-haired referee for that particular game had once been an anarchist who fought against Franco in the Spanish Civil War, because he sneered at Mr. Carrel's poor coaching, chuckled at Mitchell's antiauthoritarianism, and allowed the game to get a little rougher. I know this sounds like Hollywood fiction, but Mitchell actually ended up scoring a goal. We didn't win, but we got a tie.

In today's climate, it's likely the game would have been stopped and Mitchell summarily escorted off the field. However, I'll always remember how Mitchell's display, though perhaps too outrageous by today's standards, was just outrageous enough to be one of the most powerful morale boosts I've ever witnessed.

In fairness to the coaching profession, Mr. Carrel was more a history teacher than a coach. Actually I've met significantly more coaches who talk about morale than mental health professionals do. I've spent much of my life interacting with mental health professionals, and they almost never use words like *demoralized, dispirited,* or *broken.* Coaches, military personnel, and business managers seem to have a lot more interest in the issue of morale than mental health professionals. There are cases of military officers, coaches, and even business owners willing to offer themselves up in brave self-sacrifice for the purposes of morale or *esprit de corps.* High-ranking officers in the Civil War put their hat on their sword, raised it above their head, got out in front of the troops, and inspired them to charge. Today, coaches purposely will get thrown out of a game by a referee to motivate their team. And small business owners may, to raise their workers' morale, tweak an obnoxious customer.

We mental health professionals are certainly not taught about outrageousness and revitalization. Instead, we are taught to fear even the appearances of inappropriateness. So it is quite understandable that most mental health professionals are simply not willing to risk their professional image for the sake of raising morale.

Professional Appropriateness and Morale Building

One sixteen-year-old client of mine was talented in almost every area of life, lacking only the ability to comply with "worthless authorities" for whom he had no respect. The great nemesis in his life was a principal. The principal was deeply threatened by this teenager. A series of punishments, mostly unfair, had left this sixteen-year-old so demoralized, desperate, and agitated that he was on the verge of acting self-destructively. I said to him, "In this screwed-up society, since I have a

PhD, I sort of outrank your principal. Why not let me go to the school and tell him off?" He was a tough kid and didn't want to ask anyone for help, and he did not respond. I continued, "Look, I'm doing this to meet my own needs. In the years I spent getting a PhD, I didn't learn much, so at least it won't have been a total waste of time if I use it to put this moron back in his place." A huge part of this kid's self-esteem was about taking care of himself, and he politely rejected my offer. Then I got really animated: "Hey, I want to go to your damn school and tell this asshole off. Who the hell does he think he is, going on some power trip at the expense of kids who can't do anything about it?" He continued to politely turn down my offer, but he started to grin at how out-of-control I seemed to be—which calmed him. Then he flashed a big smile and said, "Well, I think I have another plan." Instead of dropping out of school or risking another expulsion (which would have likely prevented his graduation), he investigated how to transfer to another school, then did in fact transfer, got along well at his new school, and graduated. Fifteen years later he had built his own home and created a successful business, and we reminisced about how he had handled the conflict with his principal. He said that seeing me incensed both energized and calmed him to think more rationally, and that it felt good that someone cared enough to be that upset. He remarked, "Somehow all your wild ideas made me react more maturely. I don't know why—it just did."

If you've seen a counselor and continue to be demoralized, perhaps it will help your morale to understand why you were not helped. When I look back at my career as a clinical psychologist and my thousands of hours sitting across from the demoralized, I recognize that the times when I played it "by the book," I usually did little for the depressed except to further demoralize them.

Typical professional appropriateness is often unhelpful for the demoralized because it lacks unpredictability, surprise, and energizing drama. It is worse than being simply dull and boring. When we humans feel powerless and then get only stereotypic professional reactions, we can feel even more powerless. It is not uncommon for this to result in escalating self-destructive behaviors so as to get a rise out of someone—or giving up completely. Misery loves company, and if a helper—parent, counselor, or doctor—is doing nothing to spark you, you may try to make that helper feel as powerless and demoralized as you feel. I have found that the more frustrated and frightened doctors are, the more likely they are to be caricatures of professional appropriateness, perhaps even automaton-like. And unfortunately, it is exactly those times when we humans are most frustrating and frightening that we are often begging for a spontaneous human response.

Playing it by the book is usually more helpful when people are not deeply demoralized. Safe professional appropriateness means asking questions about symptoms, history, and current circumstances. It includes making empathic statements, confronting irrational thoughts and destructive behavior, or having patients read cognitive-behavioral therapy workbooks. These workbooks usually have tables with one column of problematic beliefs and a corresponding column of "cognitive distortions" that are self-destructive. For example:

"I'm a total loser" . . . . Disqualifying the positive

"I just can't cope with life" . . . . Overgeneralization

The problem with this approach for the completely demoralized is that "I'm a total loser" is far more compelling than the fact that it is "disqualifying the positive," and "I just can't cope with life" hits home a lot harder than the fact that it is an "overgeneralization." Imagine Vincent Van Gogh reading his cognitive therapy workbook, and reacting to this:

"I can't live without her" . . . . Exaggeration

I can imagine him cutting off his ear, wrapping it in the workbook page, and sending it off to the book's author. Then there's Sylvia Plath returning from her therapy session with her brand-new workbook, and she reads:

"I should be great" . . . . Should-ing

Somehow it's difficult to imagine that this would have turned the tide for Sylvia. I can't tell you that I could have helped Van Gogh or Plath steer away from their paths of self-destructive behavior, but I assure you that I would not have been "professionally appropriate" with them.

Of course there are truly professionally inappropriate behaviors, including exploitive behaviors (such as having a sexual relationship with a patient). However, nonexploitive, risk-taking behaviors are also sometimes labeled as inappropriate; while non-risk-taking exploitations (such as receiving money with no effort at being helpful) are often not labeled as such. Being *truly* professional means taking wise risks that energize depressed and immobilized people.

Acting As If and Imagination

In order to find answers to the conundrum of how people regain morale when they feel that they lack the energy to regain *anything*, I eventually wandered out of the psychology and psychiatry sections of bookstores. And I discovered that others were attempting creative solutions.

One book I stumbled onto was Constantin Stanislavski's *An Actor Prepares* (1936), and here is where I learned the wisdom and the power of *if*: "With the special quality of *if* . . . nobody obliges you to believe or not believe anything. Everything is clear, honest, and above-board. . . . Consequently, the secret of the effect of *if* lies first of all in the fact that it does not use fear or force, or make the artist do anything. On the contrary, it reassures him through its honesty, and encourages him to have confidence in a supposed situation."

Many depressed people have a passion for integrity. When they feel like a failure, damn if they're not going to be honest about it! If they feel miserable, damn if they are going to lie to themselves or others and say they are not! Don't ever tell them to "think positive" without expecting to turn them off. They will rebel against faking a smile when they don't feel like smiling. If they are pressured enough, compliance may come, but only with resentment, and such compliance will be short-lived. *Acting as if* is one way out of this dilemma.

With the *if*, you are not required to believe that you *are* in a good mood, or to believe that you *are* happy, or to believe that you *are* energized. *Acting as if* requires only that you genuinely and authentically *imagine* yourself in a situation that would put you in a good mood and energize you. *Acting as if* doesn't work for everyone, but even among those for whom it doesn't work, discovering unconventional solutions can give them hope—perhaps there can be other such tricks that might in fact click for them.

It's not uncommon for me to work with creative but immobilized people. Sometimes I tell them to imagine that they have special knowledge that the world is coming to an end one week from today. I emphasize that they don't have to actually believe a meteor is going to obliterate the planet, just to *act as if* it were. Some of them say, "I would just lie in bed waiting for it to happen." But others have said, "I'd telephone a friend I've lost contact with," or "I'd stop worrying about money." I remember one adolescent girl saying, "I would stop comparing myself to others and let go of self-pity," and she returned the next week in a much better mood with another idea: "I would have an end-of-the-world party."

Author Paco Ferri in *2 Running on Calm* (2006) notes, "We are born when our imagination is born and we die when it dies. . . . Imagining makes us strong." Imagination is a source of energy and is essential to sustained vitality. Many depressed people passively *fantasize* about being without misery, but *imagination* is a bridge to action. For Ferri, "Imagination is the projection of images in our interior, with the desire to transform them into real events." After many years of despair, including multiple psychiatric hospitalizations, Ferri concluded his malaise had resulted, in good part, from his ceasing to use his imagination or imagining only what he disliked. Ferri credits his recovery to rehabilitating his ability both to listen to reality and to imagine what he likes.

A Sense of Humor and Spontaneity

Voltaire said, "The art of medicine consists of amusing the patient while nature cures the disease." If you are demoralized and immobilized, there is no better nondrug stimulant than being around someone who can make you chuckle—or being with someone whom you can make chuckle.

It is difficult to be funny if you are unwilling to risk being out of control. You don't have to be a great joke teller to have a good sense of humor, but you do have to be playful, spontaneous, and unafraid of the truth. Can you think of anyone who is really funny who does not have these traits? Unfortunately, a sense of humor is no great advantage in gaining entrance to professional training, and, as noted, social risk-taking traits are often extinguished in training.

I certainly can't do stand-up comedy, and I wish I could be more "consciously funny." When I accidentally say something that generates laughter, my morale picks up, and it often has that same impact on others. When I was touring for my last book, an obviously depressed woman in the audience asked for some suggestions. I began by saying that this would take me an entire book—in retrospect, quite correct—but I realized that such a response wouldn't be helpful, and so I began talking about extricating from uncaring, distrusting, and abusive relationships and moving toward kind, caring, and loving ones. The person and the entire audience were very polite, but I sensed that I had not quite given them what they needed. Then I blurted out, "We humans are dumber than houseplants. Plants know enough to move toward the sun!" The depressed questioner smiled, and the crowd laughed. This energized me, and I suspect it had that effect on some others.

When my wife's grandfather was ninety-two, he entered a nursing home. My wife had deep affection for "Gramps," and it was sad for her to see him so unhappy in the home. He had been active with an alert mind, which had, for the most part, remained intact. But he became listless in the nursing home—which he called the "nut hatch." During one of our visits, his cough lozenges were taken away from him because they had not been "medically approved," and he sunk a little deeper into helplessness. It so happened that my wife, on that visit, had brought him his much loved pistachio nuts, and she made certain to get official approval for them. I took out my business card and wrote a "doctor's order" on it that mocked the institutional control freaks: "Patient may eat only in odd numbers." When my wife read this "prescription" to her grandfather, he busted out laughing, and all of our spirits picked up.

There is nothing more satisfying than seeing a depressed child or adult laugh. Even if what one says is not funny enough to make people chuckle but just silly enough to distract them from their own pain, it is a success. Every second outside of self-absorption is a good thing.

One does not have to be hilarious to help another's morale. What's most important is the willingness to be spontaneous. Risking inappropriateness for the sake of energizing someone feels like an act of generosity even to the severely immobilized. And felt generosity is always good for the morale.

Abraham Lincoln is one of many public figures to have used humor as an antidote to despair. In *Lincoln's Melancholy* (2005), biographer Joshua Wolf Shenk reports that Lincoln experienced two major depressive breakdowns (which included suicidal statements that frightened friends enough that they formed a suicide watch), followed by years of chronic depression. To boost his spirits, Lincoln told jokes and funny stories. A good story, said Lincoln, "has the same effect on me that I think a good square drink of whisky has to the old roper. It puts new life into me . . . good for both the mental and physical digestion." Lincoln said, "If it were not for these stories—jokes—jests I should die; they give vent—are the vents of my moods & gloom." Shenk concludes that "humor gave Lincoln protection from his mental storms. It distracted him and gave him relief and pleasure. . . . Humor also gave Lincoln a way to connect with people."

It is my experience that the depressed and immobilized often have a good sense of humor, but unlike Lincoln, they frequently don't recognize that they are capable of making others laugh, and that such laughter can in turn have an energizing impact on themselves. One way I've seen depressed people lift their own spirits is to tell stories that poke fun at their own behaviors. One man told me how six hours before a first date, he had taken an extra antidepressant pill because he was not all that excited about the date. He had just begun taking antidepressants and knew little about their side effects. Instead of getting more energized, he fell asleep right before he was to meet his date. The woman who had asked him out was, he said, very aggressive, and she came to his door when he failed to show up. This man was honest, often compulsively so, and told her that he had not been all that excited about going out with her and had thought that the extra antidepressant would help, but that instead it had made him groggy. I asked him, "Did she get hurt when you told her that you hadn't been excited about going out with her?" "Not really," he said. "She was from New York City. She just pressured me to go out with her later that week." His matter-of-fact manner of storytelling induced me to chuckle—which in turn helped him see the humor in his story and made him laugh and become energized some.

Mischief, Zyroting, and Morale

When people are completely demoralized, they routinely lack the energy to initiate any constructive behavior proactively, but it's somewhat easier to be reactive, which takes relatively little energy but can pick up the spirits.

I recall one period in my life when I was down in the dumps. Despite getting several well-known authors to endorse a book manuscript of mine, I received form-letter rejections from publishers. At the same time my book was getting rejected, I was getting an inordinate number of telemarketing phone calls in which I was regularly forced to reject others. Knowing how it felt to be turned down, it did not make me feel good to be rude—although I wanted to be. I thought surely none of these telemarketers wanted to do this for a living, and they must have been desperate for any income until they could find a less miserable line of work.

One day a telemarketer began her sales pitch by asking what I did for a living. I paused for a second, and then I told her that I was a telemarketer evangelist. At first she misunderstood, thinking I said a televangelist, and she believed I was being dishonest with her, as clearly many people told her outrageous lies. Then I explained that I was not a televangelist, that I did not evangelize on television, but that I was a telemarketer evangelist and that I ministered to telemarketers who called me. She stopped her pitch and let me continue. I told her that I believed that many telemarketers were in deep pain about what they were doing, and this was made worse by the anger they received from most people they spoke to. In a soft voice, almost sounding like she was going to cry, she agreed with me. I told her that I knew she could not stay on the phone too long, especially since I wasn't going to buy anything from her, but that I could tell she was a good person and that

I had faith she was going to get a more satisfying job. She was a religious person, and she responded, "God bless you."

I continued my telemarketer ministry for a couple of months. Some telemarketers would robotically continue with their sales pitch, but several would become more human. To these people, I would say that it was wonderful that they had not lost their humanity, and that I knew if they just hung in there, they would get a better job.

After I'd emerged from my funk, I was sitting around the dinner table with a couple of friends, and a telemarketer called. He was a young man calling from somewhere in Kansas, and he made it very clear that he hated his job and didn't even care that his supervisor was monitoring the phone call. After I did my ministering, my friends took their turn. One of my friends told the disgruntled telemarketer about my book. I had self-published it, and my friend described it in such a way that the young man from Kansas wanted a copy. He mailed me a check, and I sent him a book.

It then struck me that I had spontaneously moved into my telemarketer evangelism, had brightened a few miserable telemarketers' days, and had never bought anything from them, and, in fact, one of them actually purchased something from me. Life seemed to be instructing me that good-hearted mischief is a wise idea in helping to recover morale.

In addition to pained telemarketers, the world is filled with many other unhappy low-wage workers, and it often takes little energy to provide them with a reason to smile—which also creates energy for you. I knew one clergyman who often got deenergized by his demanding congregants but reenergized himself by "ministering" to pained restaurant servers. He would go to a dive restaurant for breakfast, treat the server with great respect, and leave a 100 percent tip.

I'd be surprised if you've heard of *zyroting*. It's not in any dictionary yet, and I am not sure I want it to be. Zyroting means giving respect, credit, support, validation, and empathy. When people get zyroted—or when they zyrote—their morale lifts.

Zyroting is decidedly not about "stroking" someone to get them to do something. That's what corporate culture does. For example, Eric Schlosser in *Fast Food Nation* (2001) reported: "For years the McDonald's Corporation has provided its managers with training in 'transactional analysis,' a set of psychological techniques popularized in the book *I'm OK—You're OK* (1969). One of these techniques is called 'stroking'—a form of positive reinforcement, deliberate praise, and recognition that many teenagers don't get at home. Stroking can make a worker feel that his or her contribution is sincerely valued. And it's much less expensive than raising wages or paying overtime." If you're stroking as a means of manipulation, you are doing the opposite of zyroting.

What is the derivation of the word *zyroting*? A few of my friends and I were discussing how the corporate manipulators had stolen one more powerful idea and were using it to control people. This was especially enraging because they were exploiting the sacred act of remoralizing. We decided that we had to come up with a new word for the old idea, since they had now ruined the old words by associating them with bad ideas. We came up with *zyroting*, because I've learned a couple of things from Big Pharma. When pharmaceutical companies name their drugs, they often want a *z* or an *x* in it. Their marketers are clever, and they know that people remember words with *z* or *x* because few words contain those letters. Thus, Prozac, Paxil, Zoloft, Celexa, Lexapro, Luvox, and Effexor—the names mean nothing but stick in our minds because of the *z* and *x* thing. So we created *zyroting*. Perhaps both our society and our language have become too corrupt to reform, and those of us who "get it" must create both a different society and a different language. We can zyrote one another, feel zyroted, and appreciate the act of zyroting.

Receiving respect and validation from a person whom you regard highly is a boost to your morale and self-worth. For zyroting to be powerful, it takes some skill. It's not really zyroting to hear a teacher call you special after you've heard that teacher say the same thing about every one of your classmates. However, if you are singled out for a mentoring relationship because of what that teacher spots in you, that can be highly zyroting.

One day I was talking to a physician who was embarrassed to admit that he resented not being given credit or respect or thanks by his patients. He said, "I shouldn't feel that way because, after all, I am getting paid." I told him, "Money does not make up for the lack of zyroting." "Zyroting?" he asked. I explained and he smiled.

Failure without Demoralization

Though Americans often hear about the "stigma of mental illness," perhaps the real stigma in the United States is being a loser. Pop culture celebrities talk at length about their mental illness and their psychiatric drugs, and Americans don't stigmatize them for it.

In the United States, you can do all kinds of things to run from your pain and not be stigmatized. You can get arrested for a DUI and still get elected president, and you can have compulsive sex and remain president. Just don't lose a war or be in office when people are losing their shirts in the stock market. Americans forgive admitted sinners, but they have no affection for losers. Extremist industrial society shames the nonproductive and inefficient. While in many traditional cultures it is taboo to lie, in American society, known liars can get elected president—but not if they appear nonproductive and inefficient.

Part of the fear of immobilization stems from the knowledge that if you can't "snap out of it," society will ostracize you for being nonproductive. Labeling the immobilized as "mentally ill" was supposed to remove the shame and stigma of being immobilized. It's now politically incorrect to disparage depressed people as long as they accept that they have a mental illness. If they admit to having an illness called "depression," and if they comply with standard forms of treatment— for example, by taking prescribed medications—they are officially granted tolerance. However, since the great shames of American culture continue to be failure, nonproductivity, and inefficiency, Americans, deep down, often shame themselves if they remain immobilized. Public relations efforts may convince the media that depression is a disease and should not be shamed, but public relations often does not convince the immobilized. At some level they know that they are violating a social taboo.

Often the immobilized overfocus on productivity, and they become ashamed of their lack of productivity, resulting in even greater immobilization. The only true way to end our stigmatization of failure, nonproductivity, and inefficiency is to replace our worship of productivity with a worship of life. When I get bummed out by my lack of productivity, I remember what Don Juan Matus (Carlos Castaneda's Yaqui mentor) said: "The things that people do cannot under any conditions be more important than the world. And thus a warrior treats the world as an endless mystery and what people do as an endless folly."

It can be especially lethal in American society to think that you have failed, that everyone besides you is walking around happy or at least not depressed, and that others have done something right while you have done everything wrong. The idea of being completely alone or in a small minority of life's losers is—to put it mildly—extremely demoralizing. People who are so seriously depressed that they become suicidal often ruminate on these thoughts.

Shame over failure, even failures that seem trivial, can trigger major depression. A mother once told me about her son, who had been a star athlete and very popular in high school. In one important football game, he committed a penalty that cost his team a winning touchdown. Her son sunk into a state of apathy and immobilization, and the mother said that even years later, as an adult, he had not fully recovered.

Many people—especially young people—can be so overwhelmed by the shame of failure that they can't imagine that much of life is double-edged, and that failure can be a gift. In this success-oriented society, we receive few positive messages about failing. I can't remember ever being told in school that the route to wisdom is learning through your own mistakes and misdirections. Failure also reminds us that we are human. When we own up to our errors and blunders, we relearn humility, and humility is something that we humans must relearn on a regular basis.

One reason why public figures are able to become and remain public figures is their resilience in the face of failure, loss, and even humiliation. One of their tricks is denial. In Cincinnati, Ohio, my home for many years, they named a major street Pete Rose Way, and kept the street name even when Pete Rose was banned from baseball. Pete is a local boy who made good, and Cincinnatians are very loyal to their own. Most knew, even before he ultimately confessed, that Pete had lied about his gambling on baseball, but they kept the street name. Part of why Pete garners so much loyalty, despite his moral failings, is his unrelenting morale. Pete lacked a powerful throwing arm, was not a fast runner, and didn't hit many home runs, but almost by sheer will, discipline, and hustle, he managed to get more hits than anybody in baseball history. How does his mind work? One day, when Pete was in his prime and leading the National League in batting average, a reporter asked him, "Pete, here you are going through a nasty divorce with your wife who is telling the entire world what a rotten guy you are, and you're hitting .340. How do you do it?" Pete looked at the reporter with an expression that said *another dumb college boy I'm going to have to explain life to,* and then he responded, "Don't you think it's a heck of a lot easier to go through a divorce when you are hitting .340 than it is when you are hitting .240?"

While resilient public figures don't all engage in denial or deception, many have learned not to take their moods too seriously. In the 2000 U.S. presidential election, Ralph Nader got rejected by more than 97 percent of the approximately 101 million Americans who voted. Worse still, an additional 100 million or so American adults rejected the entire election process and didn't even bother voting. I would have been somewhat demoralized if I were Nader. How could he not have felt like a "loser" when all the statistics were telling him that he was? In 2002, following the Enron scandal (a resounding validation of Nader's campaign message against corporate greed and irresponsibility), Nader was interviewed by the *New York Times Magazine*. He was asked why there was more resignation than outrage in America. Nader responded: "It comes from a deep sense of powerlessness. When you feel powerless, your attitude reflects apathy, withdrawal, resignation, and that is a telltale sign of the degree to which our democracy has declined in the last twenty, twenty-five years." Then Nader was asked whether he had grown more pessimistic. Nader answered: "I am not afflicted by optimism or pessimism. They are not in my lexicon. I'm not in the mood game, because moods affect your output, and the thing is you must keep striving because there is no alternative to striving for greater justice."

Noam Chomsky, the world-renowned linguist and political activist, has for more than forty years fought for genuine democracy and the sharing of power and has spoken out against totalitarianism and propaganda. In the early 1960s, when the vast majority of Americans supported U.S. involvement in Vietnam, Chomsky was one of the few

Americans actively opposing it. Looking back at this era, Chomsky reflected, "When I got involved in the anti–Vietnam War movement, it seemed to me *impossible* that [we] would ever have any effect. . . . And that was wrong. . . . So looking back, I think my evaluation of the 'hope' was much too pessimistic: it was based on a complete misunderstanding. I was sort of believing what I read." At one of his talks, a somewhat demoralized man in the audience asked Chomsky whether he too ever went through a phase of hopelessness. Chomsky responded, "Yeah, every evening. . . . If you want to feel hopeless, there are a lot of things you could feel hopeless about. If you want to sort of work out objectively what's the chance that the human species will survive for another century, [it's] probably not very high. But I mean, what's the point? . . . First of all, those predictions don't mean anything—they're more just a reflection of your mood or your personality than anything else. And if you act on that assumption, then you're guaranteeing that'll happen. If you act on the assumption that things can change, well, maybe they will. Okay, the only rational choice, given those alternatives, is to forget pessimism."

Transforming Negative Energy

The mental health industry approaches our negative emotional states in a negative way. Hopelessness, anxiety, and anger are often treated like weeds on a lawn, and these days that means using chemicals to get rid of them. However, negativity per se is not bad. It is negativity about one's negativity that is problematic. Although anger is not the most fun way in the world to get energized, I must confess that when I've had little else to motivate me, I have used anger to get a few things done. If all you are doing is mentally beating up on yourself or beating up on the world, that's still evidence of energy. The trick is turning that energy into something constructive.

If you see depression as an uncomfortable human reaction rather than a disease, you can better understand that it, like other uncomfortable human reactions, can be a motivator. Infants eventually learn the meaning and message of hunger—and its antidote—and they become adults who can enjoy a good appetite as they anticipate a wonderful meal. Most people in our culture are better at seeing the meaning and message of negative physical states than negative emotional states. If you can accept the whole of your humanity—even if it is painful—it can energize you to discover something important about yourself and about life.

I believe one reason why many writers, musicians, and other innovators have difficulty letting go of their moodiness is that they understand that the experience of emotional pain and despair can be an energizer for discovery. It can be a stimulus for seeing their experience from another angle, for organizing it differently, and for expressing it in a novel way. Many artists know that emotional pain is not wholly evil but more like fire. Fire can kill and destroy, but it can also provide warmth, cook our food, and create beautiful objects. Emotional pain can certainly be terrifying and destructive, but used wisely it can stimulate a song, a novel, or a joke. All of us, whether we are or are not professional artists, can feel oppressed by pain but also be attached to its energy.

I have talked to many depressed artists (amateur and professional). Often they've been pleasantly surprised at what they produced when they believed that they could not produce anything. It may have been a few lyrics or a small sketch that resolved a pain and ended there. Occasionally, it's a work they considered interesting enough for others. In any case, they used their dark mood to fuel concrete action—and stopped beating themselves up for being immobilized.

Emotional pain can have meaning, and meaning can provide direction and energy. Psychiatrist Viktor Frankl's *Man's Search for Meaning* (1959) has influenced and inspired many mental health professionals (though some of Frankl's later writings tarnished his reputation). In *Man's Search for Meaning*, Frankl describes a harrowing tale of his physical, psychological, and spiritual survival in Nazi concentration camps, as well as *logotherapy*—a way of helping people discover the meaning of their lives. Can meaning provide lifesaving morale? Frankl states that in the concentration camps, "the thought of suicide was entertained by nearly everyone. . . . A very strict camp ruling forbade any efforts to save a man who attempted suicide. . . . Therefore, it was all important to prevent these attempts from occurring." Frankl talks about the therapy he provided for two men who seriously talked about suicide: "In both cases it was a question of getting them to realize that life was still expecting something from them." For one man, it was a child waiting in a foreign country, and for the other, a scientist, life-saving meaning was a series of books that no one but he could complete. More than once, Frankl quotes Nietzsche's dictum: "He who has a *why* to live for can bear with almost any *how*."

While the half-life potency of a wise adage may be brief, a meaningful quote can provide the burst of energy required in moments of deep despair. The nondrug stimulant effect of a Nietzsche aphorism can be so powerful that if prescribed to the wrong person, it can result in the ugliest of violence. But Nietzsche properly self-prescribed—as in the case of Frankl—can be the inspiration required to survive a nightmarish ordeal. One cannot, as far as I know, do a medical residency or postgraduate work to become a Certified Aphorism Prescriber; one must rely on gut instincts, wisdom, and life experience.

Many Thoreau quotations transform painful truths into life-affirming stimulants, and I always try to keep a few on hand in my medicine cabinet. For mental health professionals who are demoralized not only by what their profession has become but also by what they and their "neighbor-colleagues" have become, I especially like to offer this Thoreau Rx to inspire them to reject the crowd and follow their heart: "The greater part of what my neighbors call good I believe in my soul to be bad, and if I repent of any thing, it is very likely to be my good behavior. What demon possessed me that I behaved so well?"

Perhaps nothing divides people more than how they look at tension. People can fear painful emotions, seeing them as evils or diseases to be eliminated as rapidly as possible. Or they can trust that these emotional states are natural parts of the human condition and potential sources for motivation and discovery. Depending on which side of the fence people are on, they will likely differ not only in their beliefs about depression, but also in their inclination to accept or reject the tensions that come along with genuine community and true democracy.

Changing Focus and Gaining Energy

I believe that one of the reasons people get stuck in immobilization is that they have become rigidly attached to a single way of gaining energy. It's my experience that depressive breakdowns are often nature's way of saying that there are more ways in life to get energy than what you are focusing on—you should open yourself up to more of life.

It is easiest for me to get energized by ideas. As a kid I would go into a library or a bookstore and literally get an adrenaline rush. Those of us who *rigidly* adhere to attempting to gain energy from ideas and books can eventually "crash" into a depression. It appears that nature wants us to open ourselves to getting stimulated in other ways, such as deriving energy from other people.

In contrast, there are other personalities who rigidly derive energy only from the attention of other people. However, in much of life one cannot count on this kind of energy supply. The school clown may get attention and energy for a while but will also ultimately crash. It is my experience that nature wants these personalities to expand their energy sources as well, perhaps discovering how stimulating it can be to have a passionate interest in something other than people.

Still another type of personality may rigidly derive energy from controlling life's events. Many entrepreneurs, athletes, and leader types get energized by their impact. In the same way that being stimulated by ideas or attention is not bad per se, there's nothing wrong with deriving energy from effecting change. The problem emerges when anything becomes a rigid, singular power supply. The person who is attached solely to control as a source of energy will likely "hit a wall" when parenting, as most kids will resist a parent's need to control. I believe that nature wants those people who derive energy primarily from effecting change to expand their knowledge of life—perhaps learning how energizing silliness or compassion can be.

An important way of reenergizing yourself is first recognizing what you have relied on as a source of energy and then experimenting in another zone. Is your "comfort energy zone" the attention of others? Or is it rebellion, truth, novelty, or nature? If your primary energy source has been being contrary, you might be surprised to discover that harmony can create energy. If you've derived energy only from work, you may want to experiment with play. If your fuel source has been play, discovering meaningfulness in your work may be energizing. When people are willing to experiment in a foreign zone, one of life's rewards will be renewed energy in their comfort zone. When it comes to generating energy, nothing is more important than being honest about your particular comfort zone—and experimenting in other zones.

Understanding Self-Destructive Ways

This chapter is about emotional wounds and reactions to overwhelming pain. One of these reactions is depression, which is explained as a strategy to shut down emotional pain—a strategy that ultimately can result in the depressing of one's being and a vicious cycle of more pain and repeated depression. Failed strategies to shut down pain include a wide variety of other so-called mental disorders as well as several consumer products and services, including some psychiatric treatments.

Consumer culture has increasingly become one that numbs and diverts us from pain, and I spell out the negative impact of such a culture on our ability to deal with life's trials and tribulations. I also discuss how our society actually encourages illness, and how, when it comes to genuine mental health, extreme consumer culture is unhealthy.

Depression as a Failed Strategy

Depression is a strategy for dealing with pain. By depressing your being, you feel less pain.

It is natural to temporarily protect yourself from pain so as to survive traumatic events. But it is my experience that nature does not want us to permanently anesthetize emotional pain, and depression, substance abuse, or other such anesthetizations become a new pain, often more painful than the original pain that you were trying to shut down.

If you were abused or neglected, the pain of that memory can be anesthetized by depression. However, all anesthetizations (not simply drugs and alcohol) can be addictive, and people can develop a tolerance to them. This means that if you get in the habit of using depression to protect yourself from pain (rather than healing the source), you will need to increasingly depress your being to continue to dull your pain.

People choose depression, although it doesn't feel like a choice. You may feel like a passive victim of depression, but depression is simply one more strategy. However, this strategy does not work in the long run. The act of protecting yourself from emotional pain tells you that you are incapable of handling it. Each time you do this, you feel weaker and need more protection. Depression, like all strategies to shut down emotional pain, can become a compulsion (an action that does not feel freely chosen).

Being a "depressive" can become part of one's identity. I routinely suggest to people who have not been helped by their diagnosis of depression that perhaps being a depressive is not a part of their *true* identity. Perhaps they simply discovered the shutdown strategy of depression at a younger age and—no different from someone who discovers alcohol or nicotine—developed a bad habit.

People seriously consider suicide when pain consumes their lives, when all their strategies to shut down pain fail, and when they are overwhelmed by the fear that their excruciating pain is a permanent condition. Without such a state of mind, considering suicide would go against the natural desire for life. Even when we are suffering overwhelming pain, the habit of living makes it difficult for most of us to follow through on suicidal ruminations. For those who actually do make a serious suicide attempt, certain variables tip the scales. One such variable is intoxication with alcohol or other psychotropics, which can take away our natural inhibitions, making it easier to break with our habit of living. Another such variable is easy access to a lethal method. If there's a gun or barbiturates in the house, a suicide attempt becomes easier even for those with little energy.

Pain, Loss, and Trauma

Physical and mental suffering is part of the human condition. But we are each unique. You are a unique combination of experience, temperament, sensitivity, and language, and so am I. We won't all feel torment in the same way. And even among people who may feel it similarly, they may describe it differently.

Life seems to have an infinite variety of pains, including rejection, failure, humiliation, injustice, and poverty. Pain is the death of a cherished loved one. It is a serious illness. It is being married to a husband who abuses alcohol, becomes distanced, or has affairs; or being married to a wife who has lost interest in sex or smiling. It is the memory of a mother who cared less about your need for attention than her own; or a father who cared only about his car, boat, and new girlfriend. Another great pain is loneliness. Many people are so terrified of loneliness that they often form relationships and even marriages with partners with whom they have little in common, and this can bring on the pain of disconnectedness. A basic human need is wholeness—to be connected with oneself, others, and nature. With the loss of such wholeness comes pain. In addition to past and current losses of wholeness, people often fear future losses. People often use depression and other anesthetizations to shut down the pain of fear.

Trauma consists of an injury, shock, or threat to one's very being. When one is traumatized, one routinely feels a supreme loss of control. There are dramatic, isolated traumatic episodes, but there is also the trauma of living in an ongoing, uncaring environment. People who grew up in households with substance-abusing or explosive parents often describe environments where a violation to their being could happen at any time, where there was often continuous neglect with periodic episodes of physical and/or emotional abuse. Physician Charles Whitfield in *The Truth about Depression* (2003) describes how childhood trauma is highly associated with later depression. Examining 209 studies linking childhood trauma to depression, Whitfield found that in those individuals who reported a history of significant childhood trauma, depression was from 1.6 to 12.2 times more common than in controls who did not report such trauma.

Subsequent to trauma, any loss of control, respect, or affection or even any significant tension can feel like "salt in a wound." Until wounds are healed, the tension of even minor losses can trigger an overwhelming pain resulting in depression. For some people, tension has such horrific associations that even the tension created by a loud noise or a lost watch can feel painful. Thus, when an unsophisticated cognitive-behavioral therapist tells these people that they are irrationally overreacting to a minor event, that therapist can inadvertently make matters worse. People often know that it's irrational and self-defeating to overreact to minor losses and tensions, and being confronted on their irrationality is not what they need. Their wounds need healing (detailed in chapter 4).

While psychiatry textbooks place "anxiety" and "depression" in different categories, the mind often makes no such separation. The pervasive dread of anxiety and the immobilizing shutdown of depression are part of the same arc. For many people, emotional pain routinely starts with the anticipation of an imminent loss. The tension mounts. Anticipation grows into worry, which grows into fear and dread, which can grow into an undulating wave—a physical throbbing that reaches down to the gut. We can wake up filled with dread, our body can shut itself down so as not to feel it, and we can sink into a depression—and this entire process can take place within seconds. Anxiety is the pain of anticipated overwhelming pain. Depression is the pain of the shutting down of one's being in response to that pain.

Shame

Shame is the experience of such deep unworthiness, disgrace, and dishonor that it requires condemnation. Shame is not simply "I made a mistake" but "I am a mistake." Shame is not simply "He's not attracted to me" but "I am unattractive." Shame is not simply "I am lonely" but "I am not someone people want to be friends with." Shame is the feeling that one's being or some part of it is essentially bad, unlovable, or worthless.

Shame, by its very nature, is routinely too shameful to bring up with others and possibly even with oneself. Necessary ingredients for healing are honesty and openness, and this is why the wound of shame is not so easily healed. Shame is a powerful fuel for destructive behavior. Shame occurs through the trauma of abuse and neglect. In a genuinely nonviolent culture, the shaming of another or oneself would be taboo. Thus, abuse and neglect would also be taboo.

There are several kinds of abuse. Physical abuses such as beatings, molestations, and rapes are the most concrete. The abuser's message is

"You are not a person to be cared about but an object to be used." Emotional abuse can be obvious, but it can also be subtle. Obvious examples of emotional abuse are insults said to children by parents, teachers, and peers: "You're spoiled rotten." "You'll be flipping burgers for the rest of your life." "Nobody likes you." Some people, knowing that physical and verbal abuse are wrong, shame more subtly. Nonverbal emotional abuse is insidious and can be an extremely powerful shaming force. A facial expression of disgust, a look of contempt, a mocking tone of voice, or a dismissive shrug can be lethal, especially for children. These nonverbal shaming communications can sometimes be more destructive than verbal ones because these can be more difficult to identify and confront.

There is another kind of shaming that also leads to feeling that one's being or a part of it is essentially bad, unlovable, and worthless: the shame of neglect. Neglect occurs when one's being, including one's pain, is ignored and not cared for. Those who have been neglected often believe they have been less damaged than those who have been abused. This is a self-deception. If you have been neglected, you have been passively abused, and you can feel as much shame as someone who has been actively abused. Many who grew up in an unloving environment attempted to escape abuse by being good students and well-mannered or by hiding from the world of relationships and by otherwise not revealing themselves. However, if your failings, mistakes, and inadequacies were neglected and unloved, you may have deep shame over them.

It is usually easier for people to recognize concrete offenses than to admit to withheld love. It is difficult to deny a parent's physical or emotional attacks; it is easier to deny that nobody knew who you were, which meant that nobody could care about you. Even if you experienced some affection, you still may have suffered from shaming neglect. If, for example, you were given strokes for your accomplishments but your pain was ignored, then you were neglected, and unhealed, you may have as much shame as someone who was actively abused.

People can also be shamed by what they witness. If you were surrounded by family members, teachers, or coaches who abused and neglected others, you can be infected by shame. A sister who watches as her older brother is labeled for his failings by their father as an embarrassment is as vulnerable as her brother to feeling shame over imperfections. And the little boy who sees his father get verbally abused by his mother can feel more shame than his father.

We humans can feel deep shame over any aspect of our being, from our sexuality to our hurt to our anger. For many people, the core fuel of self-destructive behavior is a shame over inadequacy. Being human, we are filled with imperfections, and many of us are ashamed of them. Commonly considered inadequacies fall into the areas of intelligence, popularity, and attractiveness. A less commonly discussed inadequacy is one of fragility.

In the Victorian era, human sexuality was shamed, but in today's rough-and-tumble, survival-of-the-fittest culture, human fragility is shamed. The word *fragile* means lacking physical or emotional strength, easily broken or destroyed. When we are infants and small children, we are by nature physically and emotionally fragile. The opposite of fragile is resilient. Not too long ago, to have a fragile daughter was nowhere near as worrisome as having a fragile son, but one unintended consequence of increasing gender equality is that today a young girl who feels fragile can experience as much shame as a young boy.

Fragility can naturally mature into resiliency; however, our society does not have the time or trust for that natural process. So society—including parents, schools, and the media—subtly and overtly shame fragility to make it go away. Many people in our society are ashamed of their fragility and thus do not want reminders of it, and they are quite willing to accept speedy superficial solutions. The fragile little boy can be shamed into acting like a tough guy and later learn how alcohol can obliterate the pain of the shame of fragility. The fragile little girl is diagnosed with "social anxiety disorder" and given a psychotropic, and the sharp pain of her fragility shame can be dulled. However, as noted with depression, whatever is used to dull the pain, more will eventually be needed. More alcohol, more pills, or more diversions. There is a sort of physics to the numbing of emotional pain: Whatever once worked, at some point won't; and more of it or something else will be necessary.

When you live with shame, you live life with a giant handicap, a giant burden. You spend much of your energy protecting yourself from even seeing it. And when you catch a glimpse of it, you spend more energy dulling the torment. You avoid intelligent risks or, under the influence of drugs and false bravado, take unwise ones. If wounds have not been allowed to heal naturally, shame festers and leaves behind a wake of self-sabotage.

People are not doomed by their past. We can heal from the shame of it and become healers ourselves. Actually, it's difficult to imagine how one can become a great healer without having once been deeply wounded and then healed. This process results in more than just a heartfelt compassion for the unhealed. The once wounded and now healed are the most equipped among us to inspire confidence that everyone can transform themselves.

Obsessions, Compulsions, and Choice

When we humans are overwhelmed by emotional pain, we are likely to do stupid and destructive things. Emotional pain can be unrelenting. One can temporarily numb it with drugs or depression, but these cannot kill it. One can temporarily overpower emotional pain with sheer force of will, but the pain of unhealed wounds will simply bide its time and wait for your weak moments. Some people, to describe this experience, use the word *demons*, which lurk in the background saying, "You can't be numb or vigilant forever."

Losing choice over one's thoughts in the extreme is called *obsessive-ness*. Losing choice over one's actions in the extreme is called *compulsiveness*. Obsessive thoughts and compulsive actions are often meaningless and destructive, and both are fueled by overwhelming emotional pain. This is why obsessive thoughts and compulsive actions often go hand in hand, and thus the term *obsessive-compulsive*. Since overwhelming pain is also the fuel for anxiety and depression, it's not uncommon for the same person to experience anxiety, depression, obsessions, and compulsions. And since alcohol or drug abuse is merely one form of compulsivity, an anxious and depressed person may well drink and/or use drugs excessively.

Many self-help pundits preach that we all have choice. This is essentially true, but for the unhealed it can be a damaging message. At some level, they know they should have choice, but they don't feel like they do. This can move them into deeper shame: "If I believe that I should have choice, and the experts are scolding me because I'm not making healthy choices, then I must be really worthless."

A generation ago, it was more common for mental health professionals to talk about healing emotional wounds. Today, talk of healing is less common. Instead psychiatrists, psychologists, and social workers take more seriously the "differential diagnoses" of specific mental disorders. I believe that mental health professionals are now increasingly concentrating on superficial distinctions rather than focusing on the genuine source of emotional malaise. So-called anxiety disorder, depression, obsessive-compulsive disorder, and substance abuse—though they present with different symptoms—are essentially flights from pain. There are those professionals who believe that the assignment of a specific illness label will relieve the shame over dysfunction. For some people this does provide relief, but for many others it does not. Many people don't accept the idea that either weakness *or* illness causes their self-destructive behaviors.

I frequently see enormous strength in people diagnosed as depressed, anxious, and obsessive-compulsive. They valiantly struggle against their unhealed wounds—demons that forever threaten: "I will force you to drink that twelve-pack, eat that entire pizza, say things you regret to a loved one. It is I who is in control. You can ward me off with willpower for a while but not forever. You will need increasingly more drugs or alcohol to numb me. I can grow so powerful that you will prefer death, and I can make you grow so angry that you couldn't care less if I cause suffering to others." I am impressed by people dominated by overwhelming emotional pain who are able to do or think *anything* that is not destructive. It takes a great deal of energy.

Shutting Down the Pain with Treatment

The American Psychiatric Association's manual of psychiatric disorders, the *Diagnostic and Statistical Manual of Mental Disorders* (*DSM*), lists hundreds of disorders, but what's telling is that psychiatry uses pretty much the same drugs for many of them. Pharmaceutical companies recommend antidepressants for far more than depression. Paxil is recommended by its manufacturer for depression, generalized anxiety disorder, obsessive-compulsive disorder, panic disorder, and social anxiety disorder. Prozac, Zoloft, and other antidepressants are also used for these disorders. Antidepressants are also prescribed for post-traumatic stress disorder, eating disorders, phobias, substance abuse, behavior problems in children, and many other official disorders—as well as for several "disorders" that haven't yet made it into the *DSM*. For example, Celexa has been touted by its manufacturer for treatment of "compulsive shopping," even though it is not an official *DSM* disorder. It is also telling that antidepressants are used for physical discomforts. Prozac manufacturer Eli Lilly took the active chemical (fluoxetine hydrochloride) in green and white Prozac pills and repackaged it in pink and lavender pills, relabeled it as Sarafem, increased the price, and recommended it for relieving premenstrual discomfort.

Discomforts can sometimes be reduced by psychotropic drugs. Antidepressant, antianxiety, antipsychotic, or illegal drugs and alcohol can "work" on the same discomfort. The discomfort of anxiety and depression can be reduced with Xanax or alcohol—both of which affect the GABA (gamma-aminobutyric acid) receptors. Or one can get relief with Wellbutrin, which enhances dopamine, or from Haldol, which actually diminishes dopamine. One can temporarily shut down emotional pain with Zoloft, Zyprexa, marijuana, cocaine, and a long list of other prescription and illegal psychotropic drugs.

Pharmaceutical companies tell us that antidepressants work by correcting a specific chemical imbalance. However, as noted in chapter 1, even antidepressant advocates now acknowledge there is no scientific evidence that depression is a consequence of any chemical imbalance we can measure. Thus, since there is no scientific proof that depression is caused by any innate chemical imbalance, the belief that psychotropics work by correcting a chemical imbalance is fetched from a far-off place. Scientifically, it is just as far-fetched as the belief that alcohol corrects the chemical imbalance that causes shyness. Rather than correcting a specific chemical imbalance, there is much more evidence that psychotropic drugs work by dampening one's emotional experiences.

Since serotonin receptors exist throughout our body, it should not be surprising that SSRIs such as Prozac, Paxil, Zoloft, Celexa, Lexapro, and Luvox (all of which enhance serotonin) affect many human functions. Specifically, studies show that anywhere from 60 to 70 percent of people using these SSRI antidepressants have diminished interest in sex, and patients commonly report that their SSRIs and other antidepressants cause memory and concentration difficulties. Simply put, psychotropics (including antidepressants, antianxieties, antipsychotics, alcohol, and marijuana) take the edge off pain—but that's not the only thing these drugs take the edge off.

I understand why people reach for psychotropic drugs. At times, I've grabbed a beer or a glass of wine to take the edge off. I don't do this too often, and I have rarely reached for anything more powerful, not because of any great moral fiber but because of what I know about psychotropic drugs. I know that by routinely using prescription or illegal psychotropics or alcohol, I will eventually have to deal with a *third* pain. In addition to the original wound and the second pain of depression or some other compulsivity, I will have to deal with the third pain *caused* by the psychotropics. In addition to diminished sex drive and cognitive difficulties, other common adverse effects of antidepressants include headaches, stomachaches, nausea, and dizziness. And, as noted, the pain of psychotropics, including antidepressants, also includes drug tolerance—the need to increase dosage over time. Tolerance means you are on your way to dependency, which means that if you decide to stop taking the drug, you are subject to the pain of withdrawal. And it may well be that immediate adverse effects, tolerance, dependency, and withdrawal are the least of our worries with antidepressants. Science now supports the possibility of potential brain damage (see notes).

Many Americans think that electroconvulsive therapy (ECT, more commonly known as electroshock) and psychosurgery have gone the way of bloodletting. But both are still regarded by American psychiatry as respected treatments, especially for patients who are "treatment resistant" to drugs.

There are various modern ECT techniques. However, the scientific reality is that for all of these techniques, without evidence of any brain malignancy, the brain is damaged. Neurologist Sidney Sament describes the process: "After a few sessions of ECT the symptoms are those of moderate cerebral contusions. . . . Electroconvulsive therapy in effect may be defined as a controlled type of brain damage produced by electrical means. . . . In all cases the ECT 'response' is due to the concussion-type, or more serious, effect of ECT. The patient 'forgets' his symptoms because the brain damage destroys memory traces in the brain, and the patient has to pay for this by a reduction in mental capacity of varying degree."

The disproportionate use of ECT on women, especially older women, once made it a feminist issue, but by 1995 *Ms.* magazine was taking psychiatry's word that ECT was no longer barbaric. Psychiatry is well aware of the bad press about ECT, including Sylvia Plath's ordeal, so today ECT is far more pleasant to observe. Patients are administered an anesthetic and a muscle relaxant drug prior to ECT so they don't writhe in agony as seizures are induced. However, the effects on the brain have not changed. In January 2007, the journal *Neuropsychopharmacology* published an article about a large-scale study on the cognitive effects (immediately after and six months later) of currently used ECT techniques. The researchers found that modern ECT techniques produce "pronounced slowing of reaction time" and "persisting retrograde amnesia" (the inability to recall events before the onset of amnesia) that continue six months after treatment.

While at one time the psychosurgery called *lobotomy* was performed with an ice pick, in the modern *cingulotomy* the scalp is frozen with a local anesthetic, a small hole is drilled in the skull, an electrode is placed directly on the brain, and tissue area approximately eight by eighteen millimeters is destroyed. Unlike other kinds of brain surgery, psychosurgery is performed on parts of the brain with no evidence of any kind of malignancy. At Massachusetts General Hospital, Reese Cosgrove, perhaps the most well-known psychosurgeon in the United States, admits, "We don't understand the pathophysiology; we have no understanding of the mechanisms of why this works."

It is not surprising to find patients and doctors who swear by ECT and psychosurgery. Two centuries ago, people reported being cured by bloodletting. Weakening the body through blood loss and damaging the brain through electricity and surgery can certainly be as or more powerful than psychotropic drugs in producing a "forgetting" of emotional pain.

Jumping to Conclusions about Bizarre Behaviors

Often patients who have been treated with ECT or psychosurgery have been diagnosed as psychotically depressed. *Psychotic* is the mental health professionals' term for losing touch with reality. Most professionals have confidence, sometimes without justification, that they can identify "delusions" and "hallucinations." If you are depressed and a psychiatrist judges you to believe, hear, or see things that the psychiatrist does not believe, hear, or see, then you will likely be diagnosed with "psychotic depression." Two of history's most famous cases of psychotic depression, at least according to standard texts, are two macho men: William Tecumseh Sherman and Ernest Hemingway.

Sherman in the early days of the Civil War was not the Union hero that he was later to become. He had difficulty sleeping, his appetite was poor, his mood was low, and he was seen as having exaggerated fears. When Sherman said that sixty thousand men were needed to drive the enemy out of Kentucky and that two hundred thousand men were required for a wider offensive, Union newspapers reported he must be "crazy" and "insane" for demanding such a large force. All this was bad for his reputation, and a distressed and depressed Sherman took leave and went home for a brief period. However, Sherman ultimately found support from a sober, sometimes depressed president named Abraham Lincoln and a not-always-sober, commanding general named Ulysses S. Grant; and so the "psychotic depressive" Sherman returned to active service. Later, Sherman was to say: "Grant stood by me when I was crazy, and I stood by him when he was drunk, and now we stand by each other always." So if not Prozac or ECT, what, besides supportive relationships, was Sherman's cure? At Shiloh, one of the bloodiest battles of the Civil War, Confederate forces surprised Union forces by launching an offensive. Sherman was wounded twice and had three horses shot out from under him. Instead of panicking, he became incensed. He displayed enormous physical courage and rallied his troops. One can only speculate what a relief it must have been for Sherman to no longer be seen as weak for fearing unseen enemies or cowardly for demanding a larger force. After Shiloh, Sherman's once-thought paranoia may well have seemed like omniscience, and historians note he became a changed man. Once known for his self-loathing, Sherman would ultimately become known for the loathing he produced among the people of the territories that his troops invaded.

A century later, Ernest Hemingway *did* receive modern psychiatric treatments for his bizarre behaviors. In *Papa Hemingway*, A. E. Hotchner recounts the sad end to Hemingway's life. Hemingway became extremely depressed, and he said things that—at the time— certainly sounded delusional. He was medicated and ultimately given ECT, but he became even more depressed and complained about the effect of the electroshock ("Well, what is the sense of ruining my head and erasing my memory, which is my capital, and putting me out of business?"). In 1961, after a second series of ECT, Hemingway used his shotgun to commit suicide. How psychotic was he? At the time, one can understand why Hotchner and others who cared about Hemingway thought he was delusional. Hemingway, believing federal agents were pursuing him, told Hotchner: "It's the worst hell. The goddamnest hell. They've bugged everything. That's why we're using Duke's car. Mine's bugged. Everything's bugged. Can't use the phone. Mail intercepted. What put me on to it was that phone call with you. You remember we got disconnected? That tipped their hand." In 1999 Hotchner reported that through the Freedom of Information Act, he had discovered that the FBI and J. Edgar Hoover had indeed bugged Ernest Hemingway's telephone.

Sherman and Hemingway are not the only cases of people labeled as delusional and psychotically depressed who turn out to be sensing a general truth, although perhaps not completely accurate in their facts. When a depressed woman believes her husband is poisoning her food, the husband is usually not in fact doing what she suspects, but her distrust of his affections often turns out to be well founded.

Bipolar disorder is the new term for what was once called *manic-depression*. These terms describe someone who gets both extremely depressed and extremely euphoric—and often behaves bizarrely. A millionaire stops sleeping, gives away all his money to the mailman, chuckles incessantly, and insults his wealthy friends, all the while believing he is as charming as they think him obnoxious. Or a middle-aged, overweight homemaker loudly demands a tryout for every National Football League cheerleading squad, disrobing each time she makes her case.

Even some people who doubt that depression is a medical disease see no other explanation besides disease for the bizarre behaviors of patients diagnosed as bipolar. However, bipolar disorder, like depression, is *not* diagnosed with any physiological markers or lab tests but with behavioral checklists. And it's a slippery slope when extreme behaviors are the only criteria for diagnosing a medical condition. What, for example, could be more extreme than murder, and what could be more ordinary than a common cold? *Common* and *ordinary* are not synonymous with *health*; and *extreme* and *bizarre* are not synonymous with *medical disease*.

People who get depressed and manic often have a heightened sensitivity to the ups and downs of life and can get overwhelmed by their emotions—both negative and positive ones. Socioeconomic data in both Europe and the United States shows that bipolar diagnoses are associated with higher social status. Ordinarily, people who are depressed get little good news in their lives, and this is especially true for those living in poverty—welfare recipients in the United States have a rate of depression approximately three times as high as that of the general population. However, depressed people in the upper classes are more likely to get an inheritance, a stock upturn, or an exciting opportunity, and perhaps this is one reason they are somewhat more likely than poor people to become manic.

Bipolar disorder, once relatively rare, is now increasingly common, and some psychiatry critics, including science journalist and author Robert Whitaker, believe that one major reason for this phenomenon is the huge increase in psychiatric drug use. Extreme agitation or mania can be chemically induced by psychostimulants such as amphetamines and cocaine. And several studies indicate that antidepressants, especially SSRIs, can trigger mania.

Television, Gambling, Heroin, and Self-Pity

In 1977 Marie Winn wrote a book about the impact of television viewing called *The Plug-In Drug*. Perhaps it's somewhat of an overstatement to compare television to psychotropic drugs, but have you ever asked yourself why you keep the television on even if you are bored by what you are watching? Television does not completely shut down pain, but it does a good enough job so that psychological addiction is possible. By the term *psychological addiction*, I mean an intense habituation to the point where it feels automatic to turn on the TV without regard to a specific program, and an unease in turning it off even if nothing interesting is on. Turning it off doesn't trigger the physical withdrawal symptoms that abruptly stopping Xanax or heroin does, but it does lead to psychological discomforts.

Television is not the only nonchemical dampener of pain. With the proliferation of lotteries and casinos, gambling is fast becoming America's national pastime. When it comes to gambling, it's difficult to deny we live in an Orwellian era—consider this passage from George Orwell's *1984* (1949): "The Lottery, with its weekly pay-out of enormous prizes, was the one public event to which the proles [proletarians or working class] paid serious attention. It was probable that there were some millions of proles for whom the Lottery was the principal if not the only reason for remaining alive."

In addition to the diversions of television and gambling, there is compulsive eating and other consumer activities. Much of why advertising for consumer products works is that it exploits our desire to divert ourselves from discomforts, boredom, and frustrations, and it persuades us to ignore the price we pay for those diversions. However, if the fix is Prozac, pot, Pick-6 Lotto, or pizza, physical and psychological tolerance often leads to dangerous super-sizing solutions.

There are also nonconsumer activities that are so effective at diverting us from our psychological pain that they can become psychologically addicting. I've met many intelligent but troubled young people who cut and burn themselves in a compulsive manner. When I ask them why, they usually tell me that it momentarily keeps them from feeling bored or diverts them from intense emotional pain.

Some people have a talent for feeling sorry for themselves in such a way that it can be addicting. They can actually achieve, albeit in a modest fashion, some of what narcotics produce in a more pronounced way. Heroin addicts often describe their experience as a "pleasurable warmth, an intense feeling of relaxation"—at least when they first begin using heroin. They say, "It feels like coming out of a lake on a hot day and feeling a warm sun dry you" or "It feels like getting underneath wonderfully cozy blankets on a cold day and getting not just warm but warm sensations." (The experience of any psychotropic cannot be absolutely predicted, as it depends on too many variables, not the least of which are the user's expectations, mood, and environment.) If you're really good at self-pity, you can achieve some of this warmth. When you feel sorry for yourself, you can get warm tears to roll down your cheeks; and while you will not likely achieve the euphoric sensations associated with heroin, you can achieve a comforting warmth without the ugly withdrawal symptoms. So when doctors say things like, "You've got to simply stop feeling sorry for yourself," they are telling you that they don't know how addicting self-pity can be. Feeling sorry for yourself is a gateway drug of sorts. I've never met a substance abuser who was not extremely comfortable with self-pity. And while you can't physically overdose on feeling sorry for yourself, I've found it easier to help heroin addicts withdraw from heroin than it is to help them—or anyone else—withdraw from their addiction to self-pity.

The Incentive for Sickness, Consumer Culture, and the Holy Grail

Despite American advances in medicine and public health, Americans are often sick. There are many reasons for this, including overeating and lack of physical activity, but one seldom-discussed reason is the incentive in modern culture to get sick.

Unless we are ill, it is not socially acceptable in our society to be nonproductive or inefficient. Our culture, unlike many traditional ones, does not encourage a regular withdrawal to reevaluate our lives.

So, in a culture where there is a taboo against nonproductivity and inefficiency, what strategy do increasing numbers of us employ to withdraw? Illness. What better way to remove the taboo against nonproductivity and inefficiency?

Given the human need to be contemplative without regard for productivity and efficiency, and given American society's taboo against nonproductivity and inefficiency, Americans, in a sense, are pushed toward illness. Americans have set up a society in which we are pushed to become ill in order to withdraw from unrelenting productivity and efficiency. Those who have a serious illness such as cancer or a heart attack are given permission to reevaluate their life and even to philosophize about the meaning of life in general; and if they are terminally ill, it is okay for Americans to do nothing but reflect and gain wisdom.

When people become ill in our efficient society, however, they must attempt to rapidly eliminate their symptoms. But since illness is one of our few socially acceptable routes to meet our needs for contemplative withdrawal, there is also a force of sorts for those treatments *not* to work in any permanent way. If all this sounds crazy to you, I'm sure that you are not alone.

If you believe, as consumer culture instructs us, that depression is wholly bad, then you try to eradicate it. You try to shut down the pain that fuels depression, but that shutdown results in depression, itself another pain. Because emotional pain is part of our humanity, the process of attempting to eradicate emotional pain results in alienation from self. This alienation results in even more suffering—and the need for greater depression.

Consumer culture is more about selling products aimed at diverting people from emotional pain than healing the source of the pain, and it promotes products that must be purchased at a significant cost owing to their unnaturalness or technological complexity (e.g., synthetic drugs). The natural crafts of transforming emotional pain to energy and healing emotional wounds are not great consumer products because they are available to us without money.

Consumer culture is, in many ways, really a culture of extended childhood. The child's fantasy is that life is lived without pain and that there are no consequences for fleeing from life's difficulties. The faith of consumer culture is that all pain, tensions, and discomfort can and should be eliminated by industrial products and services.

Traditional Lakota and Blackfoot cultures celebrate joy, attempt to remedy suffering, and have healers; however, these cultures also accept that discomfort is part of life. Instead of trying to completely eradicate pain and discomfort, many traditional peoples attempt to deal with discomfort, pain, and death in a humane and dignified manner. Adulthood, in many nonconsumer cultures, is not primarily a chronological milestone; adults are differentiated from children after they have learned not to be controlled by a fear of discomfort, pain, and death. Traditional Lakota and Blackfoot adults know about *healing, dignity, humor, courage,* and *self-control.* They also understand that pain has meaning. They understand that one can never truly know how to treat another in pain without ever having been in pain. Without pain, how does one learn *compassion, patience, duty,* and *gentleness?*

Modern psychiatry is a full member of consumer culture. Its Holy Grail is that antidepressant which can take away depression but does not destroy life. In the late nineteenth century, Freud thought he had found it with cocaine. In the middle of the twentieth century, psychiatrists thought they had found it with amphetamines. Later they thought they had found it with tricyclic antidepressants like Tofranil and Elavil. At the end of the twentieth century, there were the SSRIs and other types of antidepressants. Whatever the drug, it is introduced as a fulfillment of the dream of the Holy Grail: taking away depression without destroying life. Time after time, it is then discovered that the antidepressing effects of the drug wear off, and that when one tinkers with neurotransmitters, there is—as there is with ECT and psychosurgery—damage to life. Someone outside of our culture might see no logic in continuing this path. But there is a psycho-logic to it. It is the logic of attachment to the idea that it is possible to eradicate emotional pain without damaging life. When one is attached to an idea and it fails, one doesn't give up the idea—one tries even harder. When a single beer no longer calms, rather than considering a completely different path, one is more likely to try two beers or to add another drug.

The faith of *fundamentalist consumerism* is that one will discover an object or event that can predictably manipulate moods without any downsides. Not only does modern psychiatry not challenge fundamentalist consumerism, its practitioners have become its high priests.

A wise culture knows that pain—no less than joy—is part of life. It knows that one cannot have joy without pain, that to know one is to know the other, and to destroy one is to destroy both. A wise culture knows that the experience of life without pain is a temporary illusion. It accepts that even in a perfect society there will be pain. While it prefers joy, it respects pain as much as joy. It strives for greater harmony and attempts to reduce avoidable suffering so that life's unavoidable tensions are more tolerable. And a wise culture cares about healing wounds.

Depression in Young People: The Cultural Incubator

In the 1940s and 1950s, surveys reported that young Americans were happier than old Americans, while today young people report being *less* happy than old people—not because old people have become happier but because young people have grown increasingly unhappy. As noted, a generation ago, the average age for the first episode of depression was approximately thirty, while today it is between fourteen and fifteen.

In 2004 it was estimated that at prestigious colleges, by the time of graduation approximately 25 percent of students had been prescribed an antidepressant at the on-campus health clinic (while still other students received antidepressants from their family doctors or from their friends). I would have been depressed in college, too, if I'd been graduating with huge student loan debt (common today even among those who attend public universities). Debt is not the only pain that might have something to do with increasing rates of depression in young people.

Young people are increasingly shamed for not being academic stars, and they can be labeled as "losers" for rejecting formal education institutions. In current American society, most young people fear failing to graduate high school, and, increasingly, anxiety has spread to not gaining acceptance into a prestigious college. Crucial for such acceptance are superior grades and SAT and/or ACT scores. The achievement of consistently high grades and standardized test scores often entails doing things that young people find meaningless. For many young people, too many activities involve meaningless drudgery motivated by fear. While all of life's tasks cannot be significant ones, a life replete with meaningless tasks is likely a depressing one. And while fear is not a useless cue, using fear as a primary motivator is associated with depression.

In kindergarten and perhaps for the first few elementary grades, children are often motivated to go to school by fun and curiosity; but shortly thereafter, there is little positive except for friends and extracurricular activities to motivate many to attend. On rare occasions, a student is interested in a topic and paired up with an inspiring teacher; however, in most schools the overwhelming majority of time is not spent in such joyful circumstances.

So what do many young people really learn in school? When motivated by fear to pay attention to material that one finds meaningless—often the case in schooling—one retains little knowledge. If you had no inherent love of calculus and found it meaningless at the time you were studying it, it is not likely that you retained anything from all those class and homework hours. However, many people do retain something from their school experience: the belief that surviving depends on motivating oneself with fear so as to succeed at tasks that are meaningless. This is nothing short of a blueprint for a depressing life.

There are other pains and sources of depression. Most teenagers care passionately about their relationships, but unhealed wounds are a source of depression (and other compulsive behaviors) that can make them appear "uncool" and unattractive to their peers. If plagued by unhealed wounds, one often cannot deal with the emotional pain of others, and this destroys potentially satisfying relationships. And mutual pain can also serve as a problematic "chemistry," drawing together young people who have little in common beyond their unhealed wounds.

Why is it that so many young people have unhealed wounds? Since our consumer culture is increasingly uncomfortable when it comes to dealing with pain, many parents have difficulty dealing with their children's pain. Parents with unhealed wounds cannot deal with the wounds of their kids. Often such parents try anxiously to "fix it" with countless suggestions or, increasingly, with medication. This is a major reason why teens stop being open with their parents. And with this distance, teens feel unknown. If young people feel unknown, they may still feel some affection, but they cannot really experience deep care or love. And while this is occurring, young people are receiving increasingly more stuff. All this becomes a recipe for painful confusion.

For several years, I taught juniors and seniors at a private high school a few evening hours a week. These young people, for the most part, were children of economically successful parents. Given the school setting, it was difficult to spend significant time outside of class to get to know them in any depth. One evening in class, we were talking about the topic of caring. I announced, "Although I'm sure that I would care about many of you if I got to know you, since our contact is so limited, I don't really feel like I truly know any of you— and so how can I truly care about who you are?" A few kids laughed nervously. Then one brave seventeen-year-old girl raised her hand to say that I was the first adult she'd ever heard say that, and now she understood why she was so unhappy, concluding, "There's nobody who really knows me—so of course how can I feel anybody really cares about me or truly loves me?" I looked at the faces of her classmates, and it appeared that she spoke for many.

Kafka, Gene Mapping, and Canaries

I doubt that there is any physical or mental gift that isn't something of a double-edged sword. If you had a fantastic vertical leap and could effortlessly dunk a basketball, it would be difficult to resist using that gift often, possibly acquiring knee problems caused by so many landings from high places. Some people have fantastic emotional depths, can vividly feel what others only vaguely sense, and foresee troubles that most cannot. However, such people are often overwhelmed by what they feel and see. Great artists have these fantastic depths, and many lead troubled lives.

The writer Franz Kafka (1883–1924) saw earlier than others around him that giant bureaucratic institutions would care only about perpetuating themselves, and not about the humans who inhabited them. Kafka saw how this increasingly dehumanizing new world order would infect families and destroy human kindness. He knew that those like himself, who were especially sensitive to this reality, would be the first to feel alienated, anguished, and depressed, but that eventually so would everyone. Franz Kafka would not be surprised by our epidemic of depression.

There's a long list of artists, from Ernest Hemingway to Sylvia Plath, Charlie Parker, Janis Joplin, Phil Ochs, Kurt Cobain, and many others, who, in response to tremendous pain, either committed suicide or abused substances resulting in premature death. And there's an even longer list of people who are equally overwhelmed by their emotions, sensitivities, and intuition, but who lack the talent, support, or luck necessary to create great works.

Common sense and research suggest that we are born with different kinds of temperaments. One kind of temperament could make us more vulnerable to sensitivity and depression, another temperament could make us more vulnerable to insensitivity, dishonesty, and sociopathy, and still another to compliance and fascism.

Though we may be born with different temperaments, that does not mean that there exists a genetic link to temperament in the same simple manner that there exists for eye color. Behavioral geneticist Kennith Kendler, one of psychiatry's most revered researchers (Peter Kramer described him as a "genius"), disappointed the mental health establishment in a July 2005 *American Journal of Psychiatry* article that reviewed the evidence for "gene action in psychiatric disorders." Kendler concluded: "Although we may wish it to be true, we do not have and are not likely to ever discover 'genes for' psychiatric illness."

While parents' genes can readily be linked to their children's physical makeup, the impact of parents' genes on their children's temperaments is a very different matter. "The ultimate genetic experiment," reports psychologist Bertram Karon, "the Nazi sterilization and annihilation of [mental] patients, led to no decrease in schizophrenia in the next generation." There are other logical contradictions for the notion that a genetic link to psychological traits exists in the same manner as it exists for physical traits. For example, a large number of studies confirm the commonsense expectation of a markedly lower reproductive rate in those diagnosed with schizophrenia, major depression, and bipolar disorder as compared to the general population. From a genetic point of view, this lower reproductive rate should ultimately decrease the rate of these "disabling mental illnesses," but as noted, the rate of this population has actually increased. While critics of psychiatry sometimes neglect to mention that people's double-edged temperaments may well be innate, the mental health establishment routinely ignores evidence showing that temperament is not being passed on by parents in the same manner as physical traits.

It has been my experience (both professionally and socially) that noncompliant kids often have compliant parents, that conformist kids often have nonconformist parents, and that parents routinely report that the temperament of their child is different from their own. I've actually come to suspect that nature is more likely to give us children with different temperaments from our own—perhaps to help us grow psychologically and spiritually, or perhaps to remind us that we need community to raise children.

We know what depressed parents do that brings out their child's unhealthiest side—and not just depression. The research shows that children of depressed parents are more likely to have a host of problems, including attention difficulties, unruly behavior, anxiety, alcohol abuse, and physical ailments. Psychologist Michael D. Yapko in *Hand-Me-Down Blues* (1999) reports that depressed parents "are less able to compromise in disagreements with their children, tending to respond to even minor conflict situations with either harsh enforcement (yelling, threats of extreme punishment, verbal abuse, and even hitting) or by withdrawing completely and simply avoiding the confrontation. . . . Speak less to their children, engaging with them less frequently even during routine activities. . . . Make more negative comments when they do speak. . . . Are generally less skilled at talking to their children about their feelings, especially negative feelings." While depression can run in families, it is much more accurate to say that parenting by troubled parents is more likely to result in troubled children, some of whom will mimic the particular behavior of their parents but others of whom will exhibit different self-destructive behaviors.

While both temperament and environmental forces (such as trauma) are significant variables, an individual's own beliefs and choice of actions appear to be more important determinants of depression than either nature or nurture. Even in the case of identical twins raised together— with identical genes and in nearly identical environments—the majority of the co-twins of those who are depressed are *not* depressed.

We each have an unpleasant side, and trauma, stress, unhealed wounds, and unwise choices can bring it out. For some of us, that unpleasant—or dark—side may be deep depression, while for others it may be dishonesty and sociopathy, and for others it may be compliancy and fascism. Why has the mental health establishment been so much more passionate about discovering the genes for susceptibility to depression than discovering the genes that make us susceptible to dishonesty, sociopathy, compliancy, and fascism?

I have difficulty believing that God or biology made a mistake in creating Franz Kafka, Vincent Van Gogh, Theodore Dostoevski, Soren Kierkegaard, and others with sensitive, intuitive, and prophetic temperaments. Even before behavioral geneticists such as Kenneth Kendler were asserting that it was unlikely that genes for psychiatric disorders would ever be found, I did not accept that society would be better off if the genes for the depression-prone were discovered. What would be next—recommending to mothers carrying such fetuses to abort?

American society is already intent on weeding out pessimists. Because of research associating optimism with high achievement, the Attributional Style Questionnaire (ASQ) has, since the 1980s, been used to identify and eliminate pessimistic applicants for college, West Point, insurance jobs, and many other opportunities. Today, if you are seeking admission to a school or to be hired for a job, and you happen to be more like Franz Kafka than Tony Robbins, you may just want to fake your optimistic/pessimistic questionnaire.

I believe that in true community and a rehumanized society, we would want intuitive, prophetic, and pessimistic people. Even when people with such temperaments do not become great visionaries, they are as valuable as canaries in the mine. When the canaries, more sensitive to their surroundings than the miners, fell off their perch, the miners knew to get out of the mine as quickly as possible. The miners loved those canaries. Why don't we love those sensitive, clairvoyant people who are in touch with society before the rest of us? From my experience, they may be more prone to depression, but they are almost always right when they warn that a family, a community, a society, or a culture is in trouble. The more we see these people "falling off their perch"—and the epidemic of depression suggests that this is the case—the more we all should be concerned about what's destroying them. Even if you are neither depressed nor especially altruistic, it is no great stretch to recognize that what's getting to the canary will ultimately get to you.

Healing, Wholeness, and Choice

If your wounds are unhealed, then you are alienated from parts of yourself and thus lack the strength of wholeness. So even with morale and knowledge of what constitutes constructive behavior, you may feel unable to act on that knowledge.

In twenty-first-century psychiatry, the terms *wounds, alienation,* and *wholeness* have become mere relics. In 1986, already concerned about his profession's lack of interest in the psyche of patients, psychiatrist Morton Reiser published an article called "Are Psychiatric Educators 'Losing the Mind'?" He wrote: "I talked with some of the [psychiatric] residents and found that their approach and mind set in the interviews [were] astoundingly unpsychological. Once they had done the *DSM-III* 'inventory' and had identified target symptoms for psychopharmacology, the diagnostic workup and meaningful communication stopped. Worse than that, to my mind, so did the residents' curiosity about the patient as a person—even to the point where often there was no answer to such basic questions as why the patient came for treatment at this time and what seemed to be worrying him or her."

Since 1986, Big Pharma's influence has resulted in further biochemical reductionism in psychiatry. It became so glaring that in 2005, even the president of the American Psychiatric Association, Steven Sharfstein, told his fellow psychiatrists, "As we address these Big Pharma issues, we must examine the fact that as a profession, we have allowed the biopsychosocial model to become the bio-bio-bio model."

In this chapter, I offer two very different definitions of *healing*, only one of which I believe is ultimately helpful for the depressed. Healing as a natural process is explained, including the barriers to healing, as well as the creation of conditions that allow us to unblock these barriers. The process of self-healing, healing rituals, group healing, and the power of sacredness are also discussed. The difficulty of healing within an extremist consumer society is considered, as well as the idea that a paid therapeutic relationship may not be the ideal condition for healing.

Two Different Definitions of *Healing*

Doctors who believe that depression is a medical condition caused primarily by brain chemistry may talk about healing, but their definition of *healing* is fundamentally different from the kind of healing that I believe is helpful.

Our society's treatments for depression, as noted, are increasingly ruled by insurance companies and their managed-care organizations. Managed care demands that doctors target symptoms, select techniques for eliminating symptoms, and predict the length of treatment. The pressure to eliminate symptoms as rapidly as possible leads to brief and simplistic treatments. Symptoms are often resistant to these treatments, but even when symptoms are "fixed" by such techniques, it is my experience that it is often a temporary fix that can ultimately make matters worse. It can actually inhibit the kind of healing that makes us whole.

I am not opposed to technology. If I have a decaying tooth, I'm all for drilling away and filling the cavity. If awful noises are sounding from my car's old muffler, I'm all for replacing it. However, depression is not the same as a decayed tooth or a worn-out muffler. When dealing with depression, I don't think we can just yank something out and stick in something new.

Depression and other self-destructive compulsions can be healed by creating healing conditions. These conditions allow us to move toward wholeness. Depression is about being overwhelmed by the pain of a loss of wholeness. If we can create the conditions for healing, healing will *naturally* occur. The same cannot be said for a decayed tooth and a worn-out muffler. Much of what makes life comical or tragic comes from applying a manner of thinking that is appropriate in one mode to a completely different mode. It's silly to try to create the conditions for a worn-out muffler to naturally heal and become whole, and I believe it is tragic to treat a depressed person like a worn-out muffler.

Some time back in Western civilization, many people began to consider *everything* as mechanical objects. This meant that everything was subject to manipulation. If one believes that humans are nothing but machines filled with mechanical parts, then one replaces, manipulates, and controls whatever seems to have gone wrong. The "doctor-technician" views healing as synonymous with fixing. This may work for suturing a laceration, removing a bullet, or restoring the body from other identifiable physiological insults, but it does not work well for depression.

The technical-mechanical model is a perfect fit for a consumer society, but natural healing, which works best for transforming depression, does not fit neatly into a consumer model. Natural healing, unlike repairing, is not a top-down, vendor-to-customer kind of process. It is not unidirectional. In the natural healing process, both helper and helpee can receive healing. In the mechanical-technological consumer world, there are doctors who fix and there are patients who get fixed. It is a world of specialized authorities. Americans are often told, in this age of specialization, that we must seek experts to fix all of our problems—and this results in missed opportunities. People, by virtue of being alive, can heal and be healed. One can be in the doctor role and receive healing, and one can be in the patient role and heal; and there are all kinds of other roles where healing can take place. This truth is often denied because it plays havoc with industrialization and consumerism. If the vendor and the customer are not clearly defined, then who gets billed?

Symptoms can be seen, but a lack of emotional, interpersonal, existential, or spiritual wholeness does not show up in any lab test or X-ray. What can be intuited and known often cannot be quantified—and so in Western science is often not taken seriously. Healing the source of despair is about becoming whole, and this too cannot be scientifically measured.

With wholeness there is strength—and the gift of choice. Wholeness is about unity, harmony, and congruity. The opposite of wholeness is fracture, alienation, and falseness. If we are not whole, it is because we have been blocked. Wholeness consists of restoring conditions that allow for healing to occur naturally.

There are many kinds of fractures of wholeness. Life is large and complex and presents many ways that we and life become disconnected. There are breaks between people, such as the disconnections between spouses, friends, and siblings and between a parent and a child. And there are breakdowns in community. There are also all kinds of internal breaks to personal wholeness. When people are in denial of their pains and joys, they can lose contact with who they really are. Personal inauthenticities (for example, resenting a parent but being afraid to assert that resentment) are also internal breaks.

Wholeness is also fractured when people violate their ethical beliefs. I knew one corporate executive who regularly attended church and who genuinely believed in the Golden Rule and "Love thy neighbor." But his corporate board, fearing a hostile takeover and needing greater profits to please Wall Street analysts, decided to move production to another country. This decision cost jobs in his community but increased the price of his corporation's stock, which financially benefited him. He continued working at the corporation and became depressed. While the loss of ethical wholeness (or integrity) was not the only pain in his life, it was a major one.

Another loss of wholeness experienced by most people in consumer society is the fracture between humans and the rest of nature. In extremist industrial society, the natural world is consumed or merely serves as a pleasant diversion. In our culture, humans are superior and apart from nature. Enter that culture, and one becomes a part of that alienation from nature. Break from such a culture, and one experiences alienation from one's culture.

I believe that mental health professionals routinely suffer a loss of wholeness in their training. Much of the pain of my training was about experiencing and witnessing this process. All too often I observed psychology graduate students and psychiatry residents so afraid of not appearing "professional" that they were intimidated into shedding core aspects of their personality. For example, they would readily incorporate professional jargon at the expense of their own authentic language. This routinely rendered them impotent as healers and sometimes made them into objects of derision by their younger patients.

I also observed how the course work of mental health professionals fractured the wholeness of their knowledge. Future psychiatrists narrowly focus on brain chemistry—the bio-bio-bio model. And in the course work of both psychiatrists and psychologists, no serious attention is given to cultural, economic, and political issues. Academia can be a place of narrow, specialized turfs. Instead of freely exploring the entire landscape, academicians are often quite timid about "trespassing" onto another's domain. Among professors there are certainly rebels against this practice, and they're fond of joking, "Academia is a place where you specialize more and more about less and less with this logical endpoint: knowing absolutely everything about absolutely nothing."

An unwhole person who is *aware* of his or her condition and struggles to become whole can help another. But an unwhole person in a helper role who is ignorant of his or her condition can, I believe, be damaging. Professionals who have not actively fought to maintain or to recover their own wholeness cannot possibly actively care about their patients' wholeness.

Mental health professionals' decreasing understanding of and respect for healing and wholeness commonly result in the following unfortunate treatment: After cognitive-behavioral advice fails, the doctor proceeds to psychotropic drugs, neglecting to consider the possibility that the advice went unheeded not because of patient neurotransmitter levels, but because the person is too unwhole to make life-affirming choices.

One can approach depression with a mechanical-technical consumer model or with a concern for wholeness and a belief in natural healing. Depending on one's approach, one is going to be a very different kind of doctor—and probably a very different kind of person.

Healing Conditions

It is difficult in prose to describe emotional healing without using words that, through misuse and overuse, have come to sound sentimental and even sappy, but I will give it my best shot.

Emotional wounds heal naturally when we are not in a state of defensiveness, and healing conditions encourage this necessary openness.

These conditions are, in great part, created by kindness, gentleness, and love. Kindness includes generosity, the giving or sharing of what one has of value (such as time). Kindness is warmheartedness, a turning toward rather than away from suffering. It is tolerance, an acceptance that those in pain are often unpleasant, and it is friendliness, offering a hello before receiving one. Gentle speech, gentle movements, and gentle touch are healing (when one is noisy, erratic, and rough, others stay in a protective mode, which is not amenable to healing). Gentleness is knowing that people who are suffering have difficulty tolerating much discord. And gentle people have patience; if one feels the pressure of time, one cannot heal. Love is more difficult to define. It is certainly a deep affection for the uniqueness of another. It is a union that maintains the integrity of each, and a valuing and respect for another. It is a heartfelt concern for another's pain, and an experience of resonation to another's being. Love is also defined by its opposite, fear. If we fear that the pain of another will overwhelm us, we cannot love that person. Healing conditions also include trust, authenticity, free choice, and faith.

Some people who favor wholeness and natural healing reject the idea of calling anyone a *healer*, as that implies others are not. I have no difficulty referring to someone as a healer (or shaman) if he or she is especially gifted at providing healing conditions. But I also keep in mind that, in any given instance, any one of us can be a greater healer than the greatest of healers.

I have met only a handful of people who are exceptionally gifted healers, and they share certain important attributes. Their very presence has a soothing quality. Their facial expressions are easy on the eyes, and their speech is equally easy on the ears. All great healers are more than simply good listeners. They go beyond that. They are not reactive to negativity. They gently make certain not to let themselves get damaged, but if others are hurt, angry, frustrated, or pained in some way, this does not appear to make them anxious. Great healers are able to detach from someone else's pain, not with coldness but with warmth. Others feel that they care about their pain. None of the great healers that I have known are great joke tellers, but all have a special kind of humor that is extraordinarily sensitive. They are amazingly adept at knowing when making light of a pain lightens its burden. What clearly sets these exceptional healers apart from others is their lack of narcissism. In contrast to the majority of people who are preoccupied with their own needs, these healers can focus on life around them. All the extraordinary healers I have known were themselves wounded when young. Often the wounds were from abusive or neglectful parenting, and sometimes the wounds were also caused by society. For these extraordinary healers, their wounds became a formative positive experience, creating a deep connection and compassion for the pain of others.

When it comes to healing, we must be emotionally open. Healing requires an openness to the truth of one's pain and confusion, and this requires a faith that such openness will not destroy one's being. I have found that many people pride themselves on being open-minded (open to different opinions and new experiences), but I believe it is far easier to be open-minded than it is to be open emotionally—and this is necessary for healing.

We are often afraid to be open emotionally. For many of us, this means being vulnerable to something bad. It is difficult to be open if you feel under attack. If you are severely stressed or terrified of being nonproductive and inefficient, openness is a luxury you may believe that you cannot afford. If people around you are negative and critical, you will likely stay in a protective rather than a receptive mode.

In chapter 3, I discussed how depression and other compulsions are defenses against pain, and how defenses fail and become themselves a source of pain. Most people, at least much of the time, live in a state of defensiveness. Chronic defensiveness not only fatigues us, it also keeps us from being in a state of openness to healing and receiving more energy. We block healing by a guarded attitude: we distrust others' motives, reflexively disagree, predict and control, and are negativistic and cynical.

Some people in the midst of their fears and defensiveness receive a gift. The gift is an insight that life without any openness is not really worth living. They begin to think, "By what measure am I successful if I am always feeling the need to defend myself? Do I really need to protect myself as much as I do? If so, should I consider changing my environment, or if I am unnecessarily protecting myself, might it not be worth the risk of increasing my openness?"

The vicious cycle of the *unhealing box* parallels that of the demoralization box discussed earlier. The demoralization box exists when, without morale, people lack the energy to regain morale. The unhealing box exists when people who are unwhole are so frightened by their pain that they move quickly to defenses, protections, and shutdowns; and those very defenses, protections, and shutdowns block the process of healing. People who need healing most are in the most pain, and they are most likely to defend and protect themselves and thereby block healing.

I tell clients that it may have made sense to numb themselves when they were on the battlefield—whether that battlefield was Vietnam, Iraq, or their parents' alcoholic brawls. Their shutdown may well have helped them survive. But the problem with these shutdowns is that when people are no longer on the battlefield, they often cannot let go of what helped them survive, and their defense becomes a burden that interferes with enjoying life. There is an old Buddhist story about a man who is in danger of being killed on his side of the river. He builds a sturdy raft that gets him to the other side of the river and safety. Afterward the man comes to feel so strongly that he owes his life to the raft that he puts it on his back and carries it everywhere for the remainder of his life, interfering with his ability to experience joy.

Some people say they have faith, but their idea of faith is a belief that some day their life might improve. They may even say that they believe in healing and agree that humans naturally move toward wholeness. But they may still lack the kind of "faith in the faith" required for healing. For the unhealed, there is no convincing argument for the existence of healing. Only faith that it exists can bridge the abyss.

Ultimately, the healing of wounds expands our humanity. Many people who have healed from even horrid traumas will state: "I wouldn't wish that abuse or neglect on anyone, but I feel like a fuller, stronger person for having gone through the experience and having healed from it."

Healing is one of those phenomena that cannot be objectified, quantified, and scientifically measured. A sad irony that I observed in my professional training was that several naturally talented healers never got their PhD or MD, while many with less talent did earn their degrees. One cannot pass an exam to show a proficiency in healing, yet nothing is more important in transforming depression than healing wounds, and nothing is more helpful to healing wounds than being around someone capable of providing healing conditions.

When the conditions for healing are in place, the barriers or defenses to healing are more likely to disappear. We become open to feeling cared about, making it more likely that we can become open to caring about life beyond ourselves—and this results in healing.

Self-Healing, Self-Parenting, and Compassion

Many depressed people have never experienced nurturing parents or gifted healers, and they have a history of such traumatizing human relationships that it's extremely difficult for them to be open, at least initially, to any kind of healing involving other people. This does not mean they are doomed. If they can become more whole with any part of life, they can grow stronger—perhaps strong enough to one day risk being open to human relationships.

Depressed people who fear humans can sometimes allow themselves to be open to the healing power of the rest of nature. For example, they can care for an animal or help a plant grow and receive a healing benefit from that. I've seen children who are completely shut down when around other human beings come alive when they are around animals. By nurturing and healing anything that is alive, people heal.

Self-healing often involves "self-parenting." Good parents help their child understand that pain is natural and not to be ashamed of. Parenting for wholeness is about communicating affection and respect for a child's being. It is about nurturing pain with kindness, gentleness, and love, while setting limits on destructive behaviors. It is natural for children to become overwhelmed by their fear of not surviving, by their hurt about feeling uncared for, and by their anger with perceived injustices. Wise parenting trusts that with nurturance and limit setting, the power of fear, hurt, and anger will shrink, which will ultimately result in the child not being dominated by those painful emotions.

Self-parenting is similar to parenting another. You will remain a child in an emotional sense to the extent that fear, hurt, or anger rules you. Once you are honest with yourself about the degree to which you have emotionally remained a child, you can set about diminishing the fear-hurt-anger domination. Self-parenting, like parenting another, means nurturing pain while setting limits on the destructive behaviors it can cause. A good parent has confidence that with nurturance and limit setting, this fear-hurt-anger triumvirate will shrink in power.

When waves of pain come over people, the tendency is to struggle. The tendency is to believe that if you don't struggle against the pain, it will overwhelm you. The paradox is that as soon as you begin to struggle, the more likely it is you will feel overwhelmed. The pain is frequently the sharpest upon awakening, when you are apt to feel the most unprotected and vulnerable. When you experience emotional pain in this state, you may well panic and struggle. People struggle in different ways: they analyze the pain, they are angry about the perceived source of the pain, or they try to divert themselves with drugs, television, and so forth.

Viewing emotional pain in the following manner is helpful for some people. If a stray dog starts to bark at you and you panic and run, you have put yourself in the greatest jeopardy. The dog—like your pain—sees your panic as a provocation to attack. And the dog—like your pain—can outrun you. Samuel Johnson, the eighteenth-century British writer, actually called his dark side a "black dog." I once worked with an admirer of Samuel Johnson, a middle-aged woman who had been psychiatrically hospitalized several times. When I first saw her, she was feeling overwhelmed by her emotional pain and terrified of returning to the psychiatric ward. I asked her to make the pain something visible, and she chose to borrow Johnson's image of a black dog. I told her, "Now remember that it is not your pain—the black dog—that is causing your depression, but rather your struggle from it that leads you to torment. Let go of struggling and move toward your pain. Say calming things to your black dog in a gentle voice." Remembering her previous history with a psychiatrist who had hospitalized her against her wishes, I added, "Don't worry, this is only in your imagination. No one will probate you for petting your imaginary black dog!" She laughed—and survived without another psychiatric hospitalization.

Without faith and discipline, self-healing is unlikely. While *faith* is believing in something without empirical evidence, *discipline* is doing what you believe will be helpful despite a lack of habit. A certain discipline is required to neither panic nor struggle nor flee. A certain discipline is required to not protect yourself from emotional pain. A certain discipline is required simply to accept the pain and to be gentle, kind, and loving with it.

I have met many depressed artists and thinkers who have faith that a transcendent force loves *truth* and *beauty*. However, they often do not have faith that this transcendent force loves the *whole of life*—including their pain. To make a leap of faith that a transcendent force loves not only truth and beauty but *all* of life, they need only this simple discipline: to remind themselves that this transcendent force (God for some) loves not only truth and beauty but the whole of their humanity. When we feel our pain is loved, our pain will no longer be a demon.

Human beings seek attachments. Those who, early in life, have formed significant relationships with their fear, hurt, or anger have developed a habit of connecting to that which is painful. Depression, a way of blunting that pain, can itself become a painful experience that they can become attached to. The solution to such destructive attachments is to learn, when feeling the anxiety of disconnection, to connect with a mental experience that does not bring pain. A mental experience that suits this purpose is *compassion*—it is always available. Just as there are many reasons to experience fear, hurt, and anger, there is an endless supply of reasons for experiencing compassion for all that is alive and experiences pain.

Compassion is both altruistic and selfish. It can prompt actions that reduce pain in others, while at the same time the very experience of compassion is self-healing. Many people are so fearful of others, so hurt by others, and so angry with others that the idea of compassion toward others feels inauthentic, even absurd. They feel that if no one has cared about them, why should they have compassion toward another? This is an understandable position until one recognizes that filling one's brain and heart with compassion is an act of enlightened self-interest.

Through helping another, people are rewarded with self-healing. If parents care deeply enough for their child, it is my experience that nature "cuts them a break," allowing them to transcend their usual limitations in order to help that child become whole. Helping your child, another's child, or another adult can be self-healing.

Ultimately, the critical component of self-healing is *what we do rather than what happens to us.* While it is true that people are more likely to care about life beyond themselves if they themselves have experienced caring, it does not always follow. In contrast, while people who have never been cared about are themselves less likely to care about others, some such people do discover the self-healing force of caring about life beyond themselves. What we have experienced changes how likely we are to discover the healing force of caring about life beyond self, but our history does not guarantee our path.

Forgiveness, Acceptance, and Strength

When we forgive and accept ourselves, other people, or the world, we are essentially healing ourselves. However, even when people are aware of the importance of forgiveness and acceptance for healing, they may still resist doing so. As the writer C. S. Lewis noted, "Everyone says that forgiveness is a lovely idea until he has something to forgive."

How is it possible to overcome resistance to forgiveness and acceptance? Many people resist because they believe that forgiveness invites more hurt, as it is a sign of weakness. Yet Mahatma Gandhi pointed out, "The weak can never forgive. Forgiveness is the attribute of the strong." Once you associate forgiveness and acceptance with strength—not weakness (or forgetting or condoning that allows for further abuse)—letting go of resentments becomes easier. Though forgiveness need not necessarily lead to a reconciliation and the restoration of a relationship, the word *forgiveness* denotes exactly that for many people, and so it sounds to them like a bad idea to forgive chronically abusive people. They would rather use the word *acceptance* when it comes to letting go of resentment for uncaring, hurtful people, and they reserve *forgiveness* for caring individuals who are genuinely sorry for their hurtful behavior.

Often people privately believe that holding on to resentment provides a certain kind of *justice*. However, your resentment will be inconsequential for a person who does not care about you, and your resentment will be relished by a person who wanted to hurt you. And if the person who hurt you does in fact care about you, your resentment will be hurting a person who cares about you. So resentment creates no justice.

The path of forgiving yourself is quite similar to that of forgiving another. By holding on to self-punishment, you are not helping anyone. Self-punishment for your own misdeeds will not prevent further hurtful acts. In fact, the pain of self-punishment is likely to fuel increased compulsive destructive behaviors. Accepting that you are human and imperfect means that at times, by virtue of your insensitivity and compulsivity, you will produce pain in others and yourself. With self-forgiveness comes greater strength and control over your actions—and less hurt for others and yourself.

Sometimes the "unforgiven" is neither another person nor oneself but the *world*. The world is routinely unfair. You can reflect on your experience of the world's unfairness with bitterness and resentment—and feel weak. Or you can acknowledge the reality of the world's unfairness, forgive its imperfection, fight for justice for yourself and others—and feel strong.

Resentment, no matter what its source, is a demon. To forgive oneself, another person, or the world is to let go of a demon that can fuel depression. Letting go of resentment takes courage, and acts of courage create greater strength.

Healing through Self-Expression

Some people are convinced that they have to be a professional artist to heal through self-expression and beauty. Not true. You don't have to be a highly skilled painter, writer, musician, sculptor, actor, dancer, or any such artist to achieve healing from self-expression and beauty. I am convinced that all of us have one or more means of concrete self-expression. This is not limited to traditional art forms but can be the creation of a garden, a home, or a store. Whatever we create that allows the world to see who we are is a form of self-expression.

The poet, novelist, and screenplay writer Charles Bukowski (1920–1994) had, for much of his life, every reason to hate people and the world. As a young boy, Bukowski was beaten by his father on a regular basis; as a teenager and young man, he had a severe case of acne that cut him off from female companionship; and for much of his life, he worked at jobs that he found painfully alienating. He drank heavily, and no doubt most mental health professionals would have diagnosed him with both depression and substance abuse. But Bukowski discovered the healing power of writing, and with humor and even vulgarity he fought off both hatefulness and sentimentality. This, along with his resilience, is his appeal for many of his readers. Eventually Bukowski connected with a man who so greatly admired his work that he provided him with a stipend so he could quit his job and write. The man, John Martin, founded Black Sparrow Press and published Bukowski's books, which eventually sold well, providing Bukowski with late-in-life financial success and some fun. In Bukowski's *Barfly*, a woman in a bar tells Henry (the author's autobiographical character) that she hates people, and then asks him, "You hate them?" Henry responds, "No, but I seem to feel better when they're not around." After I had finished my training, my closest friend in graduate school, who was worried about me, said, "How are you going to remain a psychologist? You hate shrinks." Ripping off Bukowski, I replied, "I don't hate them. I just seem to feel better when they're not around." My friend was actually more right about me than I was, but she, a natural healer, pretended to believe me. She, like Bukowski, instinctively knew that an unsentimental resistance to hatefulness can be healing, and that people, if you get out of their way, can sometimes become what they aspire to be.

After exiting graduate school, I felt, perhaps because of the similarities of that experience to high school, that I had emotionally regressed to my late teens and found my heartfelt journaling to be embarrassingly adolescent. With those journals, I decided to write a coming-of-age novel in which I could give my adolescent language to adolescent characters. If I had gone instead to therapy, I doubt that I would have been as open about how truly immature I had become. But the novel form made it easy to be honest—and to care rather than judge. Thus, it was a form of self-healing, and I received added healing benefits when others resonated to it.

What happened to my friend? She eventually quit school before getting her PhD, returned to her previous profession, and, among other things, learned to make beautiful quilts. When the colors combine just right and the texture feels just right, it heals her. When she gives a quilt to someone, that heals her, too. During a particularly awful stretch in her life, she tried antidepressants, which did in fact temporarily take the edge off her anxiety but also isolated her. So she stopped the drugs and discovered quilt-making, which now connects her to other quilt-makers and to those she gives her quilts to.

A major healing aspect of concrete self-expression is that it takes our focus away from ourselves and shifts it toward what we are creating. Also, whether we are writing a book, stitching a quilt, building a house, cultivating a garden, or designing a store, there is a desire for a coherent wholeness. The more our consciousness is about wholeness, the more we are in the realm of healing. The more our focus is on creating that which revitalizes ourselves or others, the more we are in the realm of healing.

Beauty heals those who create it and those who experience it. The beauty created by a great artist is an especially powerful force in a world that has seen its natural beauty increasingly destroyed. This is one more reason why it should be unthinkable to weed out those depression-prone artistic temperaments who, better than the rest of us, can create beauty. Beauty is no trifling luxury. It is essential to life. And while the beauty produced by Van Gogh and Mozart is healing for millions of people, each of us is capable of creating beauty that can heal ourselves and one another.

Healing the Seriously Dis-Eased

In Western culture, the most serious mental diagnosis is psychosis, which, as previously noted, means losing touch or breaking with reality. Science does not know why people move into psychoses. Not too long ago, psychiatrists were convinced that certain psychoses, especially schizophrenia, were caused by too much of the neurotransmitter dopamine. Today, psychiatry admits that most people diagnosed with schizophrenia have no evidence of increased dopamine, and some actually have reduced levels of dopamine.

Lawrence Plumlee, a retired toxicologist with the Environmental Protection Agency, was diagnosed with schizophrenia as a troubled young soldier in the Army in the 1960s. He believes, "The reasons we get visions and some delusions when we're coming of age is because we're looking for meaning in life."

I believe that when people become unwhole in the extreme, a break of some kind with routine is necessary for healing. This is analogous to a broken arm that has been set incorrectly and needs to be rebroken and reset so as to heal correctly. This explanation cannot be proven in any scientific sense, but I've found that it resonates with those who have broken down. If a depressed person has become "too unwhole," and there is no community available to create a caring, ritualistic break with reality, an individual has little alternative except to create his or her own idiosyncratic break. Unfortunately, such a break, absent of healing conditions, can result in deterioration rather than healing.

The World Health Organization, in two different studies (1979 and 1992), reported that the United States and other "developed" countries are *inferior* to "developing" countries such as India, Nigeria, and Colombia in helping people diagnosed as psychotic to recover. One can only speculate why recovery rates are better in both underdeveloped nations and traditional cultures. One reason could be Western medicine's reliance on drugs, and another reason could be modern society's relative absence of gentle, supportive, healing groups.

In the late eighteenth century in England, the Quakers, a socially radical group of that era, were skeptical and distrustful of doctors, especially their treatment of the seriously mentally disturbed. The

Quakers had a completely different mind-set, as noted by Robert Whitaker in *Mad in America* (2001): "They would treat the ill with gentleness and respect, as the 'brethren' they were." Whitaker describes how the Quakers of York, England, in 1796 opened York Retreat, a small, simple home with gardens and paths for walking. The patients were provided with plentiful meals, snacks, and even wine, and Whitaker tells us: "They held tea parties, at which the patients were encouraged to dress up. During the day, patients were kept busy with a variety of tasks . . . and given opportunities to read, write, play games like chess. Poetry was seen as particularly therapeutic. . . . In this gentle environment, few needed to be confined." In our current era of restraints and chemical tranquilizers, it may surprise some to read Whitaker's account that "in its first fifteen years of operation, not a single attendant at the York Retreat was seriously injured by a violent patient." The rates of recovery at York Retreat were similar to those in modern India, Nigeria, and Colombia and approximately twice as high as those seen in modern American society.

Brooke Medicine Eagle is an author and Native American ceremonial leader. She tells us that the function of a healer is to embody wholeness of spirit in such a way as to "guide those who have fallen out of rhythm, who have stumbled into dis-ease, and help them to reestablish their balance and rhythm." She explains how an especially troubled person is healed: "[A] circle would be called together in which the diseased one would be laid at the center. The circle might begin by cleansing itself of past history through acts of personal forgiveness; then the dancers might sing songs of harmony and begin to walk in a circle. They would dance an imagined ascending spiral, calling and drawing the descending energy of the patient in the center, until the descent hesitates, stops, and begins to lift upward, carried at first by the community energy but gradually gaining its own strength. At last it would resonate fully within the newly healed one as he or she rejoined the dance. This transformation might take several days and might involve other acts of holiness as well."

In the dominant culture of Western society today, we are not completely without group healing rituals. Alcoholics Anonymous is an example of how people still help heal each other. AA is also an example of how powerful rituals can be subverted into weak consumer products. At its start, participation in AA was always a free choice, but today courts coerce drunk-driving offenders to attend AA meetings (also called Twelve Step); chemical-dependency counselors conduct "interventions" (involving friends and family) that pressure others to accept AA treatment; and for-profit hospitals use manipulative advertising to entice entrance into their AA treatments. Coercion and manipulation subvert the spiritual attitude that is necessary for healing. However, in a noncoerced AA meeting, there can be healing. Personal stories (called *leads*) about transformations from alcohol abuse to happier sobriety are told with a positive attitude. There is no attempt to coerce, manipulate, or financially profit. In such groups, the AA phrase "Take what you want, and leave the rest" is not a meaningless incantation but a sacred agreement. In such an atmosphere, a healing culture can be formed.

Healing Rituals, Sacredness, and Unusual Events

We can learn much about the degree of humanity in a particular culture by studying its rituals. Consumer culture's rituals are, of course, consumerist ones. Americans exchange gobs of Christmas presents and have Super Bowl parties, where they often focus more on the expensive commercials than they do on the game. In our culture, we still have funeral rituals, but these are often attended by relatives who've become mere acquaintances, and so even this ritual provides less and less genuine healing. Healing rituals once required time and intimacy; now they require bureaucracy and money. Contrast the following two examples, the first from modern American consumer society and the second from Native American traditional culture.

In the United States today, here is the typical procedure people follow when they are so unhappy that they seek help. They call their insurance company's mental health managed care and get the names of three doctors. They pick one name, make an appointment, and report back to a managed-care manager, who precertifies them. When they arrive at their appointment, they are given several forms to fill out. The receptionist usually seems bored from saying the same thing far too often, and it is clear that ensuring the office gets its money is extremely important. After sitting awhile in an impersonal waiting room, perhaps with a mounted television tuned to a soap opera or game show, patients are ushered into an office or an exam room. The doctor is civil but seems stressed and pressed for time. Patients are asked questions about their sleep, appetite, mood, and suicidal thoughts. Then they are probably handed a prescription for an antidepressant and asked to make a follow-up appointment.

Contrast this ritual with a Native American one. I'm no expert on Native American healing rituals, but I will tell you about a "sweat" I participated in. Prior to giving a talk on the Yakama Reservation, my wife, Bon, and I stayed at the home of a colleague, psychologist Dave Walker, and his wife, Sue. Dave introduced Bon and me to his friend Long Standing Bear Chief, a member of the Blackfoot Nation, who explained to us that among Blackfoot, coed sweats are permitted now because women are just as exposed to the world's violence as men and are therefore in need of healing. Dave, Sue, Bon, and I drove out on the reservation to the sweat lodge where Long Standing Bear Chief had been preparing to lead us. We arrived as the sun was going down, and we saw a large fire with volcanic rocks heating in it. We entered the cozy, domelike sweat lodge. Long Standing Bear Chief explained the order of the ritual, the meaning behind the foods we were to eat, and other aspects of what would occur. On his request, Dave used a pitchfork to bring six hot rocks into the sweat lodge, after which Dave covered the opening to the lodge. Then Long Standing Bear Chief gave Sue and Bon sage, cedar, and sweet grass, and with prayers, they sprinkled these on the hot rocks. Long Standing Bear Chief then poured water on the hot rocks, and we indeed began to sweat. In complete darkness and under Long Standing Bear Chief's direction, we each spoke about our fears, hopes, and desires for ourselves and others. There were four different segments, each with more hot rocks and the prayer ritual and a different opening direction. Toward the end of the sweat, we heard galloping wild horses outside the lodge. When we exited the sweat lodge, the fire was winding down, the night was crisp and clear, and stars were everywhere. We all felt relaxed, cleansed both mentally and physically, and bonds had formed among us.

There are many reasons why the power of consumer culture's healing is so weak compared to that of traditional peoples. One reason is that in consumer culture, there is an absence of the sacred. In modern Western culture, people dissect, analyze, manipulate, and consume everything without limits. If you allow extremist consumerism and industrialization to rob you of anything sacred, you rob yourself of powerful sources for healing.

Western medicine does not mock sacred spaces, but it doesn't truly appreciate them. It doesn't acknowledge how important it is to create an event and space outside of the ordinary. The Hebrew word for holiness is *kedusha*, and it means both "to sanctify" and "to set apart." When a culture agrees on that which is sacred, that culture receives a power that can heal. Once a tribe defines a place as sacred—for example, a specific mountain—that place then has the strength gained from the belief of many. This is a powerful source of healing.

For healing to succeed, it is important that the healing ritual be experienced as very different from ordinary reality. To this end, traditional people will often use fasting or herbs or retreats. Some traditional cultures try to induce a break with routine through psychotropic drugs, including peyote and mescaline. Using natural, psychotropic substances in small, unconcentrated doses within a group in special rituals provides a far different experience from sitting alone at home, attempting to get a buzz so as to kill one's pain.

The unusual event helps create a different focus of attention. It helps one come out of self-absorption by calling attention to a special external happening. Even the skeptic who believes all of healing is merely a placebo effect would agree that part of making a placebo more powerful is to make it transcend the common and the habitual. In an atmosphere with different cues, it can be easier to learn new attitudes and behaviors.

Healing rituals that build a feeling of belonging and strength need not be exotic. I knew one single mother who lacked a community but, following an ugly divorce, intuitively understood the need for a regular ritual with her young son. Every evening she made sure to read a bedtime story to him. She discovered that if her son had had a rough day, this small act was a major healing force, and in any case felt tremendously bonding for her. I've met other single parents who take their son or daughter to breakfast one day a week in a favorite restaurant and discuss significant concerns. Healing rituals that build bonds and strength are about setting apart a special place during a particular time for meaningful activities.

Love, Healing, and Money

Extremist consumer culture is, in one sense, an attempt to achieve a world where there is no pain. In such a world, love is unnecessary. One needs love to be around someone who is in pain. We need self-love to be around ourselves when we are in pain. When we are in emotional pain and we are loved, we feel more alive, more fully human.

Feeling loved when we feel pain can be a healing warmth. In chapter 3, I described the warmth one feels when taking heroin or when feeling sorry for oneself. It is easy to see why some people are attracted to such warmth, but, unlike the warmth of love, the warmth of heroin or self-pity is not healing. Love creates healing conditions. One develops tolerance to heroin and self-pity—"heroin poop-out" and "self-pity poop-out"; this is not the case with love. It is a sad fact of modernity that people often ask: "How does one love?" Extremist consumer culture barely appears to understand how to breathe and to eat in a healthy manner—and it has little wisdom about love.

Yet healing does take place in our society, sometimes even in psychotherapy. There are good therapists whose wise words hit the mark and who have deep affection for their clients, and certainly there are clients who are grateful for the help that they have received. However, the financial exchange that occurs in psychotherapy can interfere with healing. When money changes hands, some clients cannot totally trust that the therapist's efforts have anything to do with love; and so for them, the healing condition of love is absent.

I remember the first time I took money from a psychotherapy client. The best word to describe how I felt? *Icky* (a word I almost never use). I was in my early twenties doing a practicum at a community clinic. The client was twice my age, a depressed, recently empty-nested woman who dutifully arrived for her weekly appointments. My supervisor assured me that my discomfort with accepting money had to do with my lack of confidence in my competence. That made some sense, but I was not convinced. As a teenager, I had been an incompetent short-order cook (often blowing off changing the oil in the deep fryer), and I had been an incompetent New York City Parks Department seasonal worker (playing chess and cards more often than I cleaned the park), and in neither case did my incompetence cause me to feel icky about being paid.

A few years later, I became certain that it was not incompetence that caused my discomfort when taking money from therapy clients. At that same clinic where I had been a trainee, I was promoted to the rank of clinic assistant, which meant that I helped train one hundred or so neophyte therapists over a three-year period. I observed that the more competent trainees were at establishing a caring and healing relationship, the more *uncomfortable* they were with taking money; and that trainees who were the least competent in connecting with clients were also the least bothered by taking money. The majority of the senior supervisors told trainees that they needed to get more comfortable taking money, which these supervisors declared was compensation for a therapist's time and techniques. But this did not ring true for the talented trainees, who knew that their time and techniques were not bringing their clients back for additional sessions. What *was* bringing them back was care, affection, and respect. And for the talented trainees, accepting money for that kind of exchange was unsettling.

During my tenure as clinic assistant, I viewed lots of weird and violent moments with respect to money, but one stands out. A female client in her mid-twenties was in therapy with a male trainee approximately her age. The trainee thought that his client was pretty, but she believed herself to be unattractive and was quite isolated. She returned for several sessions, and he tried to be helpful, but she remained lonely and angry. She was at times bitingly sarcastic, especially about "having to pay someone to listen to her." Following one session, the trainee, holding a receipt machine, awaited her payment, both of them standing in the reception area and visible to the clinical staff. She turned her back on the trainee, crumpled up a ten-dollar bill, and threw it over her shoulder onto the floor. Then she peeked over her shoulder to watch him kneel down to pick up the money. Exiting the clinic, she laughed and said something like, "Do you guys do things like that when you see a prostitute?"

I've never seen a therapist so shaken. He entered the staff room, and the supervisor talked to him along with the other trainees. The supervisor commented on how the client was directing her anger about her life onto her therapist, and that he needed to help her express her anger rather than act it out in a hostile manner. The trainee agreed, and the discussion ended. Later, another trainee, a talented young woman who did not trust the supervisor, told me what she felt about what had happened: "I think that client *is* real angry about her life, but she's also real intelligent. And that prostitute crack . . . she is intelligent enough to hurt with a truth." She continued, "Even though we're not selling sex, we are selling . . . sort of . . . attention and maybe love, I guess . . . something that maybe we should not feel great about taking money for."

I've often wondered what would be the reaction of other mental health professionals if I placed the following advertisement in the newspaper: "Empathy Sale—50% Off Regular Price." When I have joked about it with some of my clients, they laugh. Perhaps the absurdity of it allows them—and me—to deal with the pain of the financial realities of the psychotherapeutic relationship.

While the financial clout of Big Pharma and managed care is today the most visible enemy of psychotherapy, money has always been a subtle foe of healing. Some of the best natural healers I've known are no longer psychotherapists; they have dropped out of the profession due, in part, to that icky feeling. Correlatively, some of the least talented practitioners remain in the profession. By least talented I mean those who are clueless as to how emotional wounds are healed and who believe that psychotherapy is nothing more than an array of techniques.

The psychiatrist who sells only drug prescriptions and electroshock, the psychologist who sells only cognitive-behavioral techniques, and all mental health professionals who sell only their time, in a sense, protect themselves. By *not* selling their empathy, kindness, and authenticity, they don't sell themselves. The more mechanical and impersonal they are, the more they protect themselves. At some level, many mental health professionals know this: "If I sell myself, then I become a consumer object." This is why many professionals would rather sell products or techniques. But if mental health professionals are only selling prescriptions, techniques, and their time, and if they are not offering their being, they are not healing. True healers offer their very being, but once healers take money for that, their beings become consumer objects.

The prostitute remark sticks in my mind because I've seen many talented therapists become damaged in not all that different a manner than what happens to sex-for-hire prostitutes (who are also selling a precious component of their humanity). Before practicing psychotherapy for a living, these future therapists had derived a great deal of self-esteem from their ability to selflessly care about others. However, after many years of using empathy and warmth professionally, these personal attributes became mere moneymaking tools, and lost was the self-respect they once derived from the ability to authentically, selflessly care about others.

Healthy societies engage in commerce, buying and selling certain things, but they realize that when one buys or sells that which is alive, one makes that entity less alive. When one buys or sells a person, one turns that person into an object, and when one buys or sells a precious part of our humanity, objectification also occurs—that aspect of our being that was once fully alive becomes less so.

Market-economy fundamentalists, like all religious fundamentalists, want to believe that their system is perfect. However, while the market economy might work fine in the buying and selling of widgets, it does not work for everything. People can create a culture in which healing is considered sacred and outside of the market economy, or they can try to fit *all* activities into the market economy. Increasingly, American society has chosen the latter, ultimately creating a society with diminished healing. There are mental health professionals with angst about this development. Sadly, however, the mental health profession has evolved into another industry, another component of the market economy, rather than a critic of its limitations.

Living in an extremist consumer culture and a fundamentalist market economy, it is difficult to learn how to love and heal without experiencing a grief process. Once liberated from denying that extremism and fundamentalism exist (or from resigning yourself to them), you are on your way to life-affirming rebellion. You can seek others who have similarly done so and, together, form a healing community.

Self-Absorption, Self-Acceptance, Self-Release, and Life beyond Self

Mental health professionals (and the teachers and parents whom they have influenced) are often blamed for so overemphasizing *self-esteem* that young people are now narcissistic, spoiled brats who can neither get along with others nor achieve anything. Some of that "self-esteem backlash" is probably justified, because mental health professionals have done a poor job at distinguishing between self-esteem and self-absorption. Because of this confusion about self-esteem, I will use the terms *self-acceptance, self-worth,* and *self-respect* for that which ultimately leads to connecting with the whole of life—including other people. If people don't accept themselves, it's a safe bet that they won't value and respect other people, which will likely result in relationship difficulties, the pain of which can be a source of depression.

American society and culture have not done a great job at providing the conditions that create self-acceptance, self-worth, and self-respect in children. In addition to not devoting sufficient time and energy to the issue, the problem is also one of flip-flopping between narrow views of raising children. Some pundits and parents focus exclusively on the acceptance of one's feelings and needs, while others focus exclusively on skills and accomplishments. *Whole* self-acceptance, I believe, has to do with emotions, needs, competencies, and achievements, and it also has to do with integrity, resiliency, and other components that I will discuss.

In a wise culture, self-acceptance would be not an end in itself but a step to gaining enough security to drop one's defenses. With maturity, one sees how an exclusive focus on the self subverts serenity and contentment. The adult path begins when one is secure enough to recognize that one's self-absorption is interfering with harmony and intimacy. One can then move on to the more mature process of releasing self-image and ego attachments and connecting with life beyond one's self. So few people in modern society have adequate self-acceptance, self-worth, and self-respect that talk of being secure enough to move to the next level of self-release feels almost wistful. And so I will begin with the fundamentals of self-acceptance.

Self-Acceptance: Yoohoos, Yahoos, and Emotional Perspective

While it is my experience that denying (or "being out of touch with" or "stuffing") emotions can be a source of depression, it is a mistake to think that only "feeling-stuffers" get in trouble with their emotions. Many depressed people are dominated by their feelings. Emotional well-being is about neither stuffing feelings nor being dominated by them. It's about keeping one's emotions in perspective.

When I taught and supervised beginning therapists, some of them were so filled with anxiety that they needed to simplify things. So I told them that many of the clients they would see were either *Yoohoos* or *Yahoos*, and each required a different approach. This was more than a bit reductionist, but any greater complexity would have created debilitating anxiety in these beginners. Yoohoos, I told them, are out of touch with their emotions, while Yahoos are dominated by their emotions. Both lack emotional perspective and thus create disharmony within themselves and with others.

Let's start with the Yoohoos. We humans can, at an early age, become disconnected from our emotions. The Yoohoos' hollowness creates frustrations for themselves and for others. Intimacy has to do with being emotionally open, and so if you are out of touch with your feelings, how can you form relationships? Thus, the Yoohoo carries around not only an unpleasant emptiness but also a feeling of hopelessness about ever forming intimate relationships. I've known Yoohoo substance abusers labeled by society as "losers," and I've known Yoohoo corporate managers labeled as "winners"; all were disconnected from their feelings.

I remember one Yoohoo, a likable corporate executive who called himself the "Tin Man." He identified with the character from *The Wizard of*

Oz who lacked a heart and could not feel love. He said, "I watch my little daughter talk about her favorite colors, and I don't even know what colors I like, what colors feel good to me. Do I like blue or yellow or pink or what?" I asked him how that felt, and he smiled and said, "That's the first typical shrink question you've asked me. To answer you, I guess it makes me feel a little sad. Hey, I guess I can feel something!"

There were once many skilled therapists who would spend time giving Yoohoos a safe place to get in touch with their feelings. But in today's era, this once conventional therapy has become less routine. This type of therapy is analogous to the following physical rehabilitation: if the tendons in your hand were severed and reattached, you might not be able initially to move your fingers, but slowly, without going too fast and too far, you would work to move those fingers. This is what you want to do with your emotions. After interacting with others, ask yourself how you feel.

Just as Yoohoos lack proper emotional perspective, so do Yahoos. However, rather than disconnecting from their emotions, Yahoos are overwhelmed by them. They feel hurt, fear, and anger too deeply—so much so they can't think clearly. They act self-destructively and can damage those around them. Often their hurts, fears, and angers are reasonable, but what is not reasonable is the extremeness of their reactions. Emotional well-being is about accepting our feelings as part of our humanity, neither denying emotions nor allowing for *emotional imperialism* (the takeover of one's entire being by one's emotions).

Many therapists are more comfortable confronting a feeling-stuffer than a feeling-imperialist, and I have seen Yahoos whom previous therapists had treated like Yoohoos by assisting them to get even *more* in touch with their feelings. For the friends and family of these Yahoos, these therapists took a lovable pain-in-the-butt and created a nightmare. Getting-in-touch-with-your-feelings therapy is fine for Yoohoos, but Yahoos are already too damn in touch with their feelings. Yahoos are drowned by their feelings and drowning others with them as well. Yahoos need to move beyond their emotions. They need to gain awareness of their thoughts and actions, other people, and the rest of life.

When I work with Yahoos, I don't invalidate their feelings, but I try to help them see that they don't *equal* their feelings—that they are much more than just their feelings. I often tell them that by allowing their emotions to dominate their being, they are being enslaved by those feelings; and by not focusing on others' feelings, they frighten and alienate people, creating miserable relationships or loneliness.

Depressed people are often in denial of their needs, or they exaggerate the importance of certain needs. Either way, they are out of balance, lacking acceptance of their *whole* self. Common needs that are ignored or exaggerated are security, attention, affection, exercise, sleep, emotional intimacy, physical intimacy, spontaneity, support, and self-sufficiency. Wisdom has much to do with the awareness of our human needs, a lack of shame over them, and a reasonable pursuit of them.

While keeping your emotions and needs in proper perspective is important, it is also important not to ignore other aspects of yourself.

Self-Acceptance: Competence, Skills, and Transformations

The ability to provide a product or service that others need is a significant aspect of self-worth. It is more likely that we will feel demoralized if we lack a marketable skill than if we have one. There are several causes for those statistics depicting increasing teenage depression. But one reason that American society seldom addresses is the reality that the majority of young people are either mediocre or poor students, and unless they are good at some sport, they are not likely to experience any sense of competence from school. So they turn elsewhere. Unfortunately, I've met too many adolescent boys whose only source of pride is in their ability to play a video game or roll a joint.

In 1900 in the United States, only 6 percent of young people graduated high school; today, more than 85 percent are graduating high school. For politicians, increasing high school graduation rates, like increasing gross domestic product, indicates an improving society. In reality, many students are experiencing damage to their self-worth because of an increasingly "compulsory-graduation" society, which is often meeting its own self-congratulatory needs rather than advancing the self-worth of these young people.

I have spent a great deal of time with kids who are struggling to graduate from high school, and they are frequently no less intelligent than academically inclined kids. A hundred years ago, virtually all of these nonacademics would have quit school, and fifty years ago the majority would have left before graduating. They rarely quit to become career criminals. Instead they achieved competence in areas outside of academics. They apprenticed to blacksmiths, carpenters, and other artisans or became farmers and entrepreneurs. There are many examples of nonacademic financial successes, but let's visit just a single industry—fast-food empires. Harland Sanders left school at the age of twelve, worked as a farm hand, mule tender, railway fireman, lawyer (without having a law degree), and a wide assortment of other jobs before opening up the first Kentucky Fried Chicken in 1952. Other fast-food moguls who were high school dropouts include Dave Thomas, founder of Wendy's, and Ray Kroc, who built the McDonald's empire. Not too long ago, it was not all that uncommon to be an economically successful high school dropout.

Modern society, while putting some energy into removing certain social stigmas, is creating a stigma for high school dropouts. This stigmatization is even spreading to high school graduates who don't go to college. Nonacademic young people are pushed, coerced, and shamed into staying in school, even when their school is decreasing their sense of competence. Parents are so pressured to produce academics that even when their nonacademic child is a genius in another area of life, parents don't nurture that talent. Instead, by focusing exclusively on grades, parents create lasting resentments. I have spent many counseling hours trying to convince parents to feel lucky that they had a rebellious kid who knew how to build a house or write a complex computer program; often these parents would rather have a college-bound B-student whose only skill was compliance.

If one is academically oriented, one can achieve some self-confidence in school. I was one of those kids who did well in school and achieved a sense of self-worth by getting high grades. However, A-grades were not products or services that I could sell in the marketplace but are just tokens for advancement in a relatively narrow world of academia; and once I stepped outside of that world, they were of little meaning and value. I did not attain any real sense of competence until I achieved concrete success by providing that which others found helpful.

While I was in graduate school and learning very little of use, a friend taught me how to make French onion soup. This skill gave me a greater sense of self-worth than anything I was gaining in my formal training. I'm big on learning simple things that don't seem simple to others. Cooking is one skill that doesn't require a lot of time to learn and is useful not only to yourself but to others as well.

For much of society, the word *discipline* has come to mean coercing people to do what they don't want to do. And self-discipline has come to mean forcing oneself to do what one doesn't really want to do (for example, homework). I rarely lose teenagers' attention when telling them the following about self-discipline: Self-discipline is very different from compliance. Self-discipline means overcoming your mood so as to do that which you would be proud to accomplish. If you want to play "Stairway to Heaven" so it sounds something close to "Stairway to Heaven" and you are not in the mood to pick up your guitar, self-discipline means overcoming your mood and practicing just the same. When we discipline ourselves to do something, we feel stronger; but when we have complied with something, we often feel resentful. Most lives are filled with compliance and little self-discipline. That's why many people feel weak and resentful. If you hate the word *self-discipline*, you'd better get another one that means what it is supposed to mean.

Experiencing the power of personal transformation—acquiring a good habit or getting rid of a bad one—is also good for one's self-confidence. Lacking morale, it can be difficult to acquire positive behaviors; and unhealed, it can feel impossible to break self-destructive compulsions. However, with morale and healing, people can choose to accomplish remarkable things. I have seen two-pack-a-day smokers decide to stop smoking on a certain day—and then stop for life. Actually, most people who break bad habits such as smoking or substance abuse do it on their own, without professional help (the vast majority of people who quit smoking do it on their own). Often their most powerful motivation is that nobody thinks they can.

Self-Acceptance: Work, Money, and Integrity

It should go without saying that there are various kinds of achievements, but nowadays, success and achievement all too often are synonymous with money, career, and degrees. I believe that any accomplishment that you are proud of is an achievement.

I have often thought that the "right livelihood" is, in modern society, the most difficult task of all in the Buddha's Eightfold Path (which also includes the "right knowledge, aspiration, speech, behavior, effort, mindfulness, and focus"). While there are certainly some Americans making a good living using their creativity, the leading growth jobs in the United States include cashiers, janitors, clerks, and restaurant servers. Increasing numbers of people are both bored and stressed by their jobs. Bored and stressed workers are not just from the "underclass" but among professionals such as teachers and doctors, who are increasingly oppressed by bureaucratic demands. If you are unhappy about how you make a living, I have found that it helps to forgive yourself and accept the "life challenge" of finding a nonalienating way to make a living in an increasingly alienating work world.

Given the centrality of money to American culture, most of us do feel better when we are making decent money, and we can easily get down on ourselves when we are not. I've spoken with many "counterculture nonmaterialistic" folks, and even they admit that money does matter. It's more than difficult to have well-being in our society when moneymaking is completely ignored. I have also talked with a number of financially successful people who knew that their excessive efforts at moneymaking had caused them to pay scant attention to the rest of their lives, and this was one reason why they sought therapy.

While it's true that economic survival depends in large part on providing society with what it wants, we all have beliefs as to what is good and what is bad in terms of what the world wants. Not paying attention to your beliefs and indiscriminately providing what the world wants can cause a lack of self-respect and well-being. It is called *an absence of integrity*. I have heard more than one unhappy physician say, "Hey, I don't like being a drug pusher, but if I don't give them their prescriptions, they will go elsewhere." There is of course a downside to being "market driven": people gain money but lose wholeness. They do things they don't believe in and pay a severe price in diminished self-respect. While some physicians can gain integrity simply by being less greedy, many other people find that they must completely change their line of work.

The first step to a more satisfying livelihood is finding that vector from what the world wants that you respect. The second step is discerning from that vector what you can actually provide. This process may take a while, and it is wise to have some patience. If you lack the skills to do what you respect, then begin to pick up those skills. For example, if you want to be an owner-operator of a quality food store, then perhaps you can get a part-time job in such a store to learn the business.

Many people feel so overwhelmed by financial responsibilities that they have no energy or time to consider a new career path. If you lack the time and energy to immediately begin your path toward more meaningful work, you may still have enough time and energy to do something so as to experience some integrity. While discovering a meaningful way to make a living can be a full-time endeavor, finding a meaningful way to volunteer a few hours a month can be as easy as looking in a newspaper or talking to a clergyperson whom you respect.

A preoccupation with money is not the only need that can obliterate beliefs and destroy integrity. An excessive need for ego-stroking can cause a husband or wife to engage in extramarital affairs, thereby destroying the integrity of the marriage. A common source for a loss of self-respect in parents is their absence of integrity in that role. I've often seen parents "selling out" their child to reduce tension within a marriage. A wife may ignore the sexual abuse by her husband of her child; or more commonly, I've seen spouses ignore the emotional abuse or neglect of a child to avoid marital friction.

Integrity itself is a strong need, and it is possible to actually become obsessed with it and lose perspective. For example, a father strongly believes that his teenage daughter's new boyfriend is a "worthless moron." When this father satisfies his *integrity need* by bluntly lecturing his daughter on her boyfriend's naïve ideas and unrealistic goals, that father will most likely produce resentment in his daughter. A rigid ego attachment to your beliefs at the expense of all other aspects of life will not contribute to getting along with oneself, others, or the world.

Self-Acceptance: Becoming Resilient

Even high-functioning people, those who pride themselves on their resiliency, tell me that surviving has become increasingly complex, bureaucracies have become increasingly difficult to navigate, and nothing seems easy anymore.

Resiliency is the ability to bounce back after a setback, not crumbling under pressure, and not being overwhelmed by the world's demands. Life is filled with setbacks, pressures, and demands, and for people who do not consider themselves resilient, life rarely feels friendly. Without a belief in one's resiliency, life can be a patient monster that can crush you at any time. If you don't feel resilient, the important thing to remember is that you can transform your beliefs about yourself.

There are people who, by nature, are less overwhelmed by setbacks, pressures, and demands, and this talent in many ways makes their lives easier. However, for others who are envious, keep in mind that like all natural talents, this one can be double-edged. Sometimes, those who appear to be blessed with greater strength are also born with less sensitivity, and when they experience frustration, disappointment, and hurt, they may not feel these as deeply. This may create difficulty in empathizing and connecting with others' pain, and in intimate relationships these "can-do" folks may not stir people's tenderness. If they don't acquire greater sensitivity, friendship will be difficult and intimacy unlikely.

There are also people who, temperamentally, are more sensitive to setbacks, pressures, and demands but were taught as children how to avoid being overwhelmed by life. It is easier to believe in one's resiliency when anxiety is nurtured and when coping skills are modeled by a resourceful parent. It's also easier for a child to feel resilient when that child gains a sense of mastery. When children acquire skills—mechanical, interpersonal, or otherwise—that put them less at the mercy of their environment, they are no longer as terrified of setbacks, pressures, and demands.

If as a child your anxiety went unnurtured—even if you learned coping skills—you can remain terrified by the world's demands, the pain of which can trigger depression. It may be necessary to grieve the loss of nurturance, heal that wound, and be proud that you have learned to cope.

In industrial society, people worship the machine. To the extent that we approach this ideal, society honors us, and to the extent that we fall short, society shames us. Most of us are unashamed if we lack the skills to speak Greek or play the saxophone—so why should we be ashamed if we don't feel resilient? We should approach resiliency like any other attribute. We can observe people who are resilient and model them.

Perhaps the greatest difference between those people who view themselves as fragile and those who view themselves as resilient is in their attitude toward setbacks, pressures, and demands. How would you respond to the setback of a failing business? The pressure of a time limit when you must repay a loan? The demand for a major car repair? People who perceive themselves as fragile view setbacks, pressures, and demands as threats; those who perceive themselves as resilient view them as challenges. People usually run from threats, but they meet challenges. Threats are routinely negative; challenges can be positive. Threats are more likely to cause immobilization; challenges are more likely to stimulate and energize.

People who believe that they are resilient see life more as a fun game than a serious chore. They may view life as a card game in which they get dealt good and bad hands. A good poker player sees both a bad hand and a good hand as a challenge. A bad hand can be bluffed into a winning hand, or it can be used to set up a bigger win for the next good hand. And a good hand is a challenge too—the challenge of not getting so excited that you scare everyone out of the game.

If life is not throwing you out of control at the moment, it will. Lost your job? Kids need something you can't afford? Lost half of your retirement in the stock market? Getting rejected by everyone you ask out for a date? Need money? If all these questions feel like threats, then you will be more likely to do nothing, become pained, and feel depressed. If you view these questions as challenges, it is more likely that you will come up with effective solutions. But even if you don't solve your problems, you will feel better if you view these situations as challenges rather than threats.

Once you've begun to have faith in your resiliency, you may wake up one day and discover that you have become one of those "can-do" kind of people—the kind you probably used to hate. You won't hate them anymore. Now you will accept that you had something to learn from them. Hopefully, you will also remember that your sensitivity to setbacks, pressures, and demands was nothing to be ashamed of, and you will keep in mind that emotional obtuseness is not the objective. Rather, the goal is resiliency based on deeply experiencing life without being crushed by it.

Frederick Nietzsche said, "Cold souls, mules, the blind, and the drunken I do not call brave. Brave is he who knows fear but *conquers* fear, who sees the abyss, but with *pride*." Nietzsche's provocative aphorisms are often taken out of context and misunderstood by those who aspire to *machine-man* resiliency, but a careful reading of his work reveals that he would have despised many of his admirers. While having little respect for religions or systems of any kind, Nietzsche actually called Christ the "noblest man," described Spinoza as "the purest sage," and admired Buddha's psychological brilliance. And while Nietzsche had contempt for the resiliency of the shame-based machine man, he had reverence for the resiliency of an unashamed whole human being.

Self-Acceptance: Positive and Negative Thinking

As psychotropic drugs have become the most important technology in the psychiatrist's arsenal, cognitive-behavioral therapy (CBT) is increasingly the psychologist's most valued technique. CBT is a modern term for this age-old idea: since negative thoughts and negative behaviors are associated with negative emotions, if we think and act more positively, we will automatically feel better.

I have discussed how ineffective standard CBT can be when people are severely demoralized and immobilized, and how potentially shaming and counterproductive CBT can be for the unhealed and compulsive. However, with morale and healing, we can in fact use CBT to let go of self-destructive thinking styles and behaviors.

CBT commonly consists of identifying and confronting self-defeating behaviors as well as replacing irrational, negative thoughts with rational, positive ones. I previously mentioned four jargon terms for specific kinds of irrational, negative thinking ("disqualifying the positive," "overgeneralization," "exaggeration," and "should-ing"). Examples also include:

"An A- is imperfect, thus failure" . . . . . Black-and-white thinking

"I must get an A in every class" . . . . . . Must-erbation

Negative thinking and *pessimism* are highly associated with depression, and positive thinking and *optimism* have been shown to be antidotes to depression. A major component of CBT is transforming beliefs about adverse events from pessimistic to optimistic. For example, following a poor performance on a first college exam, the optimist will say, "I just had a bad day, and it is only one course." The pessimist, by contrast, will say, "I don't have what it takes, and I'm going to do poorly in college." Pessimists tend to view a negative event as *permanent* and *pervasive*; optimists tend to view a negative event as *temporary* and *specific*. After getting turned down for a pay raise, one can pessimistically—and depressingly—conclude, "I will never make more than slave wages, and all bosses are assholes" (permanent/pervasive), or one can conclude, "My current boss doesn't appreciate me, but there are other bosses who will" (temporary/specific).

Perhaps the most well-known CBT technique is ABCDE (Adversity, Belief, Consequence, Disputation, Energization). The following is an example of how it works:

Adversity: You have always wanted to be a high school teacher whom kids liked and learned from, but when teaching your first class of teenagers, they don't pay attention to you.

Belief: I am a horrible teacher. Kids have changed, and they won't pay attention to anything unless it's on a video screen.

Consequence: I feel bad about myself, and I dislike these kids.

Disputation: Perhaps I just don't know these kids yet. Perhaps I haven't taken the time to discover what they're interested in. Perhaps what I was talking about today might be interesting to me, but not to them. They're probably interested in something that I could connect to other topics.

Energization: I am really curious as to what these kids are in fact interested in. I'm going to list some topics on the blackboard to see what sparks their interest and figure out how I can relate that to other topics. If I discover they're not interested in anything, I'm not going to feel badly about myself for not being able to teach them anything— I'm going to feel sadness rather than anger for these kids.

As much as CBT is a staple of many psychologists' repertoires, and as much as it has become known to the general public, why is it that we see no end to—and perhaps even an increase in—our irrational and negative thinking and associated malaise?

One reason, as noted, is the problem of disregarding how demoralization and an absence of healing can sabotage effort and wise choices. A second problem is that many CBT customers walk away from their three sessions and apply more positive thoughts for a while, but the approach often doesn't last. It takes a great deal of practice to develop a new attitude; and without such a transformation, cognitive distortions and negative thinking will return.

A third reason for the failure of simplistic therapies such as CBT is that life is not simplistic. One of life's interesting complexities is that there are times when "focusing on the negative" is not irrational at all. For example, editing and proofing means a vigilant focus on what's wrong. I doubt it would be satisfying to read the writing of people who examine their work only to see what's great about it. Similarly, a skilled dentist will focus on the most minute imperfections in fit and aesthetics before cementing that crown in place. Many other lines of work, from computer programming to air traffic control, demand the same negative vigilance.

People prone to depression often have a certain negative vigilance. What makes many of them likable to me is that they often see the components of increasing dehumanization in our society and culture better than so-called normals. While depressed people can look at the twentieth century and see more violent death from war and genocide than in all other centuries combined, the nondepressed are more likely to look at it and rejoice in its new technology. I once listened to the upbeat, patriotic historian Stephen Ambrose give a talk. A noticeably depressed person in the audience asked, "What's the difference between America's Manifest Destiny and the Third Reich's *Lebensraum*? Weren't both imperialistic? Didn't both ideologies justify the killing and trampling over certain peoples to steal their land?" The questioner bummed out the crowd who had come to listen to Ambrose and to feel good about the United States. Ambrose, appearing to sense that, evaded the question.

In contrast to American culture, there are cultures in which optimism does not sell books or win elections—but is considered sort of crazy. The Dobuans, located on Dobu Island off eastern New Guinea, were described by anthropologist Ruth Benedict in her classic *Patterns of Culture* (1934). Benedict reported that, in part because of food scarcities, the Dobuans lived in a "treacherous" world filled with much "jealousy" and "suspicion," where "every man's hand is against every other man." Anthropologist Meredith Small points out in *The Culture of Our Discontent* (2006), "In Dobuan society, where life was rough and no one trusted anyone, a person with an optimistic and happy personality was considered crazy."

For many depressed people, modern society is hostile, dangerous, and withholding of the necessities for survival. One depressed attorney told me: "We've been expelled from the Garden of Eden. We've all been kicked out into a world of social, economic, or actual landmines. No matter how careful we may be, we can step on a mine and have it rip off our limbs, rip out our eyes, or just rip us off. Unless we are willing to violate our integrity or somebody else's, we will become homeless—and look how our society treats the homeless."

It's difficult to disagree with him. Much of the world is a frightening and uncaring place. The wealthy and powerful walk away with millions of dollars from failing corporations and leave their workers on the street unemployed and without pensions. Politicians trump up wars to win elections and give no mind to the human cost. Never get into an argument with depressed people about how they are only looking at the dark side of things. Depending on how polite they are, they will silently think you an idiot or angrily tell you so. What did I say to that depressed, cynical attorney? "You are right that if you don't give certain institutions what they ask for, you will be crushed or abandoned. You are right to believe that impersonal institutions increasingly own much of what is necessary to survive. Your desire to withdraw and hide from such forces is certainly understandable. However, are there not other people like you who are also pained by this? If you hide from the world, will you ever meet those human beings like yourself? And won't a complete focus on protecting yourself from this hostile, withholding, frightening world make you hostile, withholding, and frightened?"

Neither positive nor negative thinking is unequivocally good or bad. Optimists have much to learn from pessimists, and vice versa. While the pessimistically depressed can benefit from more optimism, the rigidly Pollyannaish need more balance as well. Even Martin Seligman, the author of *Learned Optimism* (1991) and "positive psychology" enthusiast, acknowledges: "If your goal is to counsel others whose future is dim, do not use optimism initially. If you want to appear sympathetic to the troubles of others, do not begin with optimism, although using it later, once confidence and empathy are established, may help."

Self-Acceptance: The Physical Component

While some mental health pundits emphasize acceptance of emotions and needs to gain self-esteem, and others stress competencies and achievements, most Americans appear to be more concerned with their bodies. That concern has done little good. By 2003 approximately 65 percent of Americans were considered overweight and more than 23 percent of Americans were obese.

The problem of overweight America is a simple one: too many calories and too little physical activity. There are thousands of books, magazine articles, and television shows on how to lose weight. I can say, "Cut portions, don't eat when you're not hungry, drink more water, don't eat to meet emotional needs, blah, blah, blah." But who hasn't heard all of this before? It's boring—and boredom, ironically, is one of the reasons people overeat.

If you are increasingly inundated with weight-loss information, and you are increasingly becoming more overweight, then your problem is less likely to be lack of knowledge about how to lose weight and more likely to be caused by an absence of morale as well as unhealed pain resulting in compulsive eating. This is one more example of why remoralization and healing are so critical.

Concern over what you take into your body is wise when it comes to depression. Physical problems stemming from a poor diet can result in lethargy and depression. Many people report having allergic reactions to specific foods, and they feel better when they forgo these foods. Other people have faith in and feel energized when they take dietary supplements (such as SAMe, 5-HTP, folic acid, potassium, zinc, omega-3 fatty acids, and vitamins B_1, B_6, and B_{12}). If your diet is poor, it is possible that you might not be getting enough of the building blocks necessary for the body to create its own energy supply, but I believe that if you have a sensible diet, expensive supplements are usually unnecessary. While alternative treatments are criticized by some doctors as nothing more than placebos, there is generally far less of a downside with diet changes or supplements than there is with any kind of psychotropic drug.

With morale, you can get energized enough to become physically active, and then all kinds of positive things can happen to derail depression. A Duke University research team found that modest exercise was ultimately more effective than antidepressants for major depression. At the end of the initial study, exercise and Zoloft were equally effective; but in the six-month follow-up, exercise turned out to be superior to Zoloft. The researchers followed those subjects who had succeeded in beating depression using "Zoloft only," "exercise plus Zoloft," and "exercise only," and they discovered that the depressive symptoms had returned in 38 percent of the Zoloft-only group and in 31 percent of the exercise-plus-Zoloft group, but that depressive symptoms had returned in just 8 percent of the exercise-only group.

When we are physically active, we get all kinds of antidepressing benefits—from endorphin kicks to relaxation, a good night's sleep, a more attractive body, compliments, and flirtations. The problem is that for many people the word *exercise* feels like an unfun thing that one has to do to avoid getting fat. If you are one of those people, I suggest first getting rid of the word *exercise* and replacing it with *play* or *doing something physical.* What did you enjoy doing when you were a kid? Your body really does want to do something fun. Many activities such as walking, biking, swimming, and gardening can take some discipline to start but can become positively addicting.

Self-Release: Buddha, Jesus, and Spinoza

The more insecure people are, the more energy they must use to protect their self-image and ego. It is easy to see this in others, though not so easy to see in ourselves. It is easy to recognize when other people are expending enormous energy holding on to an image of being "good" or "smart" or "successful." We can see how they wear themselves out protecting these images, and we can feel how they wear us out. It's more difficult to see how we wear out ourselves and others. There is no greater use of honesty than applying it to our own particular ego attachment.

Your ego attachment can strangle and suffocate you. Similar to an unhealed wound, an ego attachment can be a demon. It takes away your energy and distances you from others. Moreover, since the world is so much larger and more interesting than any one of us, by spending your energy exclusively on your self-image, you become bored and boring. And for other people, there is nothing more boring than a self-absorbed person.

Ultimately, the self needs to be transcended and released. This is how we become balanced and gain a larger perspective. This is the route to becoming more whole and connecting with other aspects of life. Historically, much of wisdom is about letting go of self and ego. For some people this sounds "Eastern," while for others this sounds "Christian," and for still others it sounds "philosophical."

Much of Buddhism is about letting go of the self's narrow desires. The First Noble Truth of Buddhism is that life is *dukkha*, which is typically translated as "suffering," and Buddha goes to great lengths to describe life's pains and losses. The Second Noble Truth is that the cause of suffering is *tanha*, usually translated as "desire" or "selfish craving." The Third Noble Truth advises that the cure for suffering is a release from narrow limits of desire, self-interest, and selfishness. The Fourth Noble Truth is the previously mentioned Eightfold Path—a map for how to accomplish this release. Buddhism is about the release of ego attachments and gaining a larger perspective.

Self-release was also much of what Jesus taught. All the Gospels agree that much of Jesus's existence comprised an offering of compassion for others, ultimately leading to his selfless sacrifice of his own life. Jesus moved beyond loving thy neighbors to loving thy enemies. While there is some theological debate on exactly what loving one's enemies means, there is little debate that it was a movement away from self-absorption. Scholars have noted that Jesus was so selfless that there is no record of what Jesus ever thought about himself.

Spinoza's great work *The Ethics* is, in part, about liberation from the slavery of one's emotions. Spinoza concluded that a focus on the self's narrow needs ultimately keeps us from greater knowledge and thus sabotages our well-being. He was the rationalist who showed how narrowness of focus was a source of unhappiness. Spinoza logically explained pain as the transition from a greater state of wholeness to a lesser state. Correlatively, joy is the transition from a lesser state of wholeness to a greater state. For Spinoza, God and nature are one, and to increasingly know God—which is to know more of the whole of life—is an experience of joy.

Self-Release: Ego Attachments

The path of self-release begins, paradoxically, with a strong self. At a certain point, it becomes tiresome to use energy to protect ego and self-image, and we become bored and fatigued. In a natural process, the path of life switches from gaining self-acceptance to a more spiritual path. In the spiritual path, the self and the ego do not completely disappear. They hang around as sources of amusement. We laugh at how they interfere in our movement toward—depending on our belief system—God, wholeness, nature, unity, or nirvana. Unburdened by ego attachments, we can connect with greater and deeper aspects of life.

Earlier I mentioned how economic integrity can be a source of self-respect; however, attempting to lead a life of *perfect* economic integrity can result in a noble goal becoming a depressing demon. For many years I had been ego-attached to ridding myself of the dehumanizing financial aspects of the mental health profession. I had succeeded in small ways but not completely, and my ego attachment was driving me and others crazy. One day I had a chance encounter with just the right person at just the right time. On a trip through Tennessee, my wife and I paid a visit to her cousin and her husband, a soft-spoken, highly ethical Methodist preacher. He inquired about my life and profession, and I responded as I often did by whining about the business of being a shrink. His reply surprised me: "Bruce, we all have to make a living." Something about that jostled me, and I was forced to admit that my ego-attached ideal seemed arrogant, maybe even comical. After all, our economic system is called "capitalism," not "humanism." It also struck me as humorous that I had believed that by torturing myself with the pain of imperfection, I would behave more ethically. And once I got to the point of laughing about my arrogance and foolishness, I began to let go of my demon, which has not lessened my efforts to eliminate dehumanizing financial aspects of what I do for a living. But it has reduced my whining about it, making me more effective at articulating the problem.

If you are around people who have energy, playfulness, and some joy, you will notice that they are absorbed in other aspects of life besides their ego attachments and their narrow self. When people feel secure, they can discover the joys of not taking themselves (including their emotions, needs, achievements, looks, and other aspects of their self) so seriously. When I reflect on the people I like and when I like them most, as well as the times when others seem to enjoy my company most, I conclude that it's simply a lot easier to have fun with people when they're not taking themselves so seriously. This is very different from not taking what you are doing seriously.

Self-Release: Meditation, Prayer, and Music

There is no single technique toward a spiritual path. There are formal activities that allow us to move away from our self-images and ego attachments, but these activities themselves can become ego attachments if not performed with the right spirit. Self-release need not require an exotic path, and it is not necessary to force ourselves into any one method. I have found that moving toward something positive is much easier than trying to fight against the negative. Paths away from our narrow selves that are fun, life-affirming, and where we are fully present are paths that we stick to.

There are different theories and practices of meditation. I believe the point of meditation, as it relates to letting go of self-induced suffering, is to become more deeply mindful of the content and movement of the mind. To facilitate this process, meditation often begins with a retreat from routine into a more secluded state. Without social distractions, people are often in a more open state.

In meditation you try to quiet your mind. You notice how difficult that is. In attempting calmness and stillness, you see how uncalm and unstill your mind is. A common meditation practice involves attending to your breathing: focusing attention on the rhythm of your breathing; on the shallowness or the deepness of your inhaling and your exhaling; becoming mindful of how you can breathe joyfully versus how you can breathe joylessly; and noticing mental activities that are associated with less satisfying breathing. Meditation also can be about posture: one way to have a healthy posture is to attempt, at the same time, to have the top of your head touch the sky while your chin moves toward the earth. Another meditation practice that some people find relaxing and pleasurable is repeating a *mantra* (a primordial sound). The seclusion, the breathing, the posture, and the mantra are very pragmatic. They can actually produce an altered metabolic state (in terms of heartbeat, blood pressure, muscle tension, and stress hormones) and an altered mental state of heightened clarity.

Some people call the meditation process one of gaining *mindfulness*, others call it *quieting*, and still others call it simply *seeing*. The goal is often termed *enlightenment*. With enlightenment, we become "aware of awareness," especially of our ability to be aware of those mental events that result in suffering. With enlightenment, we gain awareness of how the mind can both enslave and free us. There is a famous Zen line: "When you are hungry, eat. When you are tired, sleep." Very simple. But in our society we often eat when we are not hungry, we are sometimes barely aware of our hunger and thirst, and few of us are getting the sleep we really need.

Prayer, for some people, has been given a bad name by religious ritualists who are more intent on displaying their orthodoxy than finding spiritual peace. Certainly there are people who practice prayer merely to enhance their egos, but genuine prayer can be a method of self-release. I believe that prayer is communing with that which is larger than oneself (called God by some people). Since none of us is God, it's pure arrogance to be self-certain what this communion should be like. For some people, God is an image of an omniscient wise soul; for others, God is all of nature. Prayer can be a deeply private experience, or it can be a powerful communal one. Prayer can produce a state of ecstasy and deeply felt love or utter clarity, serenity, and wisdom; or it can result in all of this plus something no words can describe.

Immersing oneself in great music can also be a powerful self-release. Many people believe that of all the arts, music is the most direct expression of our soul and of the divine, and that the most sublime release from self comes from listening to great music—or making music. I am a lousy guitar player and I sing just about as poorly, but during one of the worst stretches of my life, playing the guitar and writing a couple of songs was as good a release from my "sorry self" as I could find. While we all can listen to God—or that which is greater than us—few can effectively communicate to the world what we hear. I'm convinced that Beethoven was one of those few, and that is why it is a great ego-release to listen to talented musicians getting him right.

Life beyond Self: The Natural World

Released from self-absorption, one can achieve the joy of connecting with life beyond one's self.

Many people find a pleasurable release from their troubles by focusing on nonhuman life. When we are in the company of truly wild animals, their presence is so powerful that it is difficult to be self-absorbed. Most of us cannot afford an African safari, but many Americans can afford a drive to a wilderness area, and there are even less costly ways to focus on nonhuman creatures. Serious birdwatchers can achieve great transformations of consciousness. And there are cats, dogs, and other pets. Watch a cat, really watch a cat—it's hard not to smile and learn a few things. Playing with a dog can be like listening to a good banjo player—it's difficult not to feel good. Peter Kahn in *The Human Relationship with Nature* (1999) summarizes several studies showing that increased animal interactions are associated with people having improved mental and physical health.

There are many other kinds of nonhuman life that help us transcend our narrow feelings and needs. It is a rare person that doesn't enjoy growing something, whether it is a houseplant, tree, flower, or vegetable. It's difficult to remain self-absorbed when smelling a fragrant honeysuckle, observing a rosebud beginning to form petals, or harvesting a ripe tomato. Once you've become enthralled by vegetation, it's easy to become absorbed by the earth itself. Fervent composters do not think very much about their narrow selves.

When you move out into nature, you will find other attractions that make the narrow self seem sort of boring. What could be a more fun way to get out of ourselves than to watch the clouds move in, hear the thunder, see the lightning, and feel the rain? Even if your life is such that you are not around plants or animals, and even if you are nowhere near an ocean, a river, a mountain, or a forest, there is always the sky. And even if city lights blot out the stars, there are always sunsets, sunrises, and full moons.

These days, my favorite physical activity is hiking a stretch of railroad tracks through a wooded area where I often spot deer and rarely see people. The tracks have become my sanctuary, and I walk them five

135

or six times a week and always feel better for my visits. I'm not a great silent, stationary meditator, but I've found that by talking out loud and moving, I enter into a relaxed altered state in which many of my troubled thoughts appear amusing and then disappear. I should add that talking aloud to oneself and then laughing at what one says is more safely done with no police or psychiatrists around!

For much of human history, interacting with the natural world to hunt, gather, or grow food was a source of great joy, as was the communal experience of preparing and eating food. It is difficult to imagine that humans are hardwired to shop alone at a giant supermarket for a frozen dinner, which is then microwaved and eaten alone. By contrast, it is easy to feel vital when acquiring food in nature. If that's not possible, one can feel less removed from nature by shopping at a farmer's market and chatting with vendors. And one can prepare food with friends and family, "breaking bread" together, and then perhaps discover an eat-in bakery that's open at two in the morning. While eating compulsively and becoming obese can lead to depression, the joy that food brings is a lifelong antidote to depression.

Life beyond Self: Curiosity and the Present Moment

Many parents describe their children to me as once curious preschoolers who lost their love of learning by seven or eight—and were later diagnosed with depression, attention deficit hyperactivity disorder, or substance abuse. One mother told me, "My son was so curious before he went to kindergarten, but by the time he was in third grade it was like the lights in his eyes went out." There's some proof that this is a general problem. In a 2006 survey, it was found that 40 percent of children between first and third grade read every day, but by fourth grade, that rate declined to 29 percent.

Learning new things and expanding one's consciousness is a great antidote to depression, but schools, for the most part, squash curiosity more often than nurture it. There's a lengthy list of critics of American schools—including Henry David Thoreau, Mark Twain, John Dewey, Paul Goodman, John Holt, Ivan Illich, Jonathan Kozol, Alfie Kohn, and John Taylor Gatto—who have reached similar conclusions as to why the typical school experience deadens interest in learning rather than stimulating it.

It is sad when children or their parents come to believe that disliking school has anything to do with disliking learning. The vast majority of class time in most schools is spent on lectures and workbooks, both of which are turnoffs for many kids. Curiosity is kept alive by active questioning among people sharing a mutual interest. This is the opposite of what occurs in most classrooms, where students are told what questions to answer. Rewarding with As and punishing with Fs is a good way to create a compliant and conformist society, but it subverts natural curiosity and learning. When people focus on what they need to memorize in order to get a good grade, they stop asking their own questions and pursuing their own answers—and they lose their curiosity. Once the exam is over, they are likely to forget the answers to others' questions, but when they discover answers to their own questions, they are not likely to forget them. A good teacher takes seriously what a student is naturally curious about and provides the necessary stimulation to provoke even greater curiosity.

Real learning takes place by actively doing things, and school is routinely a passive experience. For many students, lengthy classroom preparation prior to doing what they are curious about only takes away enthusiasm. Those who become truly skilled in, for example, computers and programming simply start messing around with computers; and those who learn to write well, start writing. Enthusiasm for learning is natural, but many teachers and parents, by distrusting children's natural curiosity and forcing them to learn things they are not interested in, subvert this inherent component of humanity.

Depressed people are often mired in the past and obsess over the future, focusing on what has happened or what will happen. Becoming fully present means focusing on what you're doing and experiencing right now. People feel most alive when they are living fully in the present moment.

Most of us have some unpleasant, compulsory obligations. If you find yourself bored in a classroom or business meeting that you cannot leave, instead of dwelling on your resentment, try simply observing life. Look at other people's faces. Take note of their voice, tone, and expressions. Observe the features of the room such as the lighting or furniture. Pretend you are a journalist.

It is obviously more fun being present in noncompulsory events. The next time you are with someone you care about, focus totally on his or her current being. Observe what he or she is wearing. Listen carefully to what he or she is saying and how it is being said. Watch his or her movements. Don't analyze, just observe. Think nothing of your past dealings or your future expectations. Simply try to receive his or her current being. This can be an interesting self-release for you, and it can be quite satisfying for the other person.

Life beyond Self: Making Contact with People

There are many ways that people sabotage themselves from making contact with others, and this can lead to painful isolation that can result in depression.

Introverted people are increasingly being diagnosed with social anxiety disorder and prescribed antidepressants. They are seldom given the validation that their excessive anxiety is not a pathology. And it is unlikely they are told that we *all* have to transcend aspects of our temperaments either to make contact with others or to maintain relationships.

Psychologist Philip Zimbardo studied the differences between what he termed "not-shy" and shy people. While not-shy people smile, laugh, make eye contact, compliment others, ask questions, crack jokes, and make observations, shy people often view with horror the possibility that their overtures will be rejected. Many shy people believe that whatever they say must be profound or they will be viewed as stupid, or they may be so concerned about being judged as a phony that they are inhibited from taking any of the actions necessary to communicate that they are interested in another person. Shy people who desire contact with other people need to learn that initial communications can be pretty pedestrian, as the main point is to break the ice. While shy people are often intimidated by people with superior knowledge or skills, not-shy people see such encounters as opportunities for growth and new contacts. Zimbardo also observed that not-shy people both ask for favors and do favors for others, recognizing that this is an important way that we humans make contact and deepen relationships. Shy people routinely believe it is an imposition to ask for a simple favor, such as requesting the time of day, but not-shy people see the lack of having a watch as an opportunity to meet someone.

Noncommunicative people are not the only ones who push others away. So too can people who are blunt with everyone about everything and who don't see the difference between authenticity and obnoxiousness. Attached to the single dimension of honesty, they may see only the lack of candor in others—not the lack of multidimensionality in themselves. Those who are one-dimensionally attached to their truths believe that when they feel strongly enough, they can say *anything*, and that they are liberated from caring about their impact on others. Some of these people are also uniqueness addicts, demanding that the world be simultaneously shocked and attracted to their singularity. This, like all ego attachments and compulsions, tends to be, initially or ultimately, unattractive for others.

I have found that one of the best ways for people to grasp the oppressiveness of their particular ego attachment is by being around someone with their same kind of ego attachment. Rigidly shy people rarely recognize the narcissistic oppressiveness of their own lack of effort to transcend their anxiety—until they are put in a situation where they are required to deal with someone just like them. In the same manner, if someone has a one-dimensional attachment to bluntness or uniqueness, experiencing others who are similar can result in an eye-opening experience—it is not fun to be used as another's canvas.

Balance is achieved by caring about other dimensions besides those we are attached to. When shy people overcome their anxiety and risk openness, they often gain attention, respect, and intimacy. And when bluntness or uniqueness addicts stop inserting their truths and singularity into every instance and instead show regard for harmony, they too can gain relationship satisfaction.

There are other ego attachments and compulsions that repel people, and *all* of us, when insecure or under stress, have the potential for one or another of them. A skilled therapist should be able to grasp the interpersonal impact of people and be forthright and respectful in providing this information. I spend a great deal of time in my practice helping people transcend their ego attachments and compulsions so as to attain more satisfying friendships, marriages, and families. These, I believe, are significant antidotes to depression.

Life beyond Self: Maintaining Satisfying Relationships

The Interactional Nature of Depression (1999), edited by psychologists Thomas Joiner and James Coyne, documents with hundreds of studies the interpersonal nature of depression—and its interactional vicious cycle. In one study of unhappily married women who were diagnosed with depression, 70 percent of them believed that their marital discord preceded their depression, and 60 percent believed that their unhappy marriage was the primary cause of their depression. In another study, the best single predictor of depression relapse was found to be the response to a single item: "How critical is your spouse of you?"

Uncaring relationships can result in depression. And depressed people routinely act unpleasantly, which can lead to rejection from other people who may perceive the depressed person as a burden. This in turn provides more pain for that depressed person—and more fuel for depression.

For his book *Why Marriages Succeed or Fail* (1994), psychologist John Gottman studied more than two thousand marriages, and he concluded that the "Four Horsemen of the Apocalypse" associated with dissatisfying and unstable marriages are *criticism, contempt, defensiveness,* and *withdrawal.* He also found that while disagreements and even anger are an integral part of a marriage, satisfying and enduring relationships require that for each negative emotional event (such as an argument), there must be *five times* as many positive ones (such as showing interest, care, concern, appreciation, acceptance, empathy, or affection; sex; joking around; and sharing joy).

Gottman found that both emotionally volatile and emotionally constricted marriages can succeed, and that both can fail. He concluded that what separates the content from the miserable is the *ratio* of positive to negative emotional events. So the volatile couple that has five arguments for each twenty-five positive events is likely to be more content than the constricted couple that never argues but rarely has positive emotional events. Gottman reflects, "Why don't stable marriages have a positive-to-negative ratio that is more like 100 to 1 [rather than 5 to 1]? . . . Our research suggests that in the short run this may be true. But for a marriage to have real staying power, couples need to air their differences." Not airing disagreements ultimately creates resentments, and, I believe, a complete absence of negative events would reduce the credibility of the positive ones.

Although few Americans have heard of Gottman's research, my experience is that many have heard about positive communication styles. They often know about "I statements" (saying "I am upset," not "You make me upset"). They've also been taught about giving positive feedback, not harping on the negative, and sticking to a specific issue. Many have learned fair fighting rules such as not using insults. Some even know listening rules: asking for clarifications, not interrupting, not getting defensive, being patient, and empathizing with the feelings of their partner. And I have found that many can perform admirably outside of intimate involvements and are quite skilled at the beginning of their relationships. However, as they get more deeply involved, despite their array of communication skills, they stop evidencing them. I've seen many people who possess the knowledge about the importance of being positive and nonattacking but who will nevertheless behave like hysterical children when they are hurt. They completely shut down or totally explode. They know better, and are even repulsed by their own behaviors.

The reality is that while Americans are increasingly surrounded by mental health professionals, media pundits, and self-help books instructing them on how to be more positive in their relationships, there seems to be no end to failed marriages, unhappy families, and lonely people. I have found that the problem is not so much ignorance of the right way to act but rather a more profound inability to deal with the pains of relationships.

When our emotional wounds are unhealed and we are unwhole, we behave compulsively. This means choices are controlled by overwhelming pain, not by wisdom. And that is why I have spent a good part of this book talking about healing.

Compulsivity includes depression and substance abuse, but people also behave compulsively with others. When our hurt overwhelms our being, we say and do things to others that are damaging to our relationships. We withdraw and abandon or we attack and engulf. Hurt for the unhealed and unwhole feels like a threat to their entire being, and reactions routinely lack wisdom.

Intimate relationships often fail because of expectations of painlessness. In initial contact, people focus on being seen as desirable. Even if you don't manipulatively "hook" others with a false presentation, human nature instructs you to charm with your "best self." So there is, at the beginning, mostly pleasure and fun with little conflict and tension. At a certain point, the focus changes. There are other needs besides being desirable for another—for example, personal integrity, career, and parenting. And there is also the humdrum of everyday life, such as who is going to vacuum, clean the litter box, cook dinner, pay the bills, take out the garbage, and unload the dishwasher. With memories of idyllic togetherness, people often feel taken for granted and uncared about and in turn act uncaringly—and a vicious cycle begins.

To improve the quality of relationships, it is important to increase one's comfort level with conflict—and more specifically, with tension. There will be plenty of time for tensionlessness when you are dead, but while you're alive, tension is a fact of life—especially within your relationships, and even more so within your intimate ones. If you fear and resent tension, you are less likely to discover the source of the tension and how to resolve it. When you are comfortable with tension, you can distinguish between the unhealthy tension of abuse and neglect and the normal tension produced by disagreement.

Disagreements are part of any relationship, and any time people disagree with one another, there will be friction. As you become more comfortable with tension, you don't overreact to it. John Gottman concludes, "If there is one lesson I have learned from my years of research it is that *a lasting marriage results from a couple's ability to resolve the conflicts that are inevitable in any relationship*" [Gottman's emphasis].

When you are overwhelmed by the tension of conflict—especially if it goes beyond disagreement to an attack, and especially within an intimate relationship—it is difficult not to become defensive. The stress of conflict can even result in increased heart rate and blood pressure so that it can feel as if your body is instructing you to defend yourself. Thus, it is no easy matter not to defend and not to counterattack. It is easy to be positive when we are calm, but difficult when we are not.

Satisfying relationships and successful marriages have techniques to interrupt the vicious cycle of negativity, defensiveness, and counterattacks and to regain calm. Such techniques often involve first gaining awareness of the negative chain reaction. This awareness can slow down the cycle just enough that, with discipline and practice, one can choose constructive behaviors rather than simply react without wisdom.

I recall an advertising executive who told me that his wife perceived him as so manipulative that he couldn't state any opinion or assertion without her believing she was being manipulated or criticized, which caused him to become exasperated and angry, which then resulted in her becoming even more defensive. While men more often than women reject marital counseling, in this case his wife refused, and so he sought help for his marriage without her. He was fascinated by Gottman's positive-to-negative ratio of five-to-one, and we created a technique for him that we called "Five-to-One-to-Chill." When he felt frustrated, before asserting himself—which he knew his wife would perceive as an attack—he began to think "Five-to-One-to-Chill" to break up the chain reaction. Five-to-One-to-Chill reminded him that each of his "negativity-spending" behaviors better be worth it, because it would require five positive emotional events to balance it out. He told me that the flash of having to create five positives to spend one negative was like a splash of water on his face that distracted him from his emotional and physiological state of exasperation, interrupted the chain reaction, and replaced his relationship-damaging compulsive reactions with wiser choices.

William James wrote, "As the art of reading (after a certain stage in one's education) is the art of skipping, so the art of being wise is the art of knowing what to overlook." James was reflecting on the subject of reasoning, not marital bliss, but experience has convinced me that *the art of knowing what to overlook* is wise when it comes to maintaining a satisfying marriage.

While an intimate relationship should provide the safety for relaxation, informality, and risk taking, many people have a childlike fantasy that an intimate relationship means that you don't have to measure the impact of your words and behaviors prior to acting. Think about the times in your life when intimates were enjoying your company: weren't you taking a moment to consider their reaction before you said or did something?

Beyond Market-Economy Marriages

In extremist consumer culture, people are socialized to see themselves as merely an amalgam of needs. It is understandable that adolescents often can't see the difference between a frustrated need ("I want to go to a party and she doesn't") versus resentment over a violation of one's being ("I overheard him saying that he wanted to have sex with me to get back at his ex-girlfriend"). However, in modern society, many adults also can't make the vital distinction between the tension of frustration and the tension of resentment. While dissatisfaction of a need leads to frustration, disrespect (including neglect, abuse, or exploitation) results in resentment.

Unless you have rebelled from consumer culture's socialization of human beings as mere amalgams of needs, you have little chance of having satisfying intimate relationships. Why? Because whenever *any* of your needs go unmet—which will happen in every relationship, many times—you will become resentful, and the downward cycle of relationship deterioration begins. With resentment, there is distrust, and one is suspect of motives whenever one's needs go unsatisfied. He forgets to take out the garbage—"He doesn't care." She spends a bunch of money—"She's a user." He comes home late—"He's lying about something." She's upset—"She's trying to manipulate me." For a child, an unhealed adult, or a stressed-out adult, there is a failure to distinguish between frustration and resentment. For a secure person, frustration and resentment feel quite different.

Market-economy marital counseling is *exclusively* about an equitable reciprocation of needs. It is essentially a business negotiation. He needs more time watching football while she needs more time out of the house, so perhaps the couple is advised to watch the football game at a tavern, or he watches one less game a week and they go to one more restaurant a week. He wants more sex; she wants more conversation—let's make a deal. In business or in market-economy marriages, one doesn't have to respect or care about the other—just deliver the goods. While fairness around needs is important, I believe that when we are married (or intimately cohabitating), nature wants us not simply to "do business" with each other but to genuinely respect and care about each other's being.

Assembly-line relationship counseling, like other products of industrialization, is highly standardized. However, authentic and satisfying relationships are not standardized, and people can torture each other with "I statements" and can make one another feel good with "you statements." I have been pained by some people who have said, "*I* feel uncomfortable with that," and I have felt affection for others who have told me, "*You* are crazy."

I recall one middle-aged male nurse who was depressed because of his problematic marriage to a woman who almost never showed him any affection. In a very common dynamic, he had chosen to "parent her," and this made her even more dependent and hostile. He told me: "I am the only person she trusts. We have an honest relationship, although all of her honesty about me is of the negative variety. But I can handle it." I responded, "With all due respect, *you* are insane." He busted out laughing and was receptive to what I had to say. Of course, with another person—or at a different point in time with the same man—I would have produced significant resentment with my remark. There's a lot more to human communication than that which can be reduced to simplistic rules.

Communication, especially in intimate relationships, is decidedly complex. This is why a pundit's sound-bite, generic advice can make matters worse. Take a look at just one complex communication— teasing. It can be powerfully connecting or disconnecting. Teasing can be playful, enjoyable, and bonding, or it can be mocking, unpleasant, and fracturing. Slight variations in content, tone of voice, facial expression, and gesture can make all the difference. Moreover, each of us perceives language differently, and each relationship has its own history. If the relationship has a history of manipulations, this makes it more difficult to tease. If you believe that your partner adores you, put-downs can feel like positive attention.

Contentment with intimates can be challenging and fun—or it can feel impossible. Contentment with intimates is possible if you have begun to heal your wounds. It is possible if you have begun to recognize your compulsive and destructive behaviors, if you are genuinely sorry about them, and if you are moving out of them. Contentment with intimates is possible if you see the difference between your needs and your self-respect and between frustrations and resentments. It is possible when you can resolve frustrations with respect and humor. Contentment is possible when you learn to forgive the hurt caused by a caring, imperfect partner (but have the courage to leave an abusive, uncaring one). It is possible when you have become more comfortable with tension. Contentment in intimate relationships becomes challenging and fun when you are working on your own shortcomings rather than working over your partner's.

Public Passion and Reclaiming Community

Today many use the term *community* for that which is merely a locale. However, genuine community means face-to-face interactions in which there is emotional and economic interdependency. Genuine community promotes the health of individuals, their relationships, and their environs. Genuine community attempts to solve problems, and problems become an important source of energy for community building.

Depression is often associated with self-absorption and alienation, and this is why moving beyond one's private sphere can help both prevent and transform despair. Most people would like to connect with others, but they often lack direction and energy. This chapter is about discovering that direction and energy, and thus I do not shy away from social issues that can serve as springboards for forming community. It is my hope that you will grasp how public passion can energize you to form community.

The Energy to Create Community

If you are motivated *only* by a need for a social life, you will have great difficulty creating genuine community. To form and maintain enduring relationships, humans need to care about—and act on—some concern besides their loneliness. People who create community do not usually succeed because they dutifully follow instructions from self-help books about meeting people. They succeed because they care about something beyond their private world.

The energy to form community can come from a hobby, a craft, a neighborhood need, a social cause, or any passion that other people share. Decreasing numbers of Americans have such passion, and thus they are deprived of an important source of energy for forming community. However, there are people who have taken their passion and turned it into community. I have known people who love books and worked at bookstores, formed community with their coworkers, and remained connected even after leaving their job. I know a woman with a passion for beautiful fabrics who works part-time in a fabric store in exchange for materials, and she has found community there. I have a good friend who believes in food cooperatives, volunteered at one, and found community and a girlfriend there. Recently, I met someone with a passion for sustainable energy, and he is connecting with neighbors via his dream of a community windmill.

Some people who create community describe themselves as "political," but many do not. Most people who create community stop seeing their disconnectedness as bad luck and recognize that they have given away power to entities that have no regard for community. This energizes them to reclaim power, which in turn energizes them to seek out others of like mind.

People can form community through a mutual concern about neighborhood problems such as airport noise or dangerous traffic. Many neighborhoods have associations and regular meetings; and local officials routinely hold hearings on concerns, which are usually open to the public. On other issues there may be a lecture or a rally. If you attend and are bored, leave. The point is to go public with your beliefs. While authorities are often unmoved by public dissent, it is not always the case. Either way, it is an opportunity for a morale boost and social connectedness.

Many Americans have grown cynical. Given the state of the world, many doubt their capacity to change society for the better. However, even if the case can be made that it is too late to turn the world around, public passion can be the energy that forms community and leads to a more satisfying life.

Social Capital

Sociologist Robert Putnam's *Bowling Alone* (2000) is a dense and lengthy book chock-full of statistics but with a riveting message that has made it popular beyond academia. While American society has been an unparalleled success in producing financial and material capital, Putnam makes it painfully clear that it has ravaged *social capital*, his term for social connectedness.

Social capital affects virtually all aspects of our lives. It greases the wheels of human relationships and improves our ability to solve personal and social problems. It creates economic opportunities, reduces crime, and increases the quality of education. In terms of physical health, the stronger one's social ties are, the less risk of illness and disease one has; and if afflicted with ill health, the better one's chances of recovery.

With respect to depression, social capital is an antidote to the powerlessness of alienation. Putnam reports: "Low levels of social support directly predict depression, even controlling for other risk factors. . . . Countless studies document the link between society and psyche: people who have close friends and confidants, friendly neighbors, and supportive coworkers are less likely to experience sadness, loneliness, low self-esteem, and problems with eating and sleeping. . . . The single most common finding from a half-century's research on correlates of life satisfaction, not only in the United States but around the world, is that happiness is best predicted by the breadth and depth of one's social connections."

Putnam methodically details a social collapse in the United States on every level: Work life has decreasingly become a place where we find community; the informal social connections of neighbors and friends have broken down; family is a diminishing source of social capital; and the decline in membership and participation in progressive religious institutions has reduced yet another avenue for community.

In true democracy, the workplace and other societal institutions encourage connectedness; in totalitarianism, social connectedness is a threat. Putnam notes, "According to a 1999 survey by the American Management Association, two-thirds of employers record employee voice mail, e-mail, or phone calls, review computer files, or videotape workers—and such surveillance is becoming more common." Today, Americans are far less likely than their parents to join with coworkers in unions or other formal associations. I grew up in a blue-collar neighborhood in New York City, and my father, like other workers in the neighborhood, connected with fellow workers through union activities. Over the past generation, there has been a steady decline in union fellowship. Unions not only have lost power as an economic bargaining vehicle, but just as importantly, they no longer provide an entire class of people with hope and fraternity. Workplace disconnectedness is perhaps even greater for white-collar workers. When I started out in private practice, it was rare that corporate managers at blue-chip companies like IBM and Procter & Gamble were laid off, but layoffs in such places are now common. Even if not laid off, managers are often shuffled between jobs and cities, and job politics often make it unwise for them to have anything more than superficial connections with colleagues.

I know "corporate survivors" with some economic wherewithal who start planning with others another way to invest their money besides the stock market. Some have formed small businesses with family and friends. In the beginning, they didn't depend on it for income but saw it more as a vehicle for connecting with others as well as a source of meaning.

By many measures, family connectedness is less common now than ever, dramatically decreasing even from a generation ago. If time is one component of connectedness, then Americans are more connected to their cars than their children. An average American adult spends twice as much time behind the wheel every day than the average American parent spends interacting with his or her children. For most of human history, the evening meal was a family and communal experience; however, the percentage of Americans whose entire family routinely eats dinner together has declined over the last twenty years from a paltry 50 percent to a pathetic 34 percent. And between 1976 and 1997, families vacationing together fell from 53 percent to 38 percent, and families just sitting and talking together fell from 53 percent to 43 percent.

Beyond family life, another potential supply of social capital is our informal social life—and that, too, has been decimated in American society. The evidence shows that across a very wide range of activities, there has been a significant decrease in regular contact with friends and neighbors. Putnam notes, "We spend less time in conversation over meals, we exchange visits less often, we engage less often in leisure activities that encourage social interaction. . . . We know our neighbors less well, and we see old friends less often. In short, it is not merely 'do good' civic activities that engage us less, but also informal connecting."

In our culture, many people have lost the skills of how to break the ice with neighbors. For several years, my wife worked part-time at a friend's food store. At the end of the day, there sometimes would be unsold loaves of bread, which she would distribute among our neighbors, a few of whom became our friends. A client of mine who felt completely isolated gave me cookies that she'd made, which I appreciated, and I suggested that she take some to her neighbors and tell them that she'd made too many. The first time she did it, she received a smile and a thank-you—no small deal for her—and gained some hope that she could make friends in her neighborhood.

"Trends in religious life," Putnam reports, "reinforce rather than counterbalance the ominous plunge in social connectedness in the secular community." When membership and participation in progressive religious institutions decline, it is not simply religious life that disappears. Historically, progressive religious locales have been at the center of major social movements in the United States, most notably the abolition of slavery, the fight for civil rights, and antiwar activism. Such religious organizations and the buildings that house them are where the elderly and the homeless receive support, and where even the nonreligious can meet for entertainment and recreation. They are also where economically disenfranchised ethnic groups can share economic and social capital—and feel less helpless and hopeless (the frequency of church attendance is a significant predictor of whether inner-city African-American youths will have jobs and economic success). There may be good reasons for why people shun religious institutions, but the price paid for *privatizing* their spirituality is a decrease in social capital.

The fact that social capital or community has broken down is clear to many observers across the entire political spectrum. Why this is happening is not as clear. Putnam speculates that the sources for our deterioration can be attributed in the following manner: 10 percent due to increasing pressures of time and money; 10 percent due to increasing suburbanization, commuting, and sprawl; 25 percent due to effects of electronic entertainment, especially television; and 50 percent due to "generational change" in reduced caring about civic involvement (Putnam puts the remaining 5 percent in an "other" category).

Time and money pressures do seem to provide less opportunity for people to connect with one another. For example, married couples averaged fourteen *more* hours at work each week in 1998 than in 1969. Suburbs were relatively rare a few generations ago, but today almost half of the United States is suburbanized; and most observers agree with Putnam that suburbs, in contrast to small towns, reduce social contact. It is also difficult to disagree with Putnam's assessment of electronic entertainment as a major reason for the decline in social capital. Research shows that when spouses (who are already spending less time with one another) are together, they spend three to four times as much time watching television as they do talking. In 1970, 6 percent of sixth graders had a television set in their bedroom; by 1999, 77 percent of sixth graders had their own television. Approximately half of all family members report watching television while eating dinner, and nearly one-third do so during breakfast.

I have known several people who viewed themselves as so addicted to television that they felt their only option was to get rid of it. Initially, having no television created a certain anxiety, but eventually they reported being more likely to take the social risks necessary for community. Many people would benefit by at least cutting back on their television watching, unplugging it for a week, or, at the very least, setting aside two TV-free evenings a week.

Putnam allocates 50 percent of our reduction in social capital to a generational decline in civic caring. As far as I know, Martians have not come down to earth and injected each younger generation with increasing amounts of an "anticivic engagement" virus. What has happened? Major institutional, political, economic, and cultural transformations have occurred that have increased our experience of helplessness and disconnectedness. Next, I examine these problematic transformations—and what we can do to restore community.

A Relationship-Retarded Culture?

American society has come to value privacy over community. Americans build suburban houses with backyard decks rather than front porches, escaping neighbors rather than chatting with them. Americans often travel alone in isolating automobiles rather than using transportation conducive to meeting people and having face-to-face conversations. However, human beings are social creatures, and our well-being requires human contact, friendship, and intimacy. Societal and cultural arenas such as family life, mental health institutions, schools, and economic systems influence just how much value people truly place on human relationships.

It is not simply the lack of time that American families spend together that gives them an F in human relationships. More fundamentally, it is the lack of mindfulness to the complexity of relationships. Most American families are mindful of the need for money and consumer goods, and they put energy into these, but it is my experience that there is a lack of mindfulness and energy when it comes to ensuring cooperative and nonresentful family relationships. While decreased family togetherness can statistically be shown in reduced time dining together, vacationing together, and conversing with one another, there are other family disconnects that statistics can't capture. Increasingly absent, it seems to me, is any sort of "family culture." I notice that families often have no set of particular values and habits that bond them. I'm not saying that families of my childhood were more loving and caring, but they seemed to connect on *something*—a shared passion for a political ideology, a sports team, a type of food, or something. Today it's not uncommon to find families lacking even these nonintimate bonds.

Not so long ago, a mom and dad were not all a child had to rely upon. In addition to biological parents, there were grandparents, other relatives, friends, and neighbors who played with the child, nurtured pain, set limits on destructive behaviors, and essentially parented. In societies with greater humility, it was understood that raising children was a shared responsibility of the extended family and the community. It was understood that biological parents sometimes couldn't relate to their child, and vice versa. It was understood that within extended family and community, a child would likely find at least one adult who could relate to him or her.

The often-quoted traditional African proverb states: "It takes a village to raise a child." On discovering the rash of teen school shootings in the United States, it wouldn't surprise me that traditional peoples would say this about American society: "It takes a crazy village to raise a crazy child." Today, decreasing numbers of children experience any kind of village or community, and many children lack a single nurturer and limit setter—a respected adult whom they believe has deep affection for them. This is a major reason why we must have a passion for transforming our society and culture.

Psychiatry in clinical practice has never emphasized the significance of society and culture, and now it increasingly minimizes the impact of human relationships—including parenting. Psychiatrist Harold Koplewicz in *It's Nobody's Fault* (1996) makes it quite clear that inadequate parenting is unfairly blamed for mental disorders. The National Alliance for the Mentally Ill (NAMI), a staunch advocacy group for this point of view, in an extremely favorable review of *It's Nobody's Fault*, summarized Koplewicz's general views: "Parents don't cause serious mental disorders, they are responsible for getting their ill children into treatment." It's-nobody's-fault fundamentalists are not simply saying that parenting is blamed too much. They're saying that even if there was abuse and neglect in your childhood, it did not cause your depression. Psychiatrists such as Koplewicz are not at the fringe of the mental health industry but at the center; he and others like him not only are NAMI heroes but are routinely invited to White House conferences on mental health.

"It's nobody's fault" means that it is neither our fault nor our parents' fault that we are depressed, and this is a very seductive message. There is nothing so seductive as the exoneration of responsibility, in this case blaming brain chemistry rather than confronting society and human relationships. From a marketing point of view, if one wants parents to feel less threatened about taking their children to a mental health professional, then giving parenting a free ride is a brilliant idea. For Big Pharma, it is also a great idea, as it leads to drugs and profits.

But it is gravely disappointing for others who believe that American mental health institutions should be seriously confronting and transforming our relationship-retarded culture.

Why have so many people bought into the "It's nobody's fault" idea? Ironically it was the previous era of "parent shaming-and-blaming" psychiatry that created the climate for it. The "It's nobody's fault" partnership of psychiatry, NAMI, and Big Pharma is financially interconnected (while many individual members of NAMI earnestly seek better mental health treatment, NAMI itself has received substantial financial support from drug companies); and it blurs the extremely important distinction between *shaming* versus *recognizing*. It never helps to shame and blame, but it is also harmful to deny the significance of human relationships, especially parenting. In a healthy family, community, and society, healing regularly takes place within human relationships. If there were a glut of such families, and if we lived in communities within a culture that encouraged human relationships, the mental health profession would be pretty much out of business.

Schools are another significant way we are socialized to the values of society, including relationship values. In chapter 5, I discussed how standard schools for many young people do not nurture curiosity or competence. Schools have another depressing effect—most do not encourage human relationships. And this, too, fosters depression.

In most schools, cooperation is more punished than rewarded. While schools certainly punish fighting, there is little effort to socialize children to act cooperatively. Teachers may lecture about altruism, but given the rules against cooperation on homework and tests, these lectures often confuse young children. In school plays, athletics, or the occasional group project, there is some emphasis on teamwork, but when it comes to the more valued tasks associated with grade-getting—such as exams—cooperation is punished. School teaches children to compete for scant resources. Teachers often grade on a curve, which means if nobody studies for the exam and everyone does poorly, this is better for students than if some do well, so children learn to resent peers who study and do well.

Anthropologist Jules Henry described a typical Western elementary school classroom: "Boris had trouble reducing '12/16' to the lowest terms, and could only get as far as '6/8'. . . . She [the teacher] suggested he 'think.' Much heaving up and down and waving of hands by the other children, all frantic to correct him. Boris pretty unhappy, probably mentally paralyzed. . . . After a minute or two, she becomes more urgent, but there is no response from Boris. She then turns to the class and says, 'Well, who can tell Boris what the number is?' A forest of hands appears, and the teacher calls Peggy [who reduces it to 3/4]. . . . Thus Boris's failure has made it possible for Peggy to succeed; his depression is the price of her exhilaration; his misery is the occasion for her rejoicing." This, for Henry, is the standard condition of American schooling—that one child's success has been bought at the cost of another's failure and humiliation. This is quite different from the socialization of young children in cultures that value cooperation and human relationships more than Americans. Henry notes, "To a Zuni, Hopi, or Dakota Indian, Peggy's performance would seem cruel beyond belief, for competition, the wringing of success from somebody's failure, is a form of torture."

Classroom life is routinely about keeping quiet and sitting still, and children are increasingly diagnosed with attention deficit hyperactivity disorder (ADHD) if they create "classroom-management" problems for their teachers (symptoms of ADHD include a failure to keep quiet and a failure to sit still). Ritalin and Ritalin-like drugs can result in a more subdued class, as many medicated children will in fact talk less to others. Unfortunately, a 1998 study showed that the majority of medicated children also become *less interested in others*, and the U.S. Surgeon General in 1999 reported that, long term, ADHD medications do not benefit social skills and peer relationships.

People are such social creatures that even when an institution does everything possible to keep them from communicating with one another, human nature triumphs over this control. This is true in schools, prisons, and plantations. However, while the force of human nature is powerful enough to overcome institutional impediments to connecting, people often don't learn the skills and wisdom required to maintain satisfying relationships. Friendships and marriages are complex and require many skills and much wisdom. Many of us in our relationship-retarded culture increasingly don't have what it takes.

People are often unhappy and depressed to the extent that they are exclusively preoccupied with their own needs, and in any extreme consumer culture, people are socialized to be extremely self-preoccupied. It is not that our culture does not value human relationships at all. It is that our extreme industrial society values other things more than human connectedness. Rather than spending energy on family, intimacy, and friendship, Americans pour energy into efficiency, productivity, and consumption.

The nature of a society's economic system is so crucial to its survival that it determines a great deal of that society's values. For example, in the old South in the United States, slavery was crucial to the economy, and thus it was important to create a culture that made white people feel okay about having African slaves. The cultural solution for this feudalistic economy was to dehumanize Africans. A consumer economy, unlike a feudalistic economy, doesn't want slaves who lack purchasing power. An extremist industrial-consumer society requires everyone to be both a producer and a consumer. Modern culture's economic ideal is someone who consumes while he or she works, such as a salesperson using a cell phone in a car while consuming gas, phone minutes, and fast food as he or she persuades others to buy a consumer product.

Healthy families, intimacy, and friendships are not good things for an extremist consumer culture. In an extremist consumer economy, the goal is producing and buying as much as possible. A consumer economy thrives on increasing numbers of "buying units." If Americans all had happy intact families, they'd be buying far fewer televisions, refrigerators, and microwaves than if families split apart. Lots of lonely people means selling more DVDs and cable television. There is no incentive in a consumer economy to value any relationship other than a business one. In fact, anything that helps stabilize families and intimate bonds is a threat to an extremist consumer economy. Maintaining families and groups requires attention and energy, and time spent on human relationships is time taken away from production and consumption. More subtly, if you are not completely controlled by money and material goods, you become less predictable and can create havoc for the industrialized order, which needs predictability.

Prior to the worship of productivity and consumption, many traditional cultures had a strong passion for creating a culture with a minimum of resentments. Not only did people spend time on their relationships, they were deeply mindful of them. In order to truly learn about human relationships, both time and mindfulness are required, and this cannot be done without a rebellion of sorts against the worship of industrialization and consumerism.

Cultures that value human relationships are forever learning about the nuances, subtleties, and power of human communications. In such cultures, language is a source of great pleasure. However, the increasing acceptance of standardized, simplistic verbal recipes make a mockery of our intimate relationships. Lacking a passion for language, people become careless about ideas. This is a corrosive force that can dehumanize a culture. Enjoying the complexity of language is a cultural tool for promoting human relationships, making it more likely that people will enjoy connecting with one another—and will have valuable ideas worth connecting on.

Professionals: Helping or Hurting Community?

In *The Careless Society: Community and Its Counterfeits* (1995), sociologist and community activist John McKnight describes genuine community. Three features that McKnight (and de Tocqueville) observes that defined early American communities were groups of citizens who (1) claimed the power to decide what was a problem; (2) claimed the power to decide how to solve the problem; and (3) became themselves the key actors in implementing the solution.

How do you know when you are in genuine community rather than an institutionalized counterfeit? For McKnight, genuine community is distinguished by its regard for *collective effort, capacity, informality, stories, celebration*, and *tragedy*. In genuine community, the members themselves define and solve problems. In the counterfeit version, the professional provider in effect says: "*I*, the professional servicer, *am the answer. You* are not the answer. *Your peers* are not the answer" (McKnight's emphasis). McKnight notes, "While institutions and professionals war against human fallibility by trying to replace it, cure it, or disregard it, communities . . . incorporate both the capacities and the fallibilities of citizens." In genuine community there is also informality, which means that relationships are not managed and controlled by professional service providers and that "transactions of value take place without money, advertising, or hype." Genuine community utilizes stories—rather than "the foreign language of studies and reports"—to maintain its culture. And in genuine community there is meaningful celebration as well as common heartfelt grief over loss, suffering, and tragedy.

Many professionals and institutions, McKnight observes, actually preempt and destroy genuine community: "Human service professionals with special expertise, techniques, and technology push out the problem-solving knowledge and action of friend, neighbor, citizen, and association. As the power of profession and service system ascends, the legitimacy, authority, and capacity of citizens and community descend. The *citizen* retreats. The *client* advances." McKnight concludes, "Modern heretics are professional practitioners who support citizen competence." That kind of heresy has been the goal of McKnight's Center for Urban Affairs, which attempts to empower rather than de-skill communities.

McKnight tells how one community organization took health matters into its own hands and not only partially solved problems but strengthened its community. Specifically, a poor community on the West Side of Chicago, seeing no improvement in their health status after a change of management in their hospitals, sought an alternate solution. With the help of the Center for Urban Affairs, they identified their seven most common reasons for hospitalization: (1) automobile accidents; (2) interpersonal attacks; (3) accidents (nonauto); (4) bronchial ailments; (5) alcoholism; (6) drug-related problems (medically and nonmedically administered); and (7) dog bites. These health problems, it turned out, were for the most part not diseases but social problems that the community could itself attempt to solve—and by so doing, build a stronger community.

The first community-building solution was applied to dog bites, which caused about 4 percent of emergency room visits. There were packs of wild dogs in the neighborhood that the children helped identify. In one month, 160 of these dogs were captured, and dog bites decreased. Not only were children becoming community activists, but the community clearly saw that their actions—rather than those of healthcare professionals—could affect their health.

Next, they identified the site of a significant number of automobile accidents—an entrance to a department store parking lot. Here again, a health problem was defined in such a way that the community could understand it and do something to help solve it. The community negotiated with the store owner to alter the entrance, which was effective in reducing accidents. While the entrance was not the only cause of automobile accidents, taking action to define this health problem as a social problem empowered more people in the community to become politically active.

Perhaps the most interesting action was the community's response to bronchial problems. Again, the community could not control many of the factors contributing to this health issue, but they could focus on at least one variable: better nutrition. The community observed that most of their homes were two-story apartments with flat roofs, and so they built a greenhouse on one of the roofs as an experiment. In addition to being a "nutrition tool" for growing fresh fruits and vegetables, the greenhouse also became an "economic conservation tool" because the energy that escaped through the roof went into the greenhouse, where heat was needed.

The greenhouse also provided an unintended powerful antidepressant impact. Older folks at a retirement home in the community discovered the greenhouse and began coming there every day to help care for the plants. McKnight reports this transformation: "The administrator of the old people's home noticed that the attitude of the older people changed. They were excited. They had found a function. The greenhouse became a tool to empower older people—to allow discarded people to be productive."

Instead of handing all of our difficulties over to professionals, our problems can themselves become the fuel for genuine community. Genuine community may or may not effectively solve a given problem, but genuine community itself is a powerful antidote to depression.

Democracy and Community

True democracy is naturally energizing. True democracy consists of an ongoing spirited debate and discussion around values and policies, and there is an expectation that this passionate talk has potency and can ultimately lead to transforming society. Different voices, personalities, and ideologies are all heard, and opinions that win out are the ones that have the most respect (not backed by the most money). In true democracy, we feel energized by the belief that we and our neighbors have substantial impact.

True democracy means people "mix it up." In such a society, there is an incentive to have discussions with our neighbors about our community and society. There is an incentive to care about what each of us thinks because *we*, not some distant authority, have real power. Without genuine community, such discussions, essential to true democracy, are irregular or nonexistent. The absence of true democracy is another of life's double-edged swords. The pain of its absence can, history shows, result in helplessness and depression; or the pain can energize people to seek others dissatisfied with the status quo—and to form community to attempt change.

It is unnatural to withdraw from that which is energizing; and if a population has withdrawn from its political arena, even if it is labeled as *democracy*, it's not likely to be true democracy. In the United States a smaller percentage of eligible citizens vote in national elections than in most other nations that have elections (40 to 50 percent of those eligible do not vote even for president, and election turnouts are even lower for local elections). In addition to low voter turnout, since the 1970s, there has been a 30 to 40 percent decline in the percentage of Americans working for a political party, attending a political rally or speech, or attending a public meeting on town or school affairs.

Increasing numbers of Americans know that voting each November has very little to do with true democracy. In true democracy, you are not forced to choose between the "lesser of two evils," each of whom receives millions of dollars from corporations and wealthy individuals. Some Americans who have given up on voting label it a "pseudo-democratic ritual" and mock others who continue to participate. I suggest compassion. But let's also recognize that if you're depressed, voting for someone you don't respect because you "loathe the other candidate more" is not exactly going to lift you out of your malaise.

Not too long ago in the United States, it was common for people to find friends—and even future spouses—working together for a candidate or cause that they shared a passion for. While merely voting (or not voting) does little to restore morale or social capital, actively connecting with others who believe in the same candidate or cause can be quite revitalizing and community building.

True democracy means empowerment and community. If you feel that you have a voice and that you can make a significant impact on society, you will experience revitalizing energy. An absence of true democracy results in helplessness and isolation—both highly associated with depression. That is why true democracy should be important to mental health professionals. The absence of true democracy, like the absence of clean air, is in effect a public health issue.

Bigness versus Community

Large empires can enslave people, and large corporations can create standardized, assembly-line, robotic living. Until recently, it was common sense that bigness was a threat to liberty and fraternity. Over the last fifty years, social critics such as E. F. Schumacher, Kirkpatrick Sale, and Wendell Berry have kept this concern about bigness from being lost.

Before the terms *mental illness, depression,* and *learned helplessness* entered our lexicon, it was basic common sense that if a few big guys had all the power, then a lot of little guys would have none. It was also basic common sense that if you had no control over your life, no autonomy or community, then you would be unhappy. And so politics, up until recently, very much consisted of a struggle by the small guys to ensure that the big guys did not have all the power.

The American Revolution was a rebellion by the small guys against the big guys. Not only was it a revolt by colonists against a powerful monarchy, it was also a revolt of small businesspeople against large corporations such as the British East India Company. After the American Revolution, the fight between big and small continued within the United States. In the early 1800s, there were only a handful of American corporations, and government kept a watchful eye over them. Early corporate charters were limited to a fixed number of years, and their borrowing power and even their profits were sometimes limited. State legislators would revoke corporate charters if the corporations were deemed to be reducing the power of the little guy or destroying community. The fight against bigness was a major battle in American politics throughout the nineteenth century, as it was commonly known that the concentration of power—whether in the hands of a king or a corporation—would render the average person more isolated and powerless, and thus more hopeless and unhappy.

By the mid-twentieth century, the U.S. government had become less a watchdog of corporate bigness and more a partner to it. This governmental-corporate partnership convinced many Americans that opposition to big corporations was the same as opposition to free enterprise—and support for communism. In recent years, multinational corporations (existing in many countries) have become *transnational* ones, which means that such corporations are not only wealthier than many individual nation states but above the laws of once-sovereign nations. Many people who protest against global institutions (such as the World Bank, the International Monetary Fund, and the World Trade Organization) are protesting not against free trade but against transnational corporations' use of such institutions to control once-sovereign governments—and further diminish the power of communities.

A major way to create and maintain community is through how we spend our money. We can give it to impersonal transnational corporations and contribute to their profits, or, whenever possible, we can spend our money at independent merchants whom we know (and whom we can help survive). Wal-Mart and other "big-box" retail giants subvert the possibility of any of us becoming owner-operator independents and experiencing a sense of autonomy, creativity, potency, dignity, and meaning. When we spend our money at independents, we are in effect "voting" for interesting diversity rather than boring, homogeneous, depressing environments. I have never formed a significant human relationship shopping at big-box retail stores, but I have made several friends shopping in owner-operator stores. It is not uncommon for owner-operators to note their customers' absence and to be genuinely glad to see them again.

A major goal of corporate culture is convincing people to care more about acquiring a large number of goods at an inexpensive price than about community and being part of the decision-making process. Corporate culture has been successful in attaining this goal, and it is a great time for the big guy. However, the big guy for quite some time has not been an actual person. It has become a giant institution that controls not only the small guys outside of it but also the small guys who work inside of it. While there is a huge material disparity among rich and poor in the world, including in the United States, all human beings are increasingly losing control to nonhuman institutions.

When one worships industry, technology, and markets rather than people, life, and the planet, eventually it will be nonliving forces that have total control. Unless we rebel against these forces, the logical end to this progression is that the living will cede control to nonhuman institutional forces, and virtually all humans will become powerless—and depressed. According to the World Health Organization's (WHO) statistics on depression, we are well on our way toward this outcome. In 1999 WHO ranked depression as the world's fourth most devastating illness, projecting that it will climb to second place by 2020.

Maintaining Community by Resisting the Science of Control

The increasing rate of depression in the United States means growing numbers of passive Americans, making it easier for giant corporations, governmental institutions, and a few wealthy individuals to gather an increasing amount of control. It is predictable that tyrannical individuals and institutions that hold power will desire a population incapable of offering resistance. Revolutions (including the American Revolution) may be superficially about a particular ideology, but at their core they are about control and community. Revolutionaries connect with one another and actively resist the social conditions that promote helplessness. They know that once they become powerless and disconnected, they will lack the wherewithal to resist—and become depressed.

The "genius" of the current system of control is that, better than other systems, it has utilized the scientific principles of control—the technology of *behaviorism*. Every proficient behaviorist knows that the use of *only* punishment is not a long-term effective means of maintaining power. If one wants to control a rat in the laboratory, a kid in the classroom, a worker on the job, or a consumer at the mall, one needs to grasp the entire science of control. Effective long-term control is not simply about calculated punishments but is also about calculated bribes. Behaviorism means first discovering which particular reward is most associated with a desired behavior, and then calculating just how much of that reward should be meted out or withdrawn, and how often.

The science of gaining control over another human being is a far simpler science than organic chemistry or quantum physics. Most successful pimps can even articulate it, at least in their arena: (1) Be vigilant of the prostitutes' behavior and selectively reward, withdraw rewards, and punish. (2) Use powerful rewards and punishments such as money, drugs, beatings, and humiliations. (3) Be unpredictable so that the prostitutes feel completely powerless to forecast events. (4) Create an environment so that the prostitutes are no longer aware of their intrinsic being and thus make choices based exclusively on gaining pleasure and avoiding pain. A successful pimp, a control freak, or any totalitarian institution wants us disconnected from our souls and from others and at his, her, or its mercy for pleasure and pain.

It was once self-evident that a society based on behaviorism and manipulation is undesirable. As modern behaviorism has become culturally acceptable, resistance to it has increasingly been broken. Rewards have made many Americans "fatter"—in both a metaphorical and a literal sense. In addition to calculated bribes, institutional behaviorists unpredictably withdraw rewards such as jobs, and they construct environments that separate people from all that is natural while surrounding them with all that is synthetic. The Las Vegas casino is fast becoming not so much an exception of American life as an exaggeration of it.

Social critic and historian Lewis Mumford in 1951 said: "In the end [modern] civilization can produce only a mass man: incapable of choice, incapable of spontaneous, self-directed activities: at best patient, docile, disciplined to monotonous work to an almost pathetic degree, but increasingly irresponsible as his choices become fewer and fewer. . . . Ultimately, such a society produces only two groups of men: the conditioners and the conditioned; the active and the passive barbarians."

Authoritarianism, Lemons, and Lemonade

A powerful energy for forming community is antiauthoritarianism: challenging and defying illegitimate authority. Authoritarian religious institutions have labeled antiauthoritarianism as blasphemy and heresy; authoritarian governments have criminalized it; and authoritarian psychiatry has pathologized it.

After the American Revolution, Benjamin Rush, "the father of American psychiatry"—his image adorns the seal of the American Psychiatric Association (APA)—diagnosed Americans who rebelled against a centralized federal authority as having an "excess of the passion for liberty" that "constituted a form of insanity," labeling it *anarchia*. Today the *DSM*, the APA's diagnostic manual, states that a child or an adolescent who "often argues with adults" and "often actively defies or refuses to comply with adult requests or rules" suffers from *oppositional defiant disorder*. While young people once labeled as juvenile delinquents are now diagnosed with *conduct disorder*, oppositional defiant disorder is applied to those doing nothing illegal—just bucking authority.

In an earlier dark age, authoritarian monarchies partnered with authoritarian religious institutions. In today's dark age, corporations such as giant pharmaceuticals partner not with true scientists but with institutions that call themselves scientific. A 2001 editorial in Great Britain's *Lancet* (one of the most respected medical journals in the world) pointed out that the approval process of the U.S. Food and Drug Administration revealed "the extent to which the FDA, its Center for Drug Evaluation and Research (CDER) in particular, has become a servant of industry." In 2000, an article in *USA Today* titled

"FDA Advisors Tied to Industry" reported that in 55 percent of the FDA advisory meetings on drug approvals, half or more of the FDA advisers had financial connections to the interested drug company; and in 92 percent of these advisory meetings, at least one FDA adviser had a financial conflict of interest.

Many Americans are surprised to discover that before approving a drug the FDA does *not* conduct its own research on that drug but instead evaluates studies given to it by the pharmaceutical company that created the drug. Historically, when a popular antidepressant is about to lose its patent protection, Americans begin to hear reports that the drug was not all that effective and maybe even dangerous—and that a newer patent-protected drug is now available and much improved. Virtually all drug studies—those acclaiming and those discrediting—are sponsored by drug companies, and depending on the research methods (especially in terms of which subjects are excluded, the kind of placebos, and the outcome criteria), study results will vary enormously. Genuine faith in God has little to do with acceptance of authoritarian religious institutions, and genuine pursuit of scientific truth has little to do with acceptance of drug-company-sponsored studies used by the FDA for drug approval.

When the world exited from an earlier dark age and entered the Enlightenment, there was a burst of energy. Much of this revitalization had to do with risking skepticism about authoritarian and corrupt institutions and regaining confidence in one's own mind. I believe we are now in another dark age, only the institutions have changed. Americans need to be skeptical about the new authorities and regain confidence in their own common sense.

The good news is that many Americans have already begun to turn "lemons into lemonade" by forming informal information-sharing groups. Some people, for example, use Internet Listservs to become better informed about what are (and are not) safe and effective medications. Some of these "electronic relationships" can, down the road, be expanded to more satisfying face-to-face relationships. Other people, including antiauthoritarian older folks, have formed community by organizing bus trips to Canada to buy prescription drugs at significantly reduced prices.

Many people who seek my help are isolated antiauthoritarians. For one, a middle-aged woman previously diagnosed with substance abuse, depression, and several personality disorders, I "assigned" Emma Goldman's autobiography, *Living My Life* (1931). (Managed-care case managers, in an attempt to speed patients out of therapy, sometimes pressure me to refer my clientele for drugs or, more benignly, demand that I assign homework.) I had guessed that this woman would identify with the antiauthoritarian Goldman and that perhaps she would become energized by her. In the first fifty pages of *Living My Life,* Goldman tells how in the late 1880s the Haymarket martyrs provided her unhappy life with a cause, which energized her to leave her boring husband and move from Rochester, New York, to New York City, where she quickly hooked up with a lover, a mentor, and a community of like-minded souls. My antiauthoritarian client has a passion for reading and forgoes booze when captivated by a good book, and so the 993 pages of Goldman's epic provided a longer detox treatment than that provided by many insurance companies. After completing the book, my client came to believe that she would not have become depressed or abused alcohol if she, like Goldman, had found a cause and community—and she became energized in her search.

Speaking Out about Mental Health and Creating Community

My original motivations for speaking out about the mental health profession did not include forming community—though speaking out did in fact lead to community. My original motivations included an obligation to debunk pretensions, falsehoods, and myths, as well as a desire to separate myself from a profession that has become merely an industry.

There are more than a few people who are enraged by their mental health treatment. Some of them go public; most do not. I have listened to many of them and read their accounts, but I will share just one. This is a letter in the magazine *Adbusters* from Chris Black, who in 2002 went public nineteen years after extensive psychiatric treatment:

I made suicide attempts only during the three years that my mother was frightened (frightened by what my psychiatrist told her), and she insisted that I get psychiatric treatment which consisted of drugs and bullshit talk appointments with the psychiatrist. . . . I knew the drugs made me experience effects which were only detrimental to anything like a productive or even normal life. . . . My shrink made tens of thousands of dollars for himself, and for the hospital which incarcerated me. . . . I think all psychiatrists should be run through a meat grinder and left on the side of the road for the crows to eat.

Too little attention is paid to former patients who are enraged by their mental health treatment, including forced drug and ECT treatments. Some of these former patients describe themselves as "psychiatric survivors," and what angers them is not simply the failure of their treatments. What enrages them perhaps even more is the fact that the mental health establishment barely acknowledges their existence. Survivors tell me that it would go a long way in gaining their forgiveness if mental health professionals would apologize and say, "We won't make the same mistake with others that we did with you." Instead, survivors are routinely dismissed by the mental health establishment, and this dismissal threatens to strip their lives of meaning. However, there are many survivors who refuse to accept such a dismissal and have created organizations to fight for their rights. One such organization is MindFreedom International, which unites one hundred grassroots groups and several thousand members to, as it puts it, "win campaigns for human rights of people diagnosed with psychiatric disabilities. . . . Where mutual support meets human rights activism . . . and where democracy meets the mental health system." Even among those survivors resigned to less than a joyous existence, they reject the idea of having less than a meaningful life. That's why many of them speak out—especially against forced treatments.

The medical profession, with some outstanding individual exceptions, has had no great history in Western society of standing in opposition to totalitarianism and dehumanization. Historian Robert Proctor, in *Racial Hygiene: Medicine under the Nazis* (1988), tells us, "Doctors in fact joined the Nazi party earlier and in greater numbers than any other professional group." According to Proctor, these German doctors found justification for their actions in the actions of their American colleagues: "Germany's foremost racial hygiene journal reported on the refusal of the American Medical Association to admit black physicians." Historian Howard Zinn observes: "In a highly developed society, the Establishment cannot survive without the obedience and loyalty of millions of people who are given small rewards to keep the system going: the soldiers and police, teachers and ministers, administrators and social workers, technicians and production workers, doctors, lawyers. . . . They become the guards of the system. . . . If they stop obeying, the system falls."

There *are* mental health professionals concerned about the direction of mental health in the United States and the rest of the world. Many such dissident professionals have found community at the International Center for the Study of Psychiatry and Psychology (ICSPP), which describes itself as "concerned with the impact of mental health theories on public policy and the effects of therapeutic practices upon individual well-being, personal freedom, and family and community values." ICSPP (unlike the American Psychiatric Association, the National Alliance for the Mentally Ill, and other institutions in the mental health establishment) is *not* financially linked to drug companies and is supported solely by its membership.

The failure of the mental health profession in the areas of morale, healing, and social criticism has been apparent to me since I was a student. However, it was not until my late thirties that I began to realize that mental health professionals, including myself, had also omitted the powerful antidote to depression of community activism.

In 1994, fueled more by exasperation than altruism, I began my journey into the larger world. With the publication of the *DSM-IV* that year, there was yet another increase in the ever-expanding number of new psychiatric diagnoses. The number of patients placed on psychiatric drugs was skyrocketing, especially among children. Pharmaceutical companies and insurance companies were increasingly dictating treatment policy, and I was increasingly embarrassed by what the mental health profession had become. I began to publicly speak out, starting first with a letter to the editor of a national magazine, and I soon discovered that I wasn't alone in my outrage. That simple letter would ultimately result in my connecting with other mental health professionals from all over the world who shared my anger and disappointment over what had happened to our profession.

With the help of dissident mental health professionals and psychiatric survivors, my wife and I toured North America to promote my book *Commonsense Rebellion*. Not only was the traveling great fun, but connecting with like-minded people was truly energizing. Staying at our hosts' homes, we were able to get to know many activists at a deeper level. I found them to be among the most revitalizing folks I have ever met, and I formed rewarding relationships.

Some people believe that without a PhD or an MD, one cannot accomplish anything in terms of improving mental health. I have met many people who disprove this, but let me detail just one such community activist. Steve Clark took his pain and his lifelong skills and transformed them into life-affirming action. His pain? Increasing numbers of young people in his community were being labeled with psychiatric diagnoses and prescribed drugs. Clark had worked a great deal with children, but he also had a lifelong passion for bicycles. He had owned a bicycle repair shop and had served as the bicycle/pedestrian coordinator for Boulder, Colorado. Clark's concerns and skills came together in his creation of the BikeFarm, a nonlabeling approach to helping children and adolescents, which was located on forty acres in rural western Wisconsin and which Steve ran for several years. The BikeFarm offered freedom for kids to discover the world around them. They built rafts and floated them on a lake, milked goats, learned how to fix bicycles, discovered how better to get along with their peers, and gained self-discipline. Favorite activities included adventurous, self-confidence-building bike trips. I observed once unhappy, medicated kids become drug free, start smiling again, and recover a curiosity and love of life.

Robots in a One-Dimensional Society—or Community

It may surprise many Americans to discover that fifty years ago, it was *not* considered radical to voice concerns over our increasing anesthetization. In 1954, Adlai Stevenson, the Democratic candidate for president of the United States in 1952 and 1956, said, "We are not in danger of becoming slaves any more, but of becoming robots."

Rather than battling against societal sources of depression, it appears that Americans are increasingly attempting to divert themselves from the pain of their hopelessness and helplessness. Today an estimated 20 to 25 percent of Americans use psychiatric drugs; 10 to 15 percent are abusing alcohol and illegal psychotropic drugs; and 7 to 12 percent compulsively gamble. Millions more compulsively view television, video games, and pornography; play the stock market; overeat; shop for things they don't need; and flee their helplessness and hopelessness in countless other ways. Increasingly the U.S. economy is based on diversions and anesthetizations.

In the 1950s, just as a mainstream candidate for the U.S. presidency could be concerned over our becoming robots, a seminal figure in the mental health profession could be concerned over our increasing anesthetization. Erich Fromm in 1955 wrote: "Today we come across a person who acts and feels like an automaton; who never experiences anything which is really his; who experiences himself entirely as the person he thinks he is supposed to be; whose artificial smile has replaced genuine laughter; whose meaningless chatter has replaced communicative speech; whose dulled despair has taken the place of genuine pain."

Just as I try to listen to all sides in the battle over antidepressants, I try to listen to all sides of the greater political battle, including the men and women at the American Enterprise Institute (AEI) who celebrate the glories of American corporations and consumerism. Dinesh D'Souza is one such person, and his book *What's So Great about America* became an influential best seller in 2002. That year I heard D'Souza give a speech, and he told a story about his cousin back in India who unsuccessfully tried for many years to gain entrance to the United States. One day D'Souza asked him, "Why do you so badly want to come to America?" His cousin replied, "I want to go to a place where poor people are fat." D'Souza paused to let that sink in.

D'Souza's cousin was absolutely right that poor people are overweight in the United States. Obesity, a growing problem in the entire nation, is an even greater problem for America's poor. While D'Souza's cousin may well have been happy to make it to the United States, as previously noted, for other immigrants from the industrially underdeveloped world, relocation to the United States dramatically increases their probability of a major depressive episode.

When American adults were asked in 1996 to identify the elements of the "good life," 63 percent chose "a lot of money," compared to 38 percent in 1975. And from 1975 to 1996, there was a 6 percent *decrease* in Americans who valued an "interesting job" that "contributed to the welfare of society," as well as a 4 percent *decrease* in those who considered a "happy marriage" an element of the happy life. It appears that American society is increasingly becoming one-dimensional.

Moneymaking is increasingly prioritized over other dimensions, and no distinction is made between what should and should not be considered a commodity. So health care is considered a commodity today, one that is unaffordable for many people. Millions of Americans work at jobs that provide no health insurance. Many of them cannot afford to buy their own coverage and live one serious illness away from financial devastation and bankruptcy. And millions of others work at jobs that they hate just because it provides health insurance.

Teaching a class to seventeen- and eighteen-year-olds, I discovered that one of the most popular topics was "The Most Accepted Religion in the U.S." These teenagers knew that while the United States is predominantly Christian, the true religion of the majority of Americans is something quite different. The true belief system is a worship of industrialism and consumerism. This modern religion centers on the idea that salvation comes with the increasing expansion of goods and services. The commandments of Fundamentalist Industrial Consumerism are:

- Thou shalt mine all of life's resources.
- Thou shalt have unlimited growth.
- Thou shalt not be nonproductive or inefficient.

- Thou shalt worship technology.
- Thou shalt eliminate that which interferes with increased expansion of goods and services, productivity, efficiency, technology, and the mining of all of life's resources.

Industrial consumer fundamentalists reject limits on production, consumption, and technology. They see people who set limits on their growth as, in effect, *heathens* who should be marginalized and ostracized. The business expression "Grow or die" is not a mere suggestion but a commandment of this modern fundamentalism. This is why corporate executives "cook the books"—if they can't show financial growth to Wall Street analysts, they will jeopardize their careers.

Americans are socialized to dislike limits, accepting some of them only with resentment. Many Americans, for example, want to eat without limits and demand technology that makes this possible. And increasingly, Americans admire those who place no limits on money-making. However, setting limits defines abundance. And sharing what we have in abundance—whether it is food, money, or time—creates and strengthens community.

Purpose and Community

Viktor Frankl's search for meaning and purpose was not a narcissistic or self-absorbed one: "By declaring that man is a responsible creature and must actualize the potential meaning of his life, I wish to stress that the true meaning of life is to be found in the world rather than within man or his own *psyche*. . . . Human existence is essentially self-transcendence rather than self-actualization."

Frankl believed that "the striving to find a meaning in one's life is the primary motivational force in man." He considered it a dangerous misconception to assume that humans are content in a tension-free state: "What man actually needs is not a tensionless state but rather the striving and struggling for some goal worthy of him."

I agree with Frankl that each of us has our own mission. If we do not detect our purpose and act on it, we *should* feel depressed. Human beings are not mere objects that lack self-determination, and Frankl was sharply critical of not only genetic determinists but also those who see humans as mere products of familial and societal circumstances. Frankl identified himself as an "existentialist" who cared passionately about meaning, freedom, and choice. But unlike existentialists such as Sartre, who believed that we are free to invent our identity and meaning, Frankl believed that "the meaning of our existence is not invented by ourselves, but rather detected."

Modern industrialization and institutionalization have resulted not only in decreasing autonomy and community but also in diminished meaning and purpose. When a giant retail box such as Wal-Mart comes to a small town, many independent stores eventually go under. One-dimensional economists, focused solely on money and material goods, are not upset by this trend. They argue that owner-operators work long hours and often don't make much money. They are also unbothered by the decimation of family farmers, as they remind us that many of them were poor, and today their children have greater material comforts. However, one-dimensional economists fail to grasp that owner-operators and family farmers (and, even more, preindustrial people) have nonmaterial advantages that are fundamental to mental health. They routinely have a sense of purpose and a belief that what they are doing has significance. In today's work world, studies show that 80 percent of Americans consider what they do for a living to be utterly meaningless.

Frankl, Elie Wiesel, and others were somehow able to wrestle meaning and purpose from the suffering they endured in Nazi concentration camps. In his 2000 lecture "Cold Evil: Technology and Modern Ethics," Andrew Kimbrell, founder of the International Center for Technology Assessment, states that in the West, the "satanic villainy of yesteryear has been largely replaced by a technified evil which appears cold and impersonal." In Kimbrell's conception of "cold evil," communities and cultures are obliterated not by maniacal dictators but by what he calls the cold-evil ideologies of objectification (or quantification), efficiency, and competition. The struggle to find meaning and purpose in the era of cold evil is no less difficult than in those eras of satanic villainy.

There are many ways in which we can find meaning and purpose in our lives. Sometimes the most powerful public activism doesn't feel large, political, or controversial. A small act can have a great impact on increased community. It could be teaching Sunday school and talking about what you care about. Or it could be coaching kids and treating them the way you wish you had been treated. In all cases, it is about transcending your private needs and finding purpose in the world. It is acting on public concerns that you care about and giving yourself a chance to connect with like-minded people. It is transforming your negative energy into something life-affirming, and providing yourself and others with energy. It is no longer feeling helpless, hopeless, alienated, and depressed.

Just as people move naturally toward healing and personal wholeness, they also move naturally toward community and social wholeness. And just as certain barriers block our natural direction toward healing, barriers such as public apathy block our natural inclination to be in community. People with community actively care about something that others also care about. Those people working toward a better neighborhood or society may not always have great success with their stated endeavor, but they routinely succeed at gaining community.

Epilogue

After writing this book, I saw Eugene Jarecki's documentary film *Why We Fight,* about the "military-industrial complex," a term coined by Dwight Eisenhower, who devoted his farewell address in 1961 to its "grave implications." I couldn't help but see parallels between the military-industrial complex and the current "psychopharmaceutical-industrial complex," including the revolving doors of employment between government and industry. In the film, author and U.S. foreign policy critic Chalmers Johnson, in reaction to the huge growth of American military spending, states, "I guarantee you when war becomes that profitable, you are going to see more of it." In a fundamentalist market economy, when *anything*—including mental illness—becomes extremely profitable, you are likely to see more of it.

U.S. rates of depression and "disabling mental illness," as noted, have steadily increased. Those given psychiatric diagnoses are increasingly medicated. And pharmaceutical corporations' profits from psychiatric drugs are dramatically rising. Prior to the Prozac marketing blitz that began in the late 1980s, the total annual sales for *all* antidepressant and antipsychotic drugs in the United States were approximately $500 million. Two decades later, these two classes of psychiatric drugs were grossing over $20 *billion* annually. A single antidepressant such as Zoloft has grossed more than $3 billion a year, as has been the case with the single antipsychotic Zyprexa (the majority of Zyprexa is purchased via government agencies such as Medicaid).

Recently, another parallel between the military-industrial complex and the psychopharmaceutical-industrial one has become more apparent. As I write this, the United States is mired in what has become a lengthy war in Iraq, and (as previously mentioned) the head of the National Institute of Mental Health recently told *Newsweek* that newer research shows that depressed people are not necessarily underproducing serotonin or other neurotransmitters. The Bush administration told Americans that the United States must invade Iraq because of proof that Saddam Hussein had weapons of mass destruction and was connected to Al Qaeda; while the mental health establishment told us, over an even longer period of time, that depressed patients need serotonin- and other neurotransmitter-enhancing drugs because a deficiency of such chemicals caused depression. The Bush administration and the mental health establishment have now retreated from their earlier positions, but neither has spent a great deal of time or energy acknowledging errors. And since each officialdom's earlier claims were so loudly trumpeted and their later retractions so quietly whispered, many Americans continue to believe in mistaken rationales for policies and treatments that continue to affect millions of lives.

When one writes a book that is critical of the status quo, it would be naïve not to expect criticism. Criticism can be useful, and I welcome it. However, those attached to the mental health industry and consumer culture often stereotype with false attributions those of us who remain unattached. So, with apologies to the careful reader, the following restatements are meant to address common false attributions:

- Criticism of the mental health industry is not trivializing mental suffering.
- Depathologizing mental suffering is not romanticizing it.
- "Just saying *know*" to illegal and prescription psychotropic drugs means informed consent and respecting choice when it comes to drugs.
- By noting the similarities between psychiatric drugs and illegal drugs and alcohol, I am not advocating prohibition of psychiatric drugs. Rather, I am exposing hypocrisy.
- Concern over biotechnologies such as antidepressants and electroconvulsive therapy (ECT), which physiologically alter that which has *not* been identified as damaged, does not mean the rejection of biotechnologies that correct identifiable physiological damage.
- That many people say antidepressants "work" for them is not questioned. What is questioned is exactly what *working* means.

- A criticism of psychiatry does not mean a defense of psychologists, social workers, and other mental health professionals. There are psychiatrists who publicly criticize the current state of the mental health profession, and there are psychologists, social workers, and other mental health professionals who do not.
- A rejection of biochemical reductionism as the cause for depression does not mean that I reject the fact that many medical conditions can result in symptoms of depression. And certainly stress, including the stress of depression can, in turn, affect the body.
- A critical examination of psychiatric drugs does not mean an uncritical promotion of other treatments, including psychotherapy.
- Doubting the scientific value of psychotherapy as a standardized technology does not preclude believing that human relationships, including the psychotherapeutic one, can in fact be tremendously helpful.
- Noting the personal limitations of many mental health professionals does not mean that there are not exceptional psychiatrists, psychologists, social workers, counselors, and other mental health professionals who are rebelling against their professional socialization and doing wonderful work.
- Recognizing the importance of parenting is not parent blaming. It is empowering parents by helping them transform their relationship with their children—instead of helplessly sitting by and doing nothing but fill their children's prescriptions.
- Pointing out the limitations of cognitive behavioral therapy (CBT) does not mean the rejection of CBT. It is certainly a good idea to rid oneself of self-defeating thoughts and behaviors.
- Believing that a morale boost can give one the energy to begin the road back from depression does not mean that morale alone is the complete solution to depression.

- Being unafraid to be labeled as "inappropriate" means taking wise risks for severely immobilized people to help energize them. It does not mean doing damage by acting in a manner that is *truly* inappropriate (by violating or exploiting another's being).
- A refusal to *worship* technology is not the same as a rejection of all technology.
- The belief that totalitarianism results in helplessness and hopelessness does not distinguish someone in conventional political terms. When government merges with transnational corporations, *all* who care about autonomy and community have something in common.
- Understanding the influence of culture and society in creating our current epidemic of depression does not mean that we are powerless to transcend cultural and social forces.
- Finding fault with a fundamentalist market economy, industrialism, and consumerism does not mean that I am against the production and use of all material things. Rather it means that I oppose the worship of a one-dimensional value system that does not recognize that certain realms of our humanity need to be outside of markets, industry, and consumer products.
- Human beings are complex, and positive references to particular persons do not indicate my blanket approval of everything about them.
- Noting the life-affirming values of some traditional cultures is not a romanticizing of *all* aboriginal peoples and their practices.
- Finally, while I am critical of what has become of the training of psychologists, I am certainly not dismissing the study of psychology. Quite the opposite, I am trying to restore the richness of human psychology and to reconnect it to philosophy, spirituality, community, society, and culture.

To be human means that at certain times in our lives we will become demoralized and even go to that place of deep despair. How do we get revitalized? What are antidotes to demoralization? How do we let go of our demons that subvert wise choices? How do we transform ourselves to a more joyful life? And how do we create and maintain community? I began to find answers to these questions when I left the neighborhood of industrial mental health. When I moved to other neighborhoods, life once again became fascinating, meaningful, and often fun.

What if depression is *neither* a character defect *nor* a biochemical defect? The medicalization of depression, the mental health establishment told us, was supposed to eliminate the stigma of "character defect." However, it may have created the stigma of "biochemical defect." Historians note that in 1860, the general public had compassion for Abraham Lincoln's depression. Lincoln's longtime law partner William Herndon observed, "Gloom & sadness were his predominant state"; however, Lincoln's depression may have actually helped him politically more than it hurt him. Lincoln biographer Joshua Wolf Shenk concludes that Lincoln's depression gained him sympathy and drew people toward him, as it "seemed not a matter of shame but an intriguing aspect of his character, and indeed an aspect of his grand nature." In contrast, George McGovern's 1972 vice presidential running mate, Thomas Eagleton, was shoved off the ticket because of his history of medical treatment for depression. Today it continues to appear unlikely that anyone with Lincoln's temperament would receive a U.S. presidential or vice presidential nomination, especially if he or she had received antidepressant or electroconvulsive treatment.

I wrote this book for people whose gut tells them that depression is neither a character defect nor a biochemical defect but rather a normal, albeit painful, human reaction. While these people are typically unsentimental and critical thinkers, I have also found that they usually believe that the long-term solution for depression is love, especially love for those aspects of humanity that society fears.

While life can be joyful, pain is unavoidable. We can deny, shut down, or divert ourselves from pain and cause increased suffering. Or we can choose another path. We can accept that life will always bring adversity and make peace with this condition. We can build morale, heal from wounds, free ourselves from ego attachments, and transcend self-absorption. We can value intimate relationships and connect with life. We can attempt to create a saner neighborhood, society, and world, and by so doing, we can find genuine community—and be rewarded with even greater vitality.

Acknowledgments

My wife is uncomfortable with public acknowledgments, but in the interest of truth I begin with her. Bon edited, copyedited, and proofread the manuscript many times, always passionate that the book validate people's pain of living in "a world gone crazy" and provide commonsense solutions.

Three authors, each from very different worlds, read earlier versions of the book and provided invaluable criticism and enthusiasm: David Cohen, professor of social work at Florida International University; Kirkpatrick Sale, historian and decentralization activist; and Robert Whitaker, who prefers "reporter" to "award-winning science journalist." I am indebted to them and strongly recommend David's *Your Drug May Be Your Problem*, Kirk's *Human Scale*, and Bob's *Mad in America*.

Three of my closest friends, each with very different sensibilities, also read the manuscript. Lewis Kamrass, senior rabbi of the Isaac M. Wise Temple in Cincinnati, believes that the absence of community is a major cause of depression, and he wanted me to focus on community building. Russ Bozian, computer programmer, sees an increasingly unfun and boring world, and he pushed for a fun and stimulating book. Rhoda Bates, manager of clinical education at Jewish Hospital in Cincinnati, finds that depressed people have difficulty doing anything—including reading—and she encouraged me to provide both hope and an easy read.

There was a fervent debate, reflecting different sensibilities, about this book's title. Sam Levine, my father, remains certain that the best title is "Say It Ain't So," a refrain of depressed baseball fans in New York City in 1957 after discovering their beloved New York Giants and Brooklyn Dodgers had—for no purpose other than ownership greed—been taken away from them. My stepson Aaron Lichtenberg, his wife Liz, and Aaron's longtime buddy Nathan Chamberlin were most amused by "Shrinks or Shinola?" My "psychiatric survivor" friends will be encouraged to discover that the publisher seriously considered "I Am Not a Disorder." And there was more than one person who said, often with the inflection of a borscht-belt comedian, "So, Who's Not Depressed?" However, this book is about finding morale, energy, and community—and surviving America's depression epidemic; and so the title chosen, though not the catchiest one considered, is the most honest.

Nobody could have fought harder for an author and a book than my agent Timothy Wager—a genuinely good guy. Timothy found the right editor in Jonathan Teller-Elsberg, the book's initial champion at Chelsea Green. Ultimately both Jonathan and editor-in-chief John Barstow co-edited this book, and all of their suggestions were excellent ones. And I am lucky that Margo Baldwin, rare among owners of a publishing company, makes book acquisition decisions with her brain, her heart, and her soul.

I want to acknowledge several other people who provided me with morale, community, a vital fact, or a fun anecdote. First the late Kevin McCready, and then in alphabetical order: David Antonuccio, Tom Brengelman, Roland Chrisjohn, Steve Clark, Randy Cooper, Paco Ferri, Raj Finley, Leonard Roy Frank, Al Galves, Tom Gelwicks, Grace Jackson, Jay Joseph, Jeffrey Lacasse, Jonathan Leo, Long Standing Bear Chief, Lou Martinelli, Lisa McCormick, David Oaks, Silja Talvi, Dave Walker, Eddie Wern, and Rick Winkling.

Finally, I want to thank the nameless people in the clinical vignettes. I know their names, and in my countless readings of the book, I always see their faces.

Notes

Introduction

vii *Martin Seligman . . . depression epidemic:* Seligman states that the
"United States is experiencing an unparalleled epidemic of depression,"
Martin E. P. Seligman, *Learned Optimism: How to Change Your Mind
and Your Life* (New York: Knopf, 1991), 63–65. Seligman's National
Press Club talk, "Depression & Violence" (Washington, D.C.,
September 13, 1998), http://www.apa.org/releases/epidemic.html
(originally accessed June 29, 2002, reaccessed on August 15, 2005,
at http://www.nonopp.com/ar/Psicologia/00/epidemic_depersion.
htm.) Seligman's and others' assertion of a U.S. depression epidemic is
based on several epidemiological studies (such as the Epidemiological
Catchment Area and the National Institute of Mental Health
Collaborative Program) showing increasing cumulative lifetime prevalence rates of depression throughout the twentieth century in the
United States; for a review of some of these studies, see Gerald L.
Klerman and Myrna M. Weissman, "Increasing Rates of Depression,"
Journal of the American Medical Association 261:15 (1989): 2229–35;
e.g., the percentage of Americans born between 1945 and 1954 who
had a major depression by age thirty-four is 11 percent, more than five
times higher than for those born between 1925 and 1934, of whom 2
percent had a major depression by age thirty-four. Also, the percentage
of U.S. adults with major depression was 7.06 percent in 2001–2002,
more than double the 3.33 percent in 1991–1992, as described in
Wilson M. Compton et al., "Changes in the Prevalence of Major
Depression and Comorbid Substance Use Disorders in the United
States Between 1991–1992 and 2001–2002," *American Journal of
Psychiatry* 163 (December, 2006): 2141–47.

x *The book Suicide:* Paul G. Quinnett, *Suicide: The Forever Decision: For
Those Thinking about Suicide, and for Those Who Know, Love, or Counsel
Them* (New York: Continuum, 1992), 15.

xi *In 2000 it was estimated that ever year, 750,000 people:* Estimate includes
undocumented suicide attempts, in *Psychology Today*, May/June 2000,
44. U.S. Surgeon General David Satcher reports 500,000 *documented*
emergency room treatments for suicide attempts; Cox News Service,
Cincinnati Enquirer, July 29, 1999.

xi *eighth leading cause of death:* "The Surgeon General's Call to Action to Prevent Suicide, 1999" (1999), www.surgeongeneral.gov/library/calltoaction/fact1.htm (accessed July 15, 2005).

xi *third leading cause of death for teenagers . . . rate of teen male suicide has tripled:* Reported in "Depression and Suicide in Children and Adolescents," *Mental Health: A Report of the Surgeon General* (U.S. Department of Health and Human Services, 1999), http://www .surgeongeneral.gov/library/mentalhealth/chapter3/sec5. html (accessed April 4, 2004).

xii *In a 2004 study on the influence of patient expectations:* Heather V. Krell et al., "Subject Expectations of Treatment Effectiveness and Outcome of Treatment with an Experimental Antidepressant," *Journal of Clinical Psychiatry* 65:9 (2004): 1174–79. While the subject sample in this study was relatively small, the article also reviewed other studies that showed the importance of pretreatment expectations.

xv *U.S. Surgeon General . . . "Nearly two-thirds:* "The Roots of Stigma," *Mental Health: A Report of the Surgeon General* (U.S. Department of Health and Human Services, 1999), http://www.surgeongeneral.gov/library/mentalhealth/chapter1/sec1. html (accessed April 12, 2004).

xv *Gallup poll . . . "honesty and ethical standards":* Eve Bender, "Public Has Trust Issues with Psychiatrists, Survey Finds," *Psychiatric News* 42:5 (March 2, 2007): 18, http://pn.psychiatryonline.org/cgi/content/full/42/5/18 (accessed March 15, 2007). Gallup poll to which article refers: "Honesty/Ethics in Profession," December 8–10, 2006, http://www.galluppoll.com/content/default.aspx?ci=1654 (accessed March 15, 2007).

Chapter One

1 *In 2000 an ABC News poll:* "Use of Anti-Depressants Is a Long-Term Practice," ABCNEWS.com, April 10, 2000, http://abcnews.go.com/onair/WorldNewsTonight/poll000410.html (accessed February 27, 2003).

2 *(FDA) changed the rules for broadcast advertising:* Marcia Angell, *The Truth About the Drug Companies: How They Deceive Us and What to Do About It* (New York: Random House, 2004), 123–24.

2 *majority of physicians are likely to comply with requests:* In some studies as many as 90 percent of physicians comply with requests, according to Elliot S. Valenstein, *Blaming the Brain* (New York: Free Press, 1998), 231. Also, "patients' requests have a profound effect on physician pre-

scribing in major depression," concludes Richard L. Kravitz et al., "Influence of Patients' Requests for Direct-to-Consumer Advertised Antidepressants," *Journal of the American Medical Association* 293:16 (April 27, 2005): 1995–2002.

2 *Drug Firms Turn to Celebs:* Associated Press, "Drug Firms Turn to Celebs: Spots Blur Line betweeen Ads, News," *Cincinnati Enquirer,* January 3, 2001.

2 *funding advocacy organizations such as the National Alliance for the Mentally Ill:* NAMI received $11.72 million from drug companies between 1996 and mid-1999, per Ken Silverstein "Prozac.org," *Mother Jones,* November/December 1999, 22–23. In the first quarter of 2007, pharmaceutical company Eli Lilly provided NAMI with a grant of $450,000 for "Campaign for the Mind of America 2007," as well as providing various local NAMI organizations with smaller grants, in Lilly's "Grant Office 2007—1st Quarter," https://www.lillygrant office.com/docs/q1_registry_report.pdf (accessed May 22, 2007).

2 *Lilly sales representatives in Florida: 60 Minutes II,* February 19, 2003.

2 *majority of antidepressant prescriptions are written:* Primary care physicians write about 80 percent of the prescriptions for antidepressants, in Elliot S. Valenstein, *Blaming the Brain,* 183.

3 *58 percent of family practitioners . . . sales representative:* J. Greenwood, "Prescribing and Salesmanship," *HAI (Health Action International News)* 48 (1989): 1–2, 11, in Elliot S. Valenstein, *Blaming the Brain,* 166.

3 *documented by many:* Marcia Angell, *The Truth About the Drug Companies;* "Pushing Drugs to Doctors," *Consumer Reports* 57 (February 1992): 87–94; T. Bodenheimer, "Uneasy Alliance: Clinical Investigators and the Pharmaceutical Industry," *New England Journal of Medicine* 342 (2000): 1539–44; Bruce E. Levine, *Commonsense Rebellion* (New York: Continuum, 2003), 135–36, 231–34; David O. Antonuccio, David D. Burns, and William G. Danton, "Antidepressants: A Triumph of Marketing over Science?" *Prevention and Treatment* 5:25 (July 15, 2002), http://journals.apa.org/ prevention/volume5/pre0050025c.html (accessed August 15, 2005).

3 *One of Angell's examples:* Marcia Angell, *The Truth About the Drug Companies,* 103, 143.

3 *Funding university psychiatry departments:* Liz Kowalczyk, "Psychiatry Funding Questioned: Drug Firms Aid Mass. General," *Boston Globe,* May 14, 2005, in "Drugs Pay to Educate Physicians," *The National Psychologist,* July/August 2005, 2.

3 *cash gifts as high as $2,000:* Bill Brubaker, "Drug Firms Still Lavish Pricey Gifts on Doctors," *Washington Post,* January 19, 2002.

3 *Advertising in professional journals:* "Pushing Drugs to Doctors," *Consumer Reports* 57 (February, 1992): 87–94.

4   *Funding . . . professional organizations:* Peter R. Breggin, *Toxic Psychiatry* (New York: St. Martin's Press, 1991), 354–58. In the first quarter of 2007, pharmaceutical company Eli Lilly provided the American Psychiatric Association with two grants ("Improving Depression Treatments" and "Understanding the Complexity of Bipolar Mixed Episodes") totaling over $412,000, in Lilly's "Grant Office 2007—1st Quarter," https://www.lillygrantoffice .com/docs/q1_registry_report.pdf (accessed May 22, 2007).

4   *suppressing negative results:* One example is GlaxoSmithKline. Glaxo agreed to pay a fine to settle a suit brought against it by New York State Attorney General Eliot Spitzer, who had alleged that Glaxo had suppressed results of studies showing that its antidepressant Paxil, when used with children, was ineffective and increased the risk of suicidal thinking and behavior. "Glaxo Settles New York Drug Suit," *BBC News*, August 27, 2004, http://news.bbc.co.uk/2/hi/business/ 3602934.stm (accessed August 29, 2004); also, Bruce Levine, "Behind the Paxil Scandals," *Z Magazine*, April 2005, 11–13.

4   *Providing high-paying industry jobs . . . FDA:* Paul Leber, director of the FDA's division of neuropharmacological drug products, left the agency in the late 1990s to direct a consulting firm that specializes in advising pharmaceutical companies attempting to gain FDA approval for new psychiatric drugs, in Joseph Glenmullen, *Prozac Backlash* (New York: Simon & Schuster, 2000), 159–165.

4   *National Institute of Mental Health:* In 1993 Steven Paul, scientific director of the NIMH, resigned to become vice president of Eli Lilly (maker of Prozac), in Peter R. Breggin and Ginger Ross Breggin, *Talking Back to Prozac: What Doctors Aren't Telling You about Today's Most Controversial Drug* (New York: St. Martin's Press, 1994), 206.

4   *Congress:* "Billy Tauzin, a former Republican congressman from Louisiana who now heads the Pharmaceutical Research and Manufacturers of America (PhRMA) . . . helped shepherd the Medicare prescription drug law to passage as chairman of the House Energy and Commerce Committee before joining PhRMA for a reported $1 million a year or more," in Jim Drinkard, "Drugmakers Go Furthest to Sway Congress," *USA Today,* April 25, 2005, http://www.usatoday.com/money/industries/health/ drugs/2005-04-25-drug-lobby-cover_x.htm (accessed August 1, 2005); *60 Minutes* reported on April 1, 2007, that Tauzin's salary at PhRMA is $2 million a year.

4   *A 1986 poll showed that only 12 percent . . . 78 percent:* Eve Kupersanin, "Americans More Willing to Seek Out Treatment," *Psychiatric News* 37:3 (February 1, 2002), http://pn.psychiatryonline.org/cgi/ content/full/37/3/1 (accessed December 10, 2005).

4   *but by 1998, 41 percent said they would take medication for depression:* In a 1998 poll by University of Chicago investigators in which people were

asked if they would take a psychiatric drug for symptoms of depression, 41 percent of those polled said they would take the drug, in T. W. Croghan et al., "American Attitudes toward and Willingness to Use Psychiatric Medication," *The Journal of Nervous and Mental Disease* 191 (2003): 166–74.

4 *pollsters in 2000 . . . only 28 percent were willing to take antidepressants:* ABC News poll reported in Eve Kupersanin, "Americans More Willing to Seek Out Treatment," *Psychiatric News* 37:3 (February 1, 2002), http://pn.psychiatryonline.org/cgi/content/full/37/3/1 (accessed December 10, 2005).

4 *Between 1987 and 1997 . . . treatment for depression more than tripled . . . medication almost doubled:* "National Trends in the Outpatient Treatment of Depression," *Journal of the American Medical Association* 287:203 (2002), reported in Eve Kupersanin, "Americans More Willing to Seek Out Treatment," *Psychiatric News* 37:3 (February 1, 2002),http://pn.psychiatryonline.org/ cgi/content/full/37/3/1 (accessed December 10, 2005).

4 *antidepressant annual sales had grown to $11.2 billion:* Robert Whitaker, "Anatomy of an Epidemic: Psychiatric Drugs and the Astonishing Rise of Mental Illness in America," *Ethical Human Psychology and Psychiatry* 7:1 (Spring 2005): 23–35.

5 *the New York Times reassessed the value:* Erica Goode, Melody Peterson, and Andrew Pollack, "Antidepressants Lift Clouds, but Lose 'Miracle Drug' Label," *New York Times,* June 30, 2002.

5 *Andrew Solomon's The Noonday Demon:* Andrew Solomon, *The Noonday Demon: An Atlas of Depression* (New York: Touchstone, 2001), 13 (acknowledgment of bias); 119 (list of drugs he's taken); 235 ("cock-tail" [Solomon's term] that allowed him to write the book); 81 (attack on drug critics).

6 *Peter Kramer:* Peter Kramer, *Listening to Prozac* (New York: Viking, 1993), 259.

6 *Lauren Slater:* Lauren Slater, *Prozac Diary* (New York: Random House, 1998), 32 ("miracle tinged"); 120 ("Prozac poop-out" and upping dosage to 80 mg); 183 ("I am drug dependent"); 200 ("My cognition may be fraying").

6–7 *Joseph Glenmullen:* Joseph Glenmullen, *Prozac Backlash*, 8.

7 *Peter Breggin:* Peter R. Breggin, *Toxic Psychiatry*, 344 (psycho-pharmaceutical complex). Peter R. Breggin and Ginger Ross Breggin, *Talking Back to Prozac.*

8 *In April 2002, the Journal of the American Medical Association:* Hypericum Depression Trial Study Group, Jonathan R. T. Davidson, lead author of "Effect of Hypericum perforatum (St John's Wort) in Major Depressive Disorder," *Journal of the American Medical Association* 287:14 (April 10, 2002):1807–14. "Full response" is defined by a score on depression rating scales that researchers judge to be in the

normal range. Davidson's financial disclosure listing: "Dr. Davidson holds stock in Pfizer [manufacturer of Zoloft] . . . and has received speaker fees from Pfizer." Press releases of the study highlighted St. John's wort's poor showing against the placebo and omitted Zoloft's poor showing. Current spin on this study by antidepressant advocates is that it does not prove Zoloft's ineffectiveness because it used low doses of Zoloft. This is simply not true: researchers used the standard initial dose and standard target dose (subjects were given a "range from 50 to 100 mg of setraline [Zoloft]." The standard manual for psychiatric drug administration states that 50 mg of Zoloft is the recommended starting dosage; see Jerrold S. Maxmen and Nicholas G. Ward, *Psychotropic Drugs Fast Facts* (New York: W. W. Norton, 1995), 84. fifty mg of Zoloft is the recommended starting dosage and 100 mg of Zoloft is the recommended target dosage in Mary A. Whooley and Gregory E. Simon, "Managing Depression in Medical Outpatients," *The New England Journal of Medicine* 343:26 (2000): 1942–49.

9 *In July 2002, Newsweek:* David Noonan and Geoffrey Cowley, "Prozac vs. Placebos," *Newsweek*, July 15, 2002, 48–49.

9 *Prevention & Treatment . . . Kirsch:* Irving Kirsch et al., "The Emperor's New Drugs: An Analysis of Antidepressant Medication Data Submitted to the U.S. Food and Drug Administration," *Prevention & Treatment* 5:23 (July 15, 2002), http://journals.apa.org/prevention/volume5/ pre0050023a.html (accessed August 15, 2005). "57 percent of the trials funded by the pharmaceutical industry failed to show a significant difference between drug and placebo," in Irving Kirsch, Alan Scoboria, and Thomas J. Moore, "Response to the Commentaries: Antidepressants and Placebos: Secrets, Revelations, and Unanswered Questions," *Prevention & Treatment* 5:33 (July 15, 2002), http://journals.apa.org/prevention/ volume5/pre0050033r.html (accessed August 20, 2005). For an excellent summary of the Kirsch study, commentaries, and context, see Gary Greenberg, "Is It Prozac? Or Placebo?" *Mother Jones*, November/December 2003, 77–81.

9 *In 2000, a Psychiatric Times article:* David O. Antonuccio et al., "Rumble in Reno: The Psychosocial Perspective on Depression," *Psychiatric Times* 17:8 (August 2000), http://www.psychiatrictimes.com/p000824.html (accessed December 15, 2005).

9 *just one technique:* Another technique is "placebo washout," which means in a preliminary study, placebo responders are identified and excluded from the actual study. Also see the discussion of the Hamilton Depression Rating Scale later in chapter 1.

10 *STAR*D:* Shankar Vedantam, "Drugs Cure Depression in Half of Patients," *Washington Post*, March 23, 2006. Stage one STAR*D results: Madhukar H. Trivedi et al., "Evaluation of Outcomes with Citalopram for Depression Using Measurement-Based Care in

STAR*D: Implications for Clinical Practice," *American Journal of Psychiatry* 163 (January 2006): 28–40; Stage two STAR*D results: Madhukar Trivedi et al., "Medication Augmentation after the Failure of SSRIs for Depression," *New England Journal of Medicine* 354 (March 23, 2006): 1243–52; A. John Rush et al., "Bupropion-SR, Sertraline, or Venlafaxine-XR after Failure of SSRIS for Depression," *New England Journal of Medicine* 354 (March 23, 2006): 1231–42.

10 *other drugs in place of or in addition to Celexa:* In steps two, three, and four, most patients were given other antidepressants in place of or in addition to Celexa, but some patients received other kinds of psychiatric drugs (such as lithium), and a few patients in step two received cognitive-behavioral therapy.

10 *at each treatment step . . . remission occurred in less than a third of the patients:* Although the NIMH press release claimed that on step one "about a third" reached remission, on the primary measure, the Hamilton Rating Scale for Depression (HRSD, the standard scale used in most studies), only 28 percent had remission, and slightly less than 30 percent reached remission in step two. Even when STAR*D researchers combined more inflated outcome measures with the HRSD, a 36.8 percent remission rate was the best for any step, which most certainly would have been equaled or bested by a placebo control had there been one in the study.

10 *spontaneous remission:* According to a 1994 Canadian Task Force on Preventive Health Care report on depression, "Spontaneous remission can occur over 6 to 12 months in up to 50 percent of affected people,"http://www.ctfphc.org/Full_Text/Ch39full.htm (accessed June 10, 2006).

10 *STAR*D researchers . . . third and fourth treatment:* A. John Rush et al., "Acute and Longer-Term Outcomes in Depressed Outpatients Requiring One or Several Treatment Steps: A STAR*D Report," *American Journal of Psychiatry* 163:11 (November 2006): 1905–17.

10 *plummeted to below 14 percent:* STAR*D researchers reported remission rates of 13.7 percent for step three and 13.0 percent for step four.

10 *relapse rate:* Though all agree that the relapse rates were extremely high, the tables in the November 2006 *American Journal of Psychiatry* are so poorly identified that there are differences of opinion about just how high. Relapse rates were reported as 71.1 percent by Avery Johnson, "A Study Looks at Resistance to Depression Treatment," *Wall Street Journal,* November 1, 2006, but relapse rates are probably closer to 60 to 70 percent.

10 *cumulative remission rate:* A "cumulative sustained recovery rate" of 43 percent was estimated by Craig Nelson in an editorial appearing jointly with the study in the November 2006 issue of the *American Journal of Psychiatry.* Nelson notes that while STAR*D authors state that after four treatments the cumulative remission rate is 67 percent, this does

not account for relapse (which Nelson attempted to calculate), and he found "a cumulative sustained recovery rate of 43 percent." Nelson also notes that "neither the author's cumulative remission rate or my sustained recovery rate takes into account the ascending numbers of patients who discontinue treatment prematurely," in Craig Nelson, "The STAR*D Study: A Four-Course Meal That Leaves Us Wanting More," *American Journal of Psychiatry* 163:11 (November 2006): 1864–66. It would seem more likely that this discontinuing group would quit treatment because treatment wasn't working, which would further lower the true remission rate.

11 *BMJ . . . long-term outcome:* Joanna Moncrieff and Irving Kirsch, "Efficacy of Antidepressants in Adults," *BMJ* 331 (July 16, 2005): 155–57.

11 *2000 ABC News poll:* "Use of Anti-Depressants Is a Long-Term Practice," ABCNEWS.com, April 10, 2000, http://abcnews.go.com/onair/ WorldNewsTonight/poll000410.html (accessed February 27, 2003).

11 *Ecstasy to help spouses open up:* Cynthia Kuhn, Scott Swartzwelder, and Wilkie Wilson, *Buzzed: The Straight Facts about the Most Used and Abused Drugs from Alcohol to Ecstasy* (New York: W. W. Norton, 1998), 71.

11 *less easily derailed:* Richard O'Connor, *Undoing Depression* (New York: Berkley Books, 1997), 156.

12 *can better be prevented from suicide by antidepressants:* Seymour Fisher and Roger P. Greenberg, eds., *From Placebo to Panacea: Putting Psychiatric Drugs to the Test* (New York: John Wiley & Sons, 1997), 124–26, 371.

12 *"black box" warning:* Jonathan Mahler, "The Antidepressant Dilemma," *New York Times Magazine,* November 21, 2004, 59–65, 117–19.

12 *children given antidepressants were almost twice as likely:* Gardiner Harris, "Antidepressant Study Seen to Back Expert," *New York Times,* August 20, 2004, http://www.nytimes.com/2004/08/20/ science/20depress.html (accessed August 21, 2004).

12 *In 2003 . . . the MHPRA:* Erica Goode, "British Ignite Debate in U.S. on Drugs and Suicide," *New York Times,* December 16, 2003, http://www.dukehealth1.org/mental_health/British_Debate.pdf (accessed January 14, 2004).

12 *In December 2006 an FDA expert panel:* Shankar Vedantam, "Antidepressant a Suicide Risk for Young Adults," *Washington Post,* December 14, 2006.

12 *(though the FDA panel believed that risks diminish as adults age):* However, a Canadian study reported that those sixty-six and older using SSRIs were five times more likely to commit suicide during the first month of drug use than those who were using the older tricyclic antidepressants, "SSRI Antidepressants Link to Higher Suicide Risk in Seniors," CBC News, May 1, 2006, http://www.cbc.ca/health/story/ 2006/05/01/ssri-suicide060501.html (accessed May 5, 2006).

12 *in May 2007 the FDA proposed:* "FDA Proposes New Warnings about Suicidal Thinking, Behaviors in Young Adults Who Take Antidepressant Medication," *FDA News,* May 2, 2007, http://www.fda.gov/bbs/topics/NEWS/2007/NEW01624.html (accessed May 3, 2007).

12 *Critics of the FDA questioned:* Evelyn Pringle, "FDA Protects SSRI Makers with Misleading Suicide Warning," *OpEdNews.com,* May 21, 2007, http://www.opednews.com/articles/5/genera_evelyn_p_070521_fda_protects_ssri_ma.htm (accessed May 21,2007).

12 *Jeff Reardon:* "Reardon Blames Meds for Robbery," AP story on MSNBC, December 28, 2005, http://www.msnbc.msn.com/id/10613362/ (accessed January 10, 2006); "Judge Finds Reardon Not Guilty on Robbery Charge," AP story on ESPN.com, http://sports.espn.go.com/mlb/news/story?id=2564122 (accessed August 30, 2006).

13 *Spanish conquistadors . . . the Incas:* Cynthia Kuhn, Scott Swartzwelder, and Wilkie Wilson, *Buzzed,* 197.

13 *Sigmund Freud:* Ernest Jones, *The Life and Work of Sigmund Freud,* edited and abridged in one volume by Lionel Trilling and Steven Marcus (New York: Basic Books, 1953), 56–57.

13 *Alcohol was a recommended treatment:* Peter R. Breggin, *Toxic Psychiatry,* 243.

13 *psychiatrist Oscar Janiger used LSD:* AP obituary, "Oscar Janiger Died," August 17, 2001, http://www.erowid.org/culture/characters/janiger_oscar/janiger_oscar_obituary1.shtml (accessed March 3, 2004).

13 *Ecstasy was used in marital counseling:* Cynthia Kuhn, Scott Swartzwelder, and Wilkie Wilson, *Buzzed,* 71.

13 *Ecstasy . . . post-traumatic stress disorder:* Steven Kotler, "Drugs in Rehab," *Psychology Today,* March/April 2005, 28–29.

14 *The Speed Culture:* Lester Grinspoon and Peter Hedblom, *The Speed Culture: Amphetamine Use and Abuse in America* (Cambridge, MA: Harvard University Press, 1975), 51.

14 *Eric Schlosser:* Eric Schlosser, *Fast Food Nation: The Dark Side of the All-American Meal* (Boston: Houghton Mifflin, 2001), 174.

14 *Stanton Peele:* Stanton Peele, *Diseasing of America: Addiction Treatment Out of Control* (Boston: Houghton Mifflin, 1989), 96–99.

14 *Cary Grant described himself:* Carl Elliott, *Better Than Well* (New York: W. W. Norton, 2003), 42.

15 *Ricky Williams's announcement:* Fred Gardner, "Run Ricky Run Football," *Counterpunch,* August 8, 2004, http://www.counterpunch.org/gardner08072004.html (accessed August 9, 2004).

15 *In 2004 . . . Scientific American:* Roger A. Nicoll and Bradley E. Alger, "The Brain's Own Marijuana," *Scientific American,* December 2004, 69–75.

15 *Lidia Wasowicz . . . Pankaj Sah:* Lidia Wasowicz, "Pot-Like Chemical Helps Beat Fear," UPI, July 31, 2002,

http://www.upi.com/NewsTrack/Science/2002/07/31/
potlike_chemical_helps_beat_fear/7373/ (accessed August 10, 2002);
Nature article and Pankaj Sah quoted by Wasowicz.

16 *Michael Pollan:* Michael Pollan, "The Way We Live Now: Á Very Fine
Line," *New York Times Magazine,* September 12, 1999,
http://www.michaelpollan.com/article.php?id=48 (accessed January
10, 2004).

17 *psychotherapy . . . not a standardized, scientifically proven treatment:* For
summary, see Ethan Watters and Richard Ofshe, *Therapy's Delusions*
(New York: Scribner, 1999), 125–42.

17 *MD, PhD, or an MSW have no more success . . . than nonprofessionals . . .
specific technique:* Ethan Watters and Richard Ofshe, *Therapy's Delusions,*
130. Technique irrelevance, in Martin E. P. Seligman, "The
Effectiveness of Psychotherapy," *American Psychologist* 50:12
(December 1995): 965–74.

17 *more effective when there is a positive relationship:* Morris B. Parloff et al.,
"Research on Therapist Variables in Relation to Process and Outcome,"
in Sol L. Garfield and Allen E. Bergin, *Handbook of Psychotherapy and
Behavior Change: An Empirical Analysis* (New York: John Wiley &
Sons, 1978), 233–82.

17 *comparing psychotherapy to antidepressants:* David O. Antonuccio, David
D. Burns, and William G. Danton, "Antidepressants: A Triumph of
Marketing over Science?" *Prevention & Treatment,* 5:25 (July 15,
2002), http://www.antidepressantsfacts.com/2002-07-15-Antonuccio-
therapy-vs-med.htm (accessed August 20, 2005).

17 *psychotherapy results in a somewhat lower relapse rate:* David O.
Antonuccio, William G. Danton, and Garland Y. DeNelsky,
"Psychotherapy versus Medication for Depression: Challenging the
Conventional Wisdom with Data," *Professional Psychology: Research and
Practice* 26:6 (1995): 574–85.

17 *NIMH-funded study comparing Paxil to cognitive therapy:* The NIMH
study was reported at the annual meeting of the American Psychiatric
Association; Sharon Begley, "In NIMH Study, Therapy Works as Well
as Drugs for Depression," *Wall Street Journal,* May 24, 2002.

18 *psychotherapy works no better than the passage of time:* In a study at a
Kaiser Foundation Hospital in Oakland, California, therapy patients did
not improve significantly more than did the waiting-list controls, in
Martin L. Gross, *The Psychological Society* (New York: Touchstone,
1978), 18. "[T]here is no convincing evidence that psychotherapy is
more effective than placebo treatment for actual patients," in Leslie
Prioleau, Martha Murdock, and Nathan Brody, "An Analysis of
Psychotherapy versus Placebo Studies," *Behavioral and Brain Sciences* 6
(1983): 275–85.

18 *Consumer Reports reported in 1995:* "Mental Health: Does Therapy
Help?" *Consumer Reports* 60 (November 1995): 734–39.

21 *William James . . . "I take it that no man is educated who has never . . .":* John J. McDermott, ed., *The Writings of William James* (Chicago: University of Chicago Press, 1977), xx.

21 *Martin Seligman:* Martin E. P. Seligman, *Learned Optimism: How to Change Your Mind and Your Life* (New York: Knopf, 1991), 107–12.

21 *David Livingstone Smith:* David Livingstone Smith, "Natural Born Liars," *Scientific American Mind* 16:2 (2005): 16–21.

21 *Lauren Alloy and Lyn Abramson:* Lauren B. Alloy and Lyn Y. Abramson, "Judgment of Contingency in Depressed and Nondepressed Students: Sadder but Wiser?" *Journal of Experimental Psychology: General* 108:4 (1979): 441–85.

21 *Peter Lewinsohn:* Peter M. Lewinsohn et al., "Social Competence and Depression: The Role of Illusory Self-Perceptions," *Journal of Abnormal Psychology* 89 (1980): 203–12.

22 *some doctors . . . new attitude toward faith, belief, and the placebo effect:* Deepak Chopra, "The Spell of Mortality," in Richard Carlson and Benjamin Shield, eds., *Healers on Healing* (Los Angeles: Jeremy P. Tarcher, 1989), 179–84.

22 *James concluded . . . "faith in a fact can create the fact" . . . John McDermott:* William James, "The Will to Believe," in John J. McDermott, ed., *The Writings of William James*, xxvii–xxx, 717–35.

23 *In 2002, the New York Times:* Erica Goode, Melody Peterson, and Andrew Pollack, "Antidepressants Lift Clouds, but Lose 'Miracle Drug' Label," *New York Times*, June 30, 2002.

23 *a multitude of studies failed to prove this precept:* For further discussion of these issues, see Jeffrey R. Lacasse and Jonathan Leo, "Serotonin and Depression: A Disconnect between the Advertisements and the Scientific Literature," *Public Library of Science (PLOS) Medicine* 2:12 (2005), http://medicine.plosjournals.org/perlserv/%5C?request=get-document&doi=10.1371%2Fjournal.pmed.0020392#JOURNAL-PMED-0020392-T001 (accessed November 15, 2006).

23 *The American Medical Association Essential Guide to Depression:* American Medical Association Essential Guide to Depression* (New York: Simon & Schuster, 1998), 64.

23 *Elliot Valenstein:* Elliot S. Valenstein, *Blaming the Brain*, 104, 223.

23 *Newsweek . . . February 26, 2007:* Julie Scelfo, "Men and Depression: Facing Darkness," *Newsweek*, February 26, 2007, 43–49.

24 *Diagnostic and Statistical Manual of Mental Disorders: Diagnostic and Statistical Manual of Mental Disorders*, 4th ed., *DSM-IV* (Washington, D.C.: American Psychiatric Association, 1994), 327.

24 *A more glaring contradiction in the diagnosis of depression:* Benedict Carey, "Many Diagnoses of Depression May Be Misguided, Study Says," *New York Times*, April 3, 2007, http://www.nytimes.com/2007/04/03/health/psychology/03depr.html (accessed April 4, 2007); Shankar Vedantam, "Criteria for Depression Are Too Broad,

Researchers Say," *Washington Post*, April 3, 2007, http://www
.washingtonpost.com/wp-dyn/content/article/2007/
04/02/AR2007040201693.html?hpid=topnews%20http://www
.washingtonpost.com/wpdyn/content/article/2007/04/02/AR20070
40201693.html?hpid=topnews (accessed April 4, 2007).

24 *the Archives of General Psychiatry:* Jerome C. Wakefield et al.,
    "Extending the Bereavement Exclusion for Major Depression to Other
    Losses: Evidence from the National Comorbidity Survey," *The Archives
    of General Psychiatry* 64 (April 2007): 433–40.

24 *"Can Brain Scans See Depression?":* Benedict Carey, "Can Brain Scans
    See Depression?" *New York Times*, October 18, 2005,
    http://www.nytimes.com/2005/10/18/health/
    psychology/18imag.html (accessed October 19, 2005).

25 *Solomon correctly points out:* Andrew Solomon, *The Noonday Demon*, 22.

27 *German Jews . . . rate of suicide . . . fifty times higher:* Roland Chrisjohn
    and Sherri Young, *The Circle Game: Shadows and Substance in the
    Indian Residential School Experience in Canada* (Penticton, British
    Columbia: Theytus Books, 1997), 260; Raul Hilberg, *Perpetrators,
    Victims, Bystanders: The Jewish Catastrophe, 1933–1945* (New York:
    HarperCollins, 1992), 171 (Hilberg discusses Konrad Kwiet, who
    studied suicide in the German-Jewish community and estimated that in
    each of the intense years of Jewish removal from 1941 to 1943, their
    rate of suicide was massive, about 1,500 per 100,000, about fifty times
    higher than what would be considered a "high rate" of suicide of 30
    per 100,000).

27 *Roland Chrisjohn:* Roland Chrisjohn and Sherri Young, *The Circle
    Game*, 260.

27 *Native Americans have the highest suicide rate . . . second leading cause of
    death among Native American adolescents:* A. Garland and E. Zigler,
    "Adolescent Suicide Prevention: Current Research and Social Policy
    Implications," *American Psychologist* 48:2 (1993): 169–82.

27 *suicide was a rare event among aboriginal peoples:* "According to
    Aboriginal tradition, suicide was rare in Pre-Colonialism. . . . Those who
    did commit suicide were generally the sick or elderly who felt they
    could no longer contribute to their community and their deaths were
    perceived as acts of self-sacrifice. In First Nations communities today,
    suicide is more common among the young and usually results from
    feelings of hopelessness and despair," in "Aboriginal Peoples and the
    Criminal Justice System: A Bulletin," *Canadian Criminal Justice
    Association*, May 15, 2000, http://www.ccja-acjp.ca/en/aborit.html
    (accessed September 15, 2005). Also, "A study in Greenland reports
    that while in the past suicide was rare among the indigenous Inuit pop-
    ulation and restricted to old people, the suicide rate is very high among
    young Inuit men who are left behind in a society under rapid change,"
    Jorgen Thorslund, "Inuit Suicides in Greenland," *Arctic Medical*

Research 49 (1990): 25–33, summarized by Wolfgang G. Jilek, "Transcultural Psychiatry—Quo Vadis?" *Transcultural Psychiatry Newsletter* 16:1 (January 1998), www.mental health.com/newslet/tp9801.htm (accessed September 15, 2005).

28   *rate of suicide for European nations:* Erich Fromm, *The Sane Society* (1955, reprint, New York: Fawcett, 1968), 136.

28   *the Southern Literary Messenger:* Quoted in Joshua Wolf Shenk, *Lincoln's Melancholy: How Depression Challenged a President and Fueled His Greatness* (Boston: Houghton Mifflin, 2005), 77.

28   *"disabled mentally ill":* The number of disabled through 1955 is based on hospitalized mentally ill; the disability rates for 1987 and 2003 are based on the number in the United States receiving Social Security psychiatric disability payments; in Robert Whitaker, "Anatomy of an Epidemic: Psychiatric Drugs and the Astonishing Rise of Mental Illness in America," *Ethical Human Psychology and Psychiatry* 7:1 (Spring 2005): 23–35.

28   *World Health Organization . . . greater prevalence in high-income nations:* Stated by G. H. Brundtland, director general of the World Health Organization, in a general speech on mental health, Nairobi, Kenya, Mathari National Mental Hospital, April 4, 2001, http:// canberra.usembassy.gov/hyper/2001/0405/epf410.htm (accessed August 1, 2005).

28   *Oliver James:* Oliver James, "Consuming Misery," *The Ecologist,* May 2000, http://www.findarticles.com/p/articles/ mi_m2465/is_3_30/ai_62794138#continue (accessed June 12, 2005).

28   *Mexican immigrants . . . Vega:* William A. Vega et al., "Lifetime Prevalence of *DSM-III-R* Psychiatric Disorders among Urban and Rural Mexican Americans in California," *Archives of General Psychiatry* 55 (1998): 771–78. Vega quoted in Patricia McBroom, "As Mexican Immigrants Adapt to American Society, Their Mental Illness Rates Increase Dramatically," *Berkeleyan,* October 21, 1998, http://www.berkeley.edu/news/berkeleyan/1998/1021/ immigrant.html (accessed July 31, 2005).

29   *Postpartum depression:* Kwame McKenzie et al., "Learning from Low Income Countries: Mental Health," *BMJ* 329 (November 13, 2004):1138–40, http://www.bmj.com/cgi/content/full/329/7475/1138?ehom (accessed December 12, 2006).

29   *Michael Yapko notes:* Michael D. Yapko, *Hand-Me-Down Blues: How to Stop Depression from Spreading in Families* (New York: St. Martin's Press, 1999), 27.

29   *William H. Whyte.* William H. Whyte Jr., *The Organization Man* (New York: Simon and Schuster, 1956), 405 ("How to Cheat on Personality Tests"); 5, 396 (de Tocqueville); 397 (quest for normalcy).

32 *electroconvulsive therapy has made a comeback:* Kathleen Hirsch, "Shock Makes a Comeback," *Ms.* magazine, November/December 1995, 34–36.

32 *psychosurgery is no longer frowned upon:* Andrew Solomon, *The Noonday Demon,* 163–64.

32 *two-thirds of doctor visits were less than fifteen minutes:* Two-thirds of visits to doctors' offices are now less than fifteen minutes, and one-third are under ten minutes, in S. M. Schappert, "National Ambulatory Medical Care Survey: 1990 Summary," *Advance Data from Vital and Health Statistics of the National Center for Health Statistics* 213 (April 30, 1992), in Thomas J. Moore, *Prescription for Disaster: The Hidden Dangers in Your Medicine Cabinet* (New York: Random House, 1998), 169.

32 *2001 RAND Corporation survey:* Harold H. Bloomfield and Peter McWilliams, *How to Heal Depression* (Allen Park, MI: Prelude Press, 2001), 90.

32 *Hamilton Rating Scale for Depression (HRSD):* Two of many online sites to view the Hamilton Rating Scale for Depression are http://www.neuromedia.ca/en/nos_articles/tests11.asp and http://healthnet.umassmed.edu/mhealth/HAMD.pdf#search=%22%22 hamilton%20rating%20scale%20for%20depression%22%22 (accessed September 9, 2006).

32 *American Journal of Psychiatry:* R. Michael Bagby et al., "The Hamilton Depression Rating Scale: Has the Gold Standard Become a Lead Weight?" *American Journal of Psychiatry* 161 (December 2004): 2163–77.

32 *Journal of Clinical Psychopharmacology:* Mark Zimmerman et al., "Is It Time to Replace the Hamilton Depression Rating Scale as the Primary Outcome Measure in Treatment Studies of Depression?" *Journal of Clinical Psychopharmacology* 25: 2 (April 2005): 105–10.

32 *HRSD is heavily loaded with items that are most affected by psychotropic drugs:* In addition to the three insomnia items, there are three items about agitation and anxiety and two somatic items. The HRSD also excludes items that are least affected by drugs (e.g., no items about relationship satisfaction or life meaningfulness). It also excludes items such as weight gain and excessive sleep, which though standard symptoms of depression also happen to be common adverse effects of antidepressants.

35 *Fromm . . . To Have or to Be?:* Erich Fromm, *To Have or To Be?* (1976, reprint, New York: Harper & Row, 1988).

36 *Lesley Hazleton:* Lesley Hazleton, *The Right to Feel Bad: Coming to Terms with Normal Depression* (New York: Ballantine Books, 1984), 4, 5, 47, 35.

Chapter Two

39 *Siddhartha Gautama:* Huston Smith, *The Religions of Man* (New York: Harper & Row, 1965), 90–159.

49 *Constantin Stanislavski's:* Constantin Stanislavski, *An Actor Prepares* (1936, reprint, New York: Theatre Art Books, 1980), 44.

50 *Paco Ferri:* Paco Ferri, *2 Running On Calm* (Madrid: Realizacion, limited edition, 2006), 55–64, 158.

52 *Abraham Lincoln:* Joshua Wolf Shenk, *Lincoln's Melancholy: How Depression Challenged a President and Fueled His Greatness* (Boston: Houghton Mifflin, 2005), 113–16.

54 *Eric Schlosser:* Eric Schlosser, *Fast Food Nation: The Dark Side of the All-American Meal* (Boston: Houghton Mifflin Company, 2001), 74.

56 *Don Juan Matus:* Carlos Castaneda, *A Separate Reality: Further Conversations with Don Juan* (New York: Touchstone, 1971), 265.

58 *Ralph Nader:* David Wallis, "Questions for Ralph Nader," *New York Times Magazine,* June 16, 2002, 13.

58 *Noam Chomsky:* Peter R. Mitchell and John Schoeffel, eds., *Understanding Power: The Indispensable Chomsky* (New York: New Press, 2002), 139, 181.

60 *Viktor Frankl:* Viktor E. Frankl, *Man's Search for Meaning* (1959, reprint, New York: Pocket Books, 1976), 27, 125–126.

60 *Frankl's later writings:* "I have signed authorization for lobotomies without having cause to regret it. In a few cases, I have even carried out transorbital lobotomy"; Viktor E. Frankl, "'Nothing but—': On Reductionism and Nihilism," *Encounter,* November 1969, 56, cited in Thomas Szasz, *The Myth of Psychotherapy: Mental Healing as Religion, Rhetoric, and Repression* (Syracuse, NY: Syracuse University Press, 1988), 205.

Chapter Three

66 *Charles Whitfield:* Charles L. Whitfield, *The Truth about Depression* (Deerfield Beach, FL: Health Communications, 2003), 46.

70 *not uncommon for the same person:* American Medical Association *Essential Guide to Depression* (New York: Simon & Schuster, 1998), 94–99.

72 *"compulsive shopping,":* "Drug Can Help Compulsive Shoppers," CNN.com, December 12, 2000, http://www.cnn.com/2000/HEALTH/12/12/health.shopping.reut/ (accessed August 1, 2005).

72 *Sarafem:* Marcia Angell, *The Truth About the Drug Companies: How They Deceive Us and What to Do About It* (New York: Random House, 2004), 189.

73 *Since serotonin receptors exist throughout:* "In humans only 5% of serotonin is found in the brain. The other 95% is distributed throughout the rest of the body," in Joseph Glenmullen, *Prozac Backlash* (New York: Simon & Schuster, 2000), 16.

73 *60 to 70 percent of people. . . sex:* Seventy percent of SSRI users are plagued by sexual difficulty; *Psychology Today,* April 1999, 35. Joseph Glenmullen reviewed the research and concluded, "Sexual dysfunction affects 60% of people," *Prozac Backlash* (New York: Simon & Schuster, 2000), 8.

73 *Science now supports. . . brain damage:* In 1997, psychopharmacologist Ronald Pies (a member of the medical school faculties at both Harvard and Tufts and author of a textbook on psychopharmacology) wrote an editorial in the *Journal of Clinical Psychopharmacology.* Ronald Pies, "Must We Now Consider SSRIs Neuroleptics?" *Journal of Clinical Psychopharmacology* 17 (1997): 443–45, in Joseph Glenmullen, *Prozac Backlash,* 53. The mental health establishment, after many years of denying it, finally acknowledged that neuroleptics such as Thorazine and Haldol cause neurological disorders (extrapyramidal side effects such as tics, agitation, muscle spasms, and parkinsonism, termed tardive dyskinesia), that indicate brain damage. Elevated serotonin levels trigger a compensatory drop in the neurotransmitter dopamine; Joseph Glenmullen, *Prozac Backlash,* 48–50. And it's exactly this drop in dopamine levels that was widely acknowledged to be the source of the neurological damage caused by neuroleptics; Glenmullen, *Prozac Backlash,* 94–105. *Brain Research* reported abnormalities in the serotonergic neurons in rats after the administration of just four days of high doses of either Prozac, Zoloft, or Redux; M. Kalia et al., "Comparative Study of Fluoxetine, Sibutramine, Sertraline, and Dexfenfluramine on the Morphology of Serotonergic Nerve Terminals Using Serotonin Immunohistochemistry," *Brain Research* 858 (2000): 92–105. In 1997 the *Journal of the American Medical Association* published vivid photographs, taken through a microscope, revealing widespread destruction of brain cells in a monkey after just four days of the serotonin enhancer Redux; U. D. McCann et al., "Brain Serotonin Neurotoxicity and Primary Pulmonary Hypertension from Fenfluramine and Dexfenfluramine," *Journal of the American Medical Association* 278 (1997): 666–72.

74 *Sidney Sament:* Sidney Sament, *Clinical Psychiatry News,* March 1983, 11, in Leonard Roy Frank, "Electroshock: A Crime Against the Spirit," *Ethical Human Sciences and Services* 4:1 (Spring 2002): 63–71.

74 *Ms. magazine:* Kathleen Hirsch, "Shock Therapy Makes a Comeback," *Ms.* magazine, November/December 1995, 34–36.

74 *Neuropsychopharamacology:* Harold A. Sackeim et al., "The Cognitive Effects of Electroconvulsive Therapy in Community Settings, *Neuropsychopharamacology* 32 (2007): 244–54.

74 *cingulotomy . . . Reese Cosgrove:* Psychosurgery description and Cosgrove quotation in Andrew Solomon, *The Noonday Demon: An Atlas of Depression* (New York: Touchstone, 2001), 164.

75 *Sherman:* B. H. Liddell Hart, *Sherman: Soldier, Realist, American* (New York: Da Capo Press, 1993) 66, 107–11, 126–27; Richard O'Connor, *Undoing Depression* (New York: Berkley Books, 1997), 112–15.

76 *In Papa Hemingway:* A. E. Hotchner, *Papa Hemingway: A Personal Memoir* (New York: Random House, 1966), 266, 280.

76 *In 1999 Hotchner reported:* A. E. Hotchner interviewed on NPR's "Fresh Air," July 21, 1999 [I heard the live broadcast]

77 *Socioeconomic data. . .higher social status:* John J. Ratey and Catherine Johnson, *Shadow Syndromes* (New York: Pantheon, 1997), 110.

77 *welfare recipients in the United States:* K. Olsen and L. Pavetti, *Personal and Family Challenges to the Successful Transition from Welfare to Work* (Washington, D.C.: Urban Institute, 1996), in Solomon, *The Noonday Demon,* 336.

77 *Robert Whitaker:* Robert Whitaker, "Anatomy of an Epidemic: Psychiatric Drugs and the Astonishing Rise of Mental Illness in America," *Ethical Human Psychology and Psychiatry* 7:1 (Spring 2005): 23–35.

78 *Marie Winn:* Marie Winn, *The Plug-in Drug* (1977, reprint, New York: Penguin, 1985).

78 *George Orwell's 1984:* George Orwell, *1984* (1949, reprint, New York: Signet Classic, 1950), 73.

79 *Heroin addicts:* "Erowid Experience Reports: Heroin," http://www.erowid.org/experiences/subs/exp_Heroin.shtml #Glowing_Experiences (accessed August 6, 2004).

82 *In the 1940s and 1950s:* Robert D. Putnam, *Bowling Alone: The Collapse and Revival of American Community* (New York: Touchstone, 2000), 263.

82 *25 percent of students:* Peter Kramer reports this estimate from a Steven Hyman colloquium, "Ethical Issues in the Psychopharmacology of Mood" (New York Academy of Science, New York, July 13, 2004), in Peter D. Kramer, *Against Depression* (New York: Viking, 2005), 257.

85 *Common sense and research. . . .temperaments:* James Garbarino, *Lost Boys* (New York: Free Press, 1999), 36, 71–74. Also Alexander Thomas and Stella Chess, *Temperament and Development* (New York: Brunner/Mazel, 1977).

85 *Kennith Kendler, one of establishment psychiatry's most revered researchers:* Peter Kramer states, "Ken was the genius of our residency group," Peter D. Kramer, *Against Depression* (New York: Viking, 2005), 125.

85 *American Journal of Psychiatry article . . . Kendler:* Kennith Kendler, "'A Gene for. . .': The Nature of Gene Action in Psychiatric Disorders," *American Journal of Psychiatry* 162:7 (July 2005): 1243–52.

85 *Bertram Karon:* Bertram P. Karon, "The Tragedy of Schizophrenia without Psychotherapy," *Journal of American Academy of Psychoanalysis and Dynamic Psychiatry* 31 (2003): 89–118.

86 *large number of studies confirm. . .lower reproductive rate:* Matthew C. Keller and Geoffrey Miller, "Resolving the Paradox of Common, Harmful, Heritable Mental Disorders: Which Evolutionary Genetic Models Work Best?" *Behavioral and Brain Sciences 29* (2006), 385–452, table 2: "Available Fertility Estimates (1960–2005) of Common Mental Disorders"; includes lower fertility rates in "affective disorders" and "bipolar disorders,"http://www.matthewckeller.com/Keller_Miller_MentalDisorderEvolution_2006.pdf (accessed July 25, 2007).

86 *children of depressed parents . . .host of problems:* A. J. Sameroff, R. Seifer, and M. Zax, "Early Development of Children at Risk for Emotional Disorder," *Monographs of the Society for Research in Child Development* 47:7 (1982), in Solomon, *The Noonday Demon,* 181–182. Leonard Milling and Barbara Martin, "Depression and Suicidal Behavior in Preadolescent Children" in C. E. Walker and M. C. Roberts, eds., *Handbook of Clinical Child Psychology,* 2nd ed. (New York: John Wiley, 1992), in Solomon, *The Noonday Demon,* 181–82.

86 *Michael D. Yapko:* Michael D. Yapko, *Hand-Me-Down Blues: How to Stop Depression from Spreading in Families* (New York: St. Martin's Press, 1999), 156–61.

87 *Even in the case of identical twins:* "Four of ten co-twins of the depressed are depressed" and "depression has a heritability of 35 to 40 percent" are common assertions of the mental health establishment, reiterated by Peter Kramer in *Against Depression,* 126. In twin studies, *heritability* is a statistic found by comparing identical twins to same-sex fraternal twins and is supposedly meant to tease out environmental influence. One problem with comparing identical twins to fraternal twins to tease out environmental influences and to find "heritability" is that it's incorrect to assume that the environmental influence on identical and same-sex fraternal twins is equal. Biologists R. C. Lewontin and Steven Rose and psychologist Leon Kamin report how identical twins—as compared to same-sex fraternal twins—are often treated more similarly by parents, peers, and teachers; have more similar friends; do more similar things; and spend more time with one another. For instance, in one study, 40 percent of identical twins reported that they usually studied together, compared to only 15 percent of fraternal same-sex twins; R. C. Lewontin, Steven Rose, and Leon Kamin, *Not in Our Genes: Biology, Ideology, and Human Nature* (New York: Pantheon

Books, 1984), 115. Furthermore, 35 to 40 percent heritability for depression is not very impressive; for example, the social/political attitude of *conservatism* was found in two major twin studies to have heritability of 62 percent and 65 percent; Thomas J. Bouchard and Matt McGue, "Genetic and Environmental Influences on Human Psychological Differences," *Journal of Neurobiology* 54:1 (2002): 4–45.

87   *Because of research associating optimism:* Martin E. P. Seligman, *Learned Optimism: How to Change Your Mind and Your Life* (New York: Knopf, 1991), 102–03, 151–53.

Chapter Four

89   *Morton Reiser:* Morton Reiser, "Are Psychiatric Educators 'Losing the Mind'?" *American Journal of Psychiatry* 145 (1988), in Elliot S. Valenstein, *Blaming the Brain* (New York: Free Press, 1998), 240.

89   *Steven Sharfstein:* Steven S. Sharfstein, "Big Pharma and American Psychiatry: The Good, the Bad, and the Ugly," *Psychiatric News* 40:16 (August 19, 2005): 3, http://pn.psychiatryonline.org/cgi/content/full/40/16/3 (accessed August 23, 2005).

102 *Charles Bukowski:* Charles Bukowski, *The Movie: Barfly* (Santa Rosa, CA: Black Sparrow Press, 1987), 46–47. For Bukowski background, Bukowski: *Born into This*, directed by John Dullaghan (2003).

104 *no evidence of increased dopamine:* Acknowledged by biopsychiatrist John Ratey, in John Ratey and Catherine Johnson, *Shadow Syndromes* (New York: Pantheon, 1997), 5.

104 *Lawrence Plumlee:* "Are Psychiatric Drugs Overused?" Reuters News, March 24, 2003, http://www.msnbc.com/news/890143.asp (accessed April 11, 2004).

104 *The World Health Organization. . .studies:* Robert Whitaker, *Mad in America: Bad Science, Bad Medicine, and the Enduring Mistreatment of the Mentally Ill* (Cambridge, MA: Perseus, 2001), 226–32.

105 *Quakers:* Robert Whitaker, *Mad in America*, 22–24.

105 *Brooke Medicine Eagle:* Brooke Medicine Eagle: Brook Medicine Eagle, "The Circle of Healing," in *Healers on Healing*, Richard Carlson and Benjamin Shield, eds. (Los Angeles: Tarcher, 1989), 58–62.

Chapter Five

117 *In 1900. . .graduated high school:* For 1900, see *The World Almanac and Book of Facts 1999* (Mahwah, NJ: World Almanac Books/Primedia 1998),

242. For 2004, see "Statewide Planning E-News: Rhode Island's Electronic Newsletter," which notes, "According to new data released by the Census Bureau titled 'Educational Attainment in the United States: 2004,' 85 percent of persons twenty-five years of age and older reported they had completed high school," http://www.planning.ri.gov/news/oldnewsletters.pdf (accessed December 12, 2005).

118 *examples of nonacademic financial successes:* Eric Schlosser, *Fast Food Nation: The Dark Side of the All-American Meal* (Boston: Houghton Mifflin, 2001), 22–23, 33.

119 *quit smoking:* As high as 95 percent according to Stanton Peele, *Diseasing of America: Addiction Treatment Out of Control* (Boston: Houghton Mifflin, 1989), 25.

120 *leading growth jobs:* U.S. Bureau of Labor Statistics estimate of job growth from 1994 to 2005, in *Wall Street Journal Almanac 1998* (New York: Ballantine, 1997), 302.

124 *Frederick Nietzsche:* Walter Kaufmann, *The Portable Nietzsche* (New York: Viking Press, 1968), 62, 400.

125 *Negative thinking and pessimism:* Martin E. P. Seligman, *Learned Optimism: How to Change Your Mind and Your Life* (New York: Knopf, 1991).

127 *The Dobuans:* Ruth Benedict, *Patterns of Culture* (1934, Reprint, New York: Mentor, 1956), 120–59.

127 *Meredith Small:* Meredith F. Small, *The Culture of Our Discontent: Beyond the Medical Model of Mental Illness* (Washington, D.C.: Joseph Henry Press, 2006), 107.

128 *Even Martin Seligman:* Martin E. P. Seligman, *Learned Optimism*, 209.

128 *Americans. . . overweight:* "U.S. Centers for Disease Control and Prevention finds that 65 percent of adults are overweight—up 9 percent from 2000—and 23 percent are obese, an 8 percent increase since 1998," in "Six Mindful Ways to Shed Pounds," *Psychology Today*, January/February 2003, 72–74.

129 *A Duke University research team:* Duke study lead author James A. Blumenthal in *Psychosomatic Medicine*, September/October 2000, http://www.hbns.org/newsrelease/exercise9-12-00.cfm (accessed April 19, 2005).

131 *Much of Buddhism:* Huston Smith, *The Religions of Man* (New York: Harper & Row, 1965), 110–15.

131 *For Spinoza, God and nature are one:* There is some philosophical/theological controversy as to whether Spinoza was a pantheist (God = nature) or a panentheist (God = nature + x). Nature for Spinoza refers not just to visible nature, but also to the divine laws and principle of it; Paul Edwards, ed., *The Encyclopedia of Philosophy,* vol. 7 (New York: MacMillan, 1967), 530–41.

135 *Peter Kahn:* Peter H. Kahn Jr., *The Human Relationship with Nature: Development and Culture* (Cambridge, MA: MIT Press, 1999).

136 *2006 survey. . . children. . .read every day:* Peg Tyre and Karen Springen, "Fourth-Grade Slump," *Newsweek*, February 19, 2007, 47.

138 *Philip Zimbardo:* Philip G. Zimbardo and Shirley L. Radl, *The Shy Child: Overcoming and Preventing Shyness from Infancy to Adulthood* (New York: Doubleday/Dolphin, 1982), 204–10.

140 *The Interactional Nature of Depression:* Thomas Joiner and James C. Coyne, eds., *The Interactional Nature of Depression: Advances in Interpersonal Approaches* (Washington, D.C.: American Psychological Association, 1999).

140 *In one study, unhappily married women:* Ibid., 275

140 *In another study, the best single predictor:* Ibid., 329–30.

140 *Why Marriages Succeed or Fail:* John Gottman, *Why Marriages Succeed or Fail* (New York: Simon & Schuster, 1994), 56–67.

142 *John Gottman concludes, "If:* Ibid., 28.

143 *William James wrote:* William James, *The Principles of Psychology,* volume 2 (1890, reprint, New York: Henry Holt, 1950), 369.

Chapter Six

148 *Bowling Alone:* Robert D. Putnam, *Bowling Alone: The Collapse and Revival of American Community* (New York: Touchstone, 2000).

149 *In terms of physical health:* Ibid., 329.

149 *With respect to depression:* Ibid., 332.

149 *American Management Association:* Ibid., 92.

150 *twice as much time behind the wheel:* Ibid., 212.

150 *For most of human history, the evening meal:* Ibid., 100–101.

150 *Putnam notes, "We spend:* Ibid., 115.

151 *"Trends in religious life," Putnam reports:* Ibid., 79; membership and participation in progressive religious institutions decline, 75–79.

151 *the frequency of church attendance:* Ibid., 321.

151 *Putnam speculates that the sources:* Ibid., 283–84.

152 *married couples average fourteen:* Ibid., 191.

152 *almost half of the United States is suburbanized:* Ibid., 206–7.

152 *four times as much time watching television:* Ibid., 224.

152 *In 1970, 6 percent of sixth graders:* Ibid., 223.

152 *Approximately half of all families. . . television:* Ibid., 227.

154 *Harold Koplewicz:* Harold Koplewicz, *It's Nobody's Fault: New Hope and Help for Difficult Children and Their Parents* (New York: Random House, 1996). NAMI review of *It's Nobody's Fault,* http://www.nami.org/books/ItsNobodysFault.html (accessed August 15, 2003). Peter R. Breggin reports that Koplewicz, at the 1999 White House Conference on Mental Health, said that "absent fathers" and

"bad childhood traumas" don't cause emotional disturbances in children, quoted in Peter R. Breggin, *Talking Back to Ritalin: What Doctors Aren't Telling You about Stimulants and ADHD* (Cambridge, MA: Perseus, 2001), 18.

155 *NAMI, and Big Pharma. . . interconnected:* NAMI received $11.72 million from drug companies between 1996 and mid-1999. Ken Silverstein, "Prozac.org," *Mother Jones,* November/December 1999, 22–23. In the first quarter of 2007, pharmaceutical company Eli Lilly provided NAMI with a grant of $450,000 for "Campaign for the Mind of America 2007," as well as providing various local NAMI organizations with smaller grants, in Lilly's "Grant Office 2007—1st Quarter," https://www.lillygrantoffice.com/docs/q1_registry_report.pdf (accessed May 22, 2007).

155 *Jules Henry:* Jules Henry, "In Suburban Classrooms," in Ronald and Beatrice Gross, eds., *Radical School Reform* (New York: Simon & Schuster, 1969), 83–84.

156 *a 1998 study showed that the majority of medicated children:* "Talks less to others" in 50 percent of children and "uninterested in others" in 75 percent of children, in P. Firestone et al., "Short-Term Side Effects of Stimulant Medications in Preschool Children with Attention-Deficit/Hyperactivity Disorder: A Double-Blind Placebo Controlled Study," *Journal of Child Adolescent Psychopharmacology* 8 (1998): 13–25.

156 *the U.S. Surgeon General in 1999:* "However, psychostimulants do not appear to achieve long-term changes in outcomes such as peer relationships, social or academic skills, or school achievement," in "Attention-Deficit/Hyperactivity Disorder," *Mental Health: A Report of the Surgeon General* (U.S. Department of Health and Human Services, 1999), http://www.surgeongeneral.gov/library/mentalhealth/chapter3/sec4.html (accessed March 2, 2000).

158 *In The Careless Society:* John McKnight, *The Careless Society: Community and Its Counterfeits* (New York: Basic Books, 1995), 117 (three features . . . critical features of early American communities); 170–72 (collective effort, capacity, informality, stories, celebration); 46 (I, the professional servicer); 170 (while institutions and professionals war, transactions of value); 171 (the foreign language of studies); 105–6 (human service professionals . . . The client advances); 49 (support citizen competence); 81–85 (how one community organization took health matters into its own hands); 85 (the administrator of the old people's home).

161 *In the United States a smaller percentage. . . vote:* Robert Putnam, *Bowling Alone,* 31.

161 *election turnouts are even lower for local elections:* Steven Hill discussing his book *Fixing Elections* (New York: Routledge, 2002) on C-SPAN, September 7, 2002 [I watched the broadcast].

161 *30 to 40 percent decline:* Robert D. Putnam, *Bowling Alone,* 45.

163 *Early corporate charters:* David C. Korten, *When Corporations Rule the World* (West Hartford, CT: Kumarian Press, 1995), 56–57.

164 *According to the World Health Organization:* WHO defines "devastating illness" in terms of total years of healthy life stolen by death or disability, in Donna Foote and Sam Selbert, "The Age of Anxiety," *Newsweek,* Spring/Summer 1999, 68–72.

166 *Lewis Mumford:* Lewis Mumford, *The Conduct of Life* (New York: Harcourt, Brace & Company, 1951), in Erich Fromm, *The Sane Society* (1955, reprint, New York: Fawcett, 1968), 195–96.

166 *Benjamin Rush:* Daniel J. Boorstin, *The Lost World of Thomas Jefferson* (Boston: Beacon, 1948), 182.

166 *Lancet:* Richard Horton, "Lotronex and the FDA: A Fatal Erosion of Integrity," *Lancet.* 357 (May 19, 2001): 1544–45.

166 *an article in USA Today:* Dennis Cauchon, "FDA Advisors Tied to Industry," *USA Today,* September 25, 2000, in Marcia Angell, *The Truth About the Drug Companies: How They Deceive Us and What to Do About It* (New York: Random House, 2004), 210.

168 *Living My Life:* Emma Goldman, *Living My Life* (1931, reprint, New York: Dover Publications, 1970).

168 *Chris Black:* Chris Black, letter to the editor, *Adbusters,* November/December 2002.

170 *Robert Proctor:* Robert N. Proctor, *Racial Hygiene: Medicine under the Nazis* (Cambridge, MA: Harvard University Press, 1988), 65, 286.

170 *Howard Zinn:* Howard Zinn, *A People's History of the United States* (New York: Harper Perennial, 1995), 622.

172 *Adlai Stevenson:* Erich Fromm, *The Sane Society,* 96.

172 *20 to 25 percent of Americans use psychiatric drugs:* Conservative estimates of 20 percent; Andrew Kimbrell (founder and director of the International Center for Technology Assessment) says 25 percent, in Andrew Kimbrell, "Breaking the Job Lock," *Utne Reader,* January/February 1999, 47–49.

172 *10 to 15 percent are abusing alcohol:* There are widely varying estimates due to different definitions of what constitutes abuse, with 11.3 percent reported for "any substance abuse/dependence" in "1991 National Comorbidity Survey," *Substance Abuse and Mental Health Statistical Sourcebook* (U.S. Department of Health and Human Services, 1995).

172 *12 percent compulsively gamble:* The 12 percent figure comes from the National Council on Compulsive Gamblers, in Stanton Peele, *Diseasing of America: Addiction Treatment Out of Control* (Boston: Houghton Mifflin, 1989), 25. "Problem and pathological gambling" increased in New York State to 7.3 percent in 1996, in *Wall Street Journal Almanac 1998* (New York: Ballantine, 1997), 934.

172 *Erich Fromm:* Erich Fromm, *The Sane Society,* 24, 312.

172 *Dinesh D'Souza:* Dinesh D'Souza, *What's So Great about America* (New York: Regnery, 2002).

173 *Obesity. . . greater problem for America's poor:* "Overweight and obesity are particularly common among minority groups and those with a lower family income," in "Disparities and Prevalence," *2001 Surgeon General's Report on Overweight and Obesity,* http://www.surgeongeneral.gov/topics/obesity/calltoaction/1_5.htm (accessed November 10, 2005).

173 *When American adults were asked in 1996:* All statistics in this paragraph from Robert D. Putnam, *Bowling Alone,* 272–73.

174 *Viktor Frankl's search:* Viktor E. Frankl, *Man's Search for Meaning* (1959, reprint, New York: Pocket Books, 1976), 175 ("By declaring that man . . . essentially self-transcendence rather than self-actualization"); 154 ("the striving to find meaning . . ."); 166 ("not a tensionless state"); 205 (sharply critical of . . . determinists . . . psychological and sociological conditions); 157 ("the meaning of our lives . . . detected").

175 *Wal-Mart comes to a small town:* Bill Quinn, *How Wal-Mart Is Destroying America* (Berkeley, CA: Ten Speed Press, 1998), xii.

175 *work world. . . 80 percent of Americans. . .meaningless:* Andrew Kimbrell, "Breaking the Job Lock," *Utne Reader,* January/February 1999, 47–49.

175 *Andrew Kimbrell:* Andrew Kimbrell, *Cold Evil: Technology and Modern Ethics* (Great Barrington, MA: E. F. Schumacher Society, 2002), 12.

Epilogue

177 *annual sales for all antidepressant and antipsychotic drugs:* Robert Whitaker, "Anatomy of an Epidemic: Psychiatric Drugs and the Astonishing Rise of Mental Illness in America," *Ethical Human Psychology and Psychiatry* 7:1 (Spring 2005): 23–35.

181 *Lincoln's depression:* Joshua Wolf Shenk, *Lincoln's Melancholy: How Depression Challenged a President and Fueled His Greatness* (Boston: Houghton Mifflin, 2005), 216 ("Gloom & sadness were his predominant state"); 167 (helped more than it hurt); 221 (not a matter of shame).

Index

the politics and practice of sustainable living

CHELSEA GREEN PUBLISHING

Chelsea Green Publishing sees books as tools for effecting cultural change and seeks to empower citizens to participate in reclaiming our global commons and become its impassioned stewards. If you enjoyed *Surviving America's Depression Epidemic*, please consider these other great books.

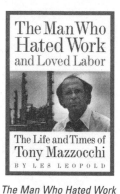

Exposed: The Toxic Chemistry of Everyday Products and What's at Stake for American Power
MARK SCHAPIRO
HC | $22.95 | ISBN: 978-1-933392-15-8

The Man Who Hated Work and Loved Labor
LES LEOPOLD
PB | $24.95 | ISBN: 978-1-933392-64-6
HC | $40.00 | ISBN: 978-1-933392-63-9

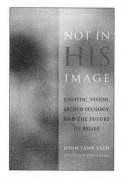

The Culture of Make Believe
DERRICK JENSEN
PB | $25.00 | ISBN: 978-1-931498-57-9

Not in His Image: Gnostic Vision, Sacred Ecology, and the Future of Belief
JOHN LAMB LASH
PB | $21.95 | ISBN: 978-1-931498-92-0
HC | $35.00 | ISBN: 978-1-933392-40-0

CHELSEA GREEN PUBLISHING
the politics and practice of sustainable living

For more information or to request a catalog, please visit **www.chelseagreen.com** or call **802.295.6300**